82 *distinctive* HOUSES

from Architectural Record

PUBLISHED BY F. W. DODGE CORPORATION

INTRODUCTION

THE EVOLUTION, or perhaps revolution, which has been occurring in American house design is mirrored in this book. Here is inscribed the work of many of our leading residential architects, a coast-to-coast sampling that conveys, I believe, a significant picture of contemporary work.

The best of our modern houses are rarely seen from highways or trafficked streets. There is more good modern than most of us realize because so much is deliberately screened from public view. This collection serves a useful purpose by bringing together as it does so many significant examples of good modern work.

In this collection of houses selected for publication in *Architectural Record* over the past five years, no attempt has been made to prove a "trend" or a "movement" in American home planning or design. Yet it must be apparent that significant change has occurred. Comparison with a similar collection of as late as ten years ago would show a vigorous—perhaps startling—progression in design, planning, and in the basic concept of modern living as served by construction techniques.

These houses show, it seems to me, a greater appreciation by architects of the hospitality of the out-of-doors. While providing the mechanical equipment, services, and comforts Americans value so highly, they also seem to place the family in much more direct everyday contact with nature, its trees, sunshine, and changing seasons. These houses are more direct, simple, and natural. There is much use of local wood and masonry, with little ornamentation. There appears a feeling that the purpose of a house is not to stifle or enclose, but to liberate and open out. Space is lightly divided, with rooms separated from gardens, trees, and lawns by thin panels of glass. There is greater flexibility of plan and use—and escape from the closed box and restricting tradition.

Progress in this field, which is so closely linked to the habits, customs, and traditions of people, is necessarily a continuing and fluid thing. This collection indicates a direction that will continue—a course leading to more agreeable homes honestly and thoughtfully suited to American living.

Joseph B. Mason

Executive Editor, Architectural Record

TWO HOUSES

George Nemeny and A. W. Geller, Architects

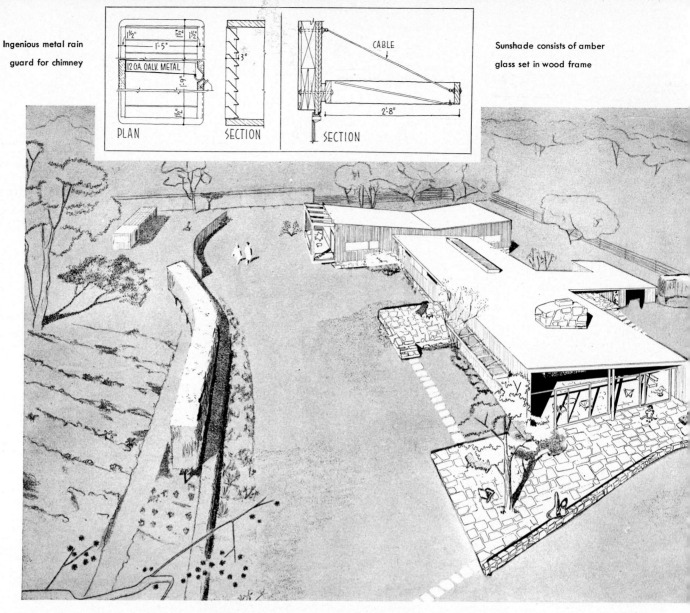

PLAN   SECTION   SECTION

1½" 1½" 1½"
1'-5"
12 GA. GALV. METAL
1'-9"
1½"

3"

CABLE

2'-8"

Rendering by Stanley M. Sherman

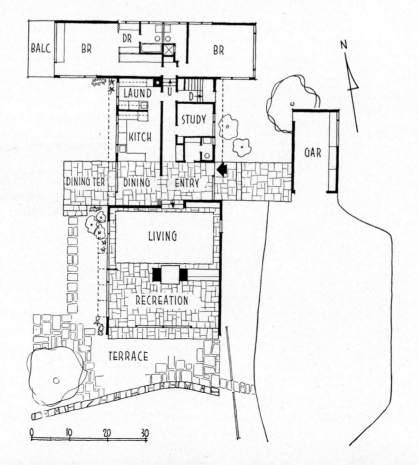

BALC   BR   DR   BR

LAUND   U   D

KITCH   STUDY

DINING TER   DINING   ENTRY   GAR

LIVING

RECREATION

TERRACE

N

0   10   20   30

OPENNESS WITH PRIVACY
FOR A THREE ZONE PLAN

House for Mr. & Mrs. Jack Diamond

Hewlett Neck, Long Island, N. Y.

George Nemeny & A. W. Geller, Architects

By JUDICIOUSLY PLACING the house against the far northeast zoning limit of the plot, all principal rooms can face southwest to a maximum size garden area, which in turn is screened from neighboring houses by fences and planting. Privacy from the northeast is gained by the detached garage and minimum fenestration in this direction, as well as by raising the bedroom element to provide a playroom below grade.

The glass-ended entry which divides the living and utility zones (see plan) yields an outside vista in its two main directions as well as a glimpse of the outdoors through and around the open fireplace in the third direction.

Exterior materials: bluestone paving and walks; gray stained vertical cedar boards; flush doors, glass frames and overhangs painted white.

Garden fence, blank wall and separated garage (below) serve as visual block to the east. Motor court in foreground can accommodate six cars

Ezra Stoller

Kitchen (left) has pass-through to dining area beyond; birch shelves above can be opened from either side. Both kitchen and dining areas orient to southwest

Glass walled entry (facing page) carries flagstone and cedar boards inside — demonstrates how detached garage blocks view of neighbors, creates open feeling

THE DIAMOND HOUSE

Ezra Stoller

Passage to bedroom zone (above) becomes a skylighted gallery for owner's paintings. Fluorescent tubes between skylight panels provide light at night

Birch panels in living-recreation zone (left) serve as foil for owner's treasured oriental rugs. Adjustable brass lighting fixture was designed by architects

Ezra Stoller

THE DIAMOND HOUSE

Master bedroom contains built-in ma-hogany desk unit under window; cabinet for radio, phone and books at head of beds; special wardrobe units — all archi-tect designed. Door leads to canti-levered balcony, which features adjust-able canvas sun screen

THE DESIGN APPROACH
AND THE BANK ACCOUNT

THE process by means of which these two houses came into being and the question of whether the architects' bank account became as a result fatter or leaner are points of interest architects at large may ponder.

As for the process, George Nemeny and A. W. Geller, designers of the houses, feel that the kind of architecture represented by them requires a great amount of personal, continuous attention and follow through. In starting a

which they regard as the synthesis or crystallization of their best thought at that time. They regard each house as a new experience and a lesson — not as a further example in the unfolding of a personal style. To engender a more creative attitude, they, like certain others, try to free their minds of the current clichés and too direct influences. They prefer "the open road." They keep the basic solution and all of its elements flexible as

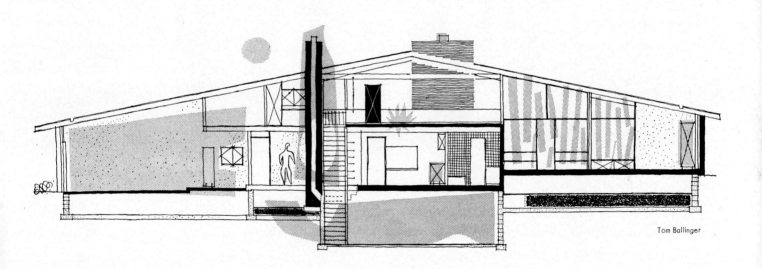

Tom Ballinger

house, their first step is a careful analysis of the client family's needs, tastes and budget. As an example, the program for the Diamond house amounted to six, single-spaced, typewritten pages. As the design is then slowly developed, client education and persuasion are often involved in the process, as well as time consuming discussions of unconventional construction and unusual details. As for drawings, the set for the Diamond house comprised thirty sheets, of which twenty were details. The foregoing examples are typical.

Philosophically, these architects try to avoid a formulated approach — they like to mix the ingredients, stir the pot, and see what happens. They explore all the avenues they think might lead to a possible solution, and after trying many of them finally arrive at an answer

long as possible, even to a point where changes are sometimes made on the job in order to secure the desired effect.

In answer to our question, "can this kind of highly personalized practice be conducted at a profit charging minimum Institute rates?" their answer was that if such a practice consisted entirely of houses, it would have a tough struggle indeed, and might not be able to survive. However, these architects find that if their commissions are in the ratio of 60 per cent residential to 40 per cent other types, they can get along well enough. Aside from that, though, Nemeny and Geller feel that the satisfaction they derive from doing the most creative job they are capable of, plus the owner's pride in his home, is much more important than making an assured profit.

Ezra Stoller

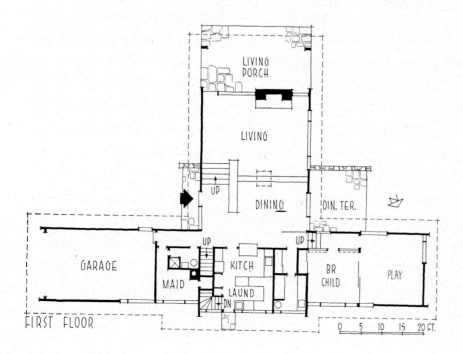

LIVING
PORCH

LIVING

UP

DINING   DIN. TER.

GARAGE

MAID   KITCH   UP   BR   PLAY
LAUND   CHILD

DN

FIRST FLOOR

0   5   10   15   20 FT.

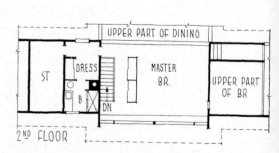

UPPER PART OF DINING

ST   DRESS   MASTER
BR.   UPPER PART
B   OF BR
DN

2ND FLOOR

A GENTLY SLOPING ROOF SHELTERS THREE LEVELS

House for Mr. & Mrs. Morton G. Mack
North Newstead, South Orange, N. J.
George Nemeny & A. W. Geller, Architects

HERE IS A HOUSE DESIGN that capitalizes on a two-story, sloping-roof building restriction by playing it up and making it the theme for a dramatic effect. An interesting T shaped plan in three levels is thus pulled into spatial unity by the single, continuous, pitched roof that shelters it — this feeling further emphasized by the simple device of painting the entire ceiling and exterior soffit a soft, sky-blue color.

The structure is honestly expressed in the living-dining-porch wing of the T: simple triangular trusses with steel tie rods, spaced 14 ft on centers.

Exterior glass frames, doors, and roof overhang fascias are painted white to contrast with the vertical redwood siding; fireplace brick is a light warm gray. Interior walls are all painted white; interior cabinets are mahogany; kitchen cabinets are white oak.

Direct elevation of living porch (opposite page) assumes an almost Mondrianesque quality in relationships of glass, brick and wood. In photo above, unity created by the single roof becomes apparent

PORCH LIVING DINING MBR

KITCH

Looking down from the master bedroom (left page) the three-level relationship can be seen best; trusses express the structure

Master bedroom bookcase (below) becomes balcony railing. Privacy is obtained by closing sliding panels; top triangle glazed

Ezra Stoller

From entry (left) five risers ascend to spacious living area which in turn opens out to sheltered porch beyond

View from living area (above) shows the bedroom balcony over kitchen-laundry

Ezra Stoller

THE MACK HOUSE

Photos above show (left) child's bedroom and playroom; (right) the kitchen and laundry.

When standing near the ground level entrance (right) one can see through to the outdoors ahead and can enter either dining area at same level or can turn left to ascend to living area. Straight through is passage to child's quarters; at near right the kitchen passthrough projects

DIAGONAL TRUSSES PERMIT FOUR-WAY VIEW

Residence of Mr. and Mrs. Arch Ekdale, San Pedro, California

Sumner Spaulding—John Rex—Architects

C. Gordon DeSwarte—Structural Engineer

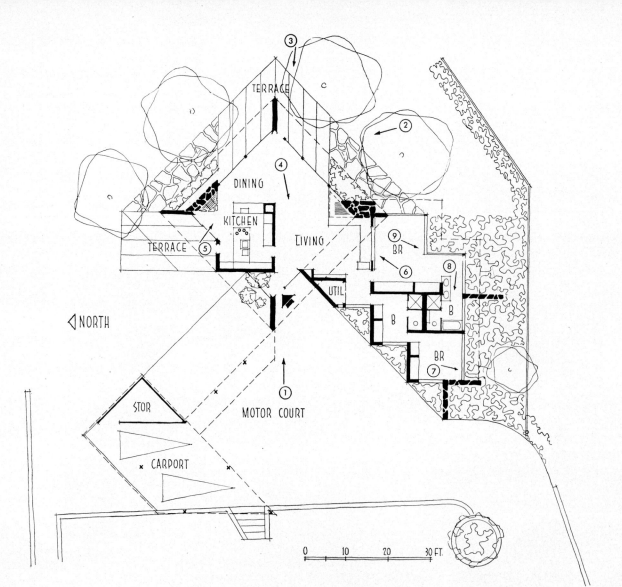

TERRACE

DINING

KITCHEN

TERRACE ⑤

LIVING

UTIL

BR ⑨

⑥

⑧

B

B

BR ⑦

③

②

④

◁ NORTH

STOR

CARPORT

MOTOR COURT

①

0 10 20 30 FT.

HOUSE WITH FOUR-WAY VIEW

1

THE SITE, high in the palos Verdes hills, commands a panoramic view in almost every direction. Given a free hand by the owner, the architect met these rare conditions by designing a high, square, glass-walled enclosure for the living area, and subordinating the other parts of the house to this dominant element. The boxiness of this unit is relieved by a roof of unique design — an inverted pyramid with its apex suspended over the center of the room and its sides sloping upward and outward until they meet the eaves 6 ft beyond the glass walls. The roof is formed by two diagonal steel trusses, supported at the four corners of the room. Solid wall fins extend from the corners out to the ends of the trusses, providing structural bracing and visual interest. The effect of this roof on the interior space is to emphasize its loftiness and its four-directional view.

High square glass-walled bay dominates the design. Bedroom wing kept low and attached to living area where it does least harm to view. Bedrooms stepped back in plan for cross ventilation and better view

2

3

4

Julius Shulman

5

Above: living room extends back into low-ceiling bedroom wing. Right: charcoal grill supplements kitchen range; not shown is soda fountain, another feature of kitchen

Below: southeast elevation. Exterior materials are redwood and fieldstone picked up on site. Carpentry is by shipwrights; all finish materials screwed and doweled

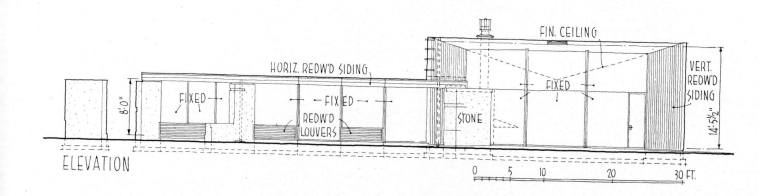

Below: sliding panels open master bedroom to living room. Sun lamps are installed in ceiling over each bed, and an intercommunication system is incorporated in headboard

6

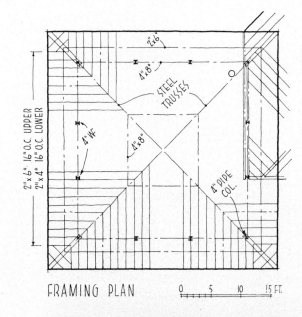

4" SLOPE

4'-9"

4"x8" A

ST 4 B 5.0   2"x6"

L 1½"x1½"x³∕₁₆"

L 1½"x1½"x³∕₁₆"

L 2"x2"x³∕₁₆"

4" ST. PIPE

1½" ST. PIPE

B   ST 4 B 5.0

2"x6"

5 EQUAL SPACES = 20'-2"

0   5 FT.

13"x13"x¼" PL.

1" SHEATHING

2"x6"

2"x6"   2"x6"
16" O.C.   CONT.

SECTION A

2"x4"   2"x6"
16" O.C.   CONT.

2"x4"

1" SHEATHING

SECTION B

2"x6"

4"x8"

STEEL TRUSSES

2"x6" 16" O.C. UPPER
2"x4" 16" O.C. LOWER

4" WF

4"x8"

4" PIPE COL.

FRAMING PLAN

0   5   10   15 FT.

Left: roof framing plan and detail of truss. Roof is 39 ft square, enclosed area 28 ft square. Ceiling 9 ft 7 in. at center of room, 13 ft 6 in. at walls. Bedroom ceilings 8 ft. Below: guest room. Opposite page, above: master bath; floors and walls terrazzo; hot water pipes form towel bars. Opposite page, below: master bedroom, looking toward lavatory. Terrazzo floors used throughout house for easy maintenance. Bedrooms ventilated by sliding panels below fixed glass. Heating is forced warm air, oil fired

HOUSE WITH FOUR-WAY VIEW

7

8

9

Samuel R. Lewis and Associates
Mechanical Engineers

Edward H. Bennett
Landscape Architect

Living room and terrace from west, shown above
in detail and below in relation to rest of house

Joseph Molitor

MOUNTAIN RIDGE

Residence of Mr. and Mrs. Edward H. Bennett

Tryon, North Carolina

Schweikher and Elting, Architects

THIS house in the mountains of North Carolina was designed for the winter use of a semi-retired city-planner and his wife. The sloping site is heavily wooded and commands a fine view to the west across a valley to the mountains. The plan permits all major rooms to enjoy the view. Separate but adjoining apartments, each with a fireplace, are provided for the owners. They share a terrace on the east, screened from the motor court by a brick wall. The big living room with terrace on two sides, has distinct areas for dining, lounging, and study. The maid's room, at the end of the service wing, has a fireplace and is practically a duplicate of the master bedroom at the other end of the house. There is no garage nor any carport in the usual sense. Instead, a projecting roof along most of the entrance side of the house, can shelter several cars at once. It also provides a covered walk to the entrance door. Entrance side of house has no glass except at dining area. The roof pitches in a single direction, upward from the entrance side. The masonry walls opposite the entrance and between study and pantry are carried above the roof to the same height as the chimneys.

Left: general view of entrance side of house seen from drive. Service wing at right, bedroom wing at left. Below: main entrance, with skylight over dining area. In foreground, terrace outside bedroom wing, separated by brick wall from entrance court

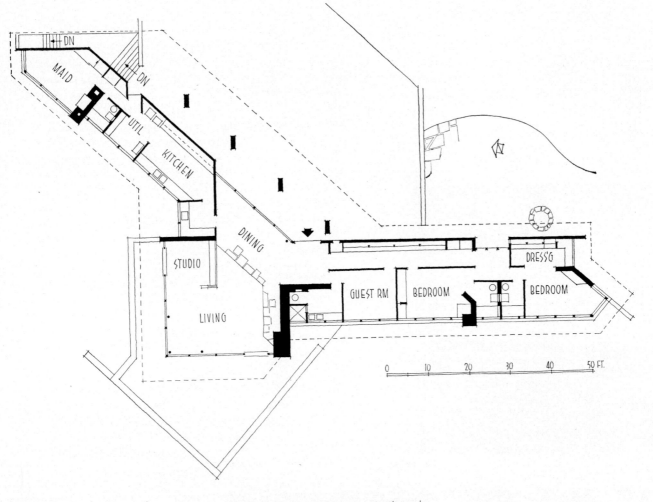

Ventilation in bedroom wing is through
single giant louver below the windows.
Bottom-hinged doors on interior drop
down to hang flush with wall

Joseph Molitor

Right: living room fireplace, terrace beyond. Below: dining area overlooking entrance court. Since roof extends almost 18 ft beyond glass wall, skylight is provided. Door to pantry at left. In both views intersecting ceiling boards give illusion of ridge or mitre; ceiling is actually one plane

End of bedroom wing, seen from outside (above) and inside (below). Bottom of page: living room terrace. Foreshortened wall is same shown on p. 20

Joseph Molitor

HOUSE ON MOUNTAIN RIDGE

Since buildings must be designed for use, restrictions of one sort or another are an inseparable part of architecture. The conditions imposed by the site, the requirements of the owner, and the limitations of the budget are all restrictions in a sense. When we speak of an architect's design as a "solution," we are referring to the problem presented by these restrictions.

Although architecture without restrictions is inconceivable, too many restrictions can easily stifle it. Up to a certain point, restrictions may actually be beneficial, by challenging the architect to do his utmost. But where the restrictions are so severe that they dictate the design of the building, they may be fatal to architecture.

In residential design the deadliest of all restrictions is an insufficient budget. This in itself is a serious obstacle, but normally not insurmountable. It is the indirect effect that is most to be feared. Where the owner must borrow heavily in order to build, the resale value of his house becomes all-important. In such a case the design of the house is often determined, not by the architect and not by the needs of the owner, but by the mortgage lender's idea of its resale value.

On the brighter side is the fact that now and then an architect has the good fortune to be able to carry an architectural idea through to fulfillment without having to compromise on any essential point. If the architect is clear in his own mind as to what he wants to say and if he has the skill to say it clearly, the result will be interesting architecture, at the very least. If what the architect has to say is important, the result may be great architecture.

The Ekdale house is a brilliant example of what can happen when site, client, and architect are all exceptional, and restrictions are not severe. A clear-cut architectural idea has been skilfully stated and carried through without compromise. The same is true of the Bennett and the Palmer houses. The Poetker house differs from these only in that its successful result was achieved in spite of extreme difficulties. Possibly this is a case where the numerous obstacles stimulated the architect and resulted in a better design than would otherwise have occurred.

Hedrich-Blessing

SITE CHOSEN FOR VIEW DESPITE DRAWBACKS

Residence of Mr. and Mrs. Joseph G. Poetker

Mt. Adams, Cincinnati, Ohio

Garriott, Becker & Bettman, Architects

O. W. Motz, Mechanical Engineer

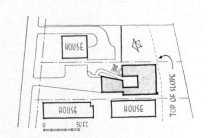

DESIGNING A HOUSE to exploit the dramatic view afforded by a site high above the city, presented many difficulties. The narrow, deep lot, in a built-up and by-passed section of the city, was hemmed in on the west by two high and ungainly frame tenements. To the east, however, lay only the unused backyard of a house built close to the street. The U-shaped plan with entrance through the court, blank west wall, and bedroom facing east, was the direct result of these site conditions.

The partially covered entrance court, adopted by necessity, proved to be one of the pleasantest features of the house. The small sheltered area is an effective contrast to the big living room with its magnificent view. The view can be enjoyed even from the court, as shown in the illustration on page 28.

Floors and walks are paved with an old local brick of a dark purplish red color. In addition to hot-water radiant heat in the floor slab, a separate hot-air system blankets the 40-ft glass wall in the living room from slots in the floor. An 8-ft roof overhang keeps out the summer sun.

SITE CHOSEN FOR VIEW

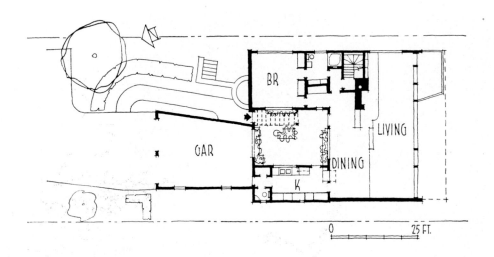

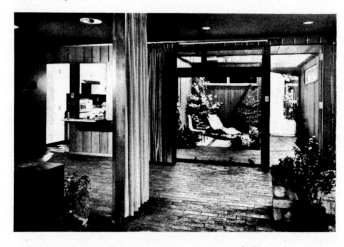

Hedrich-Blessing

House is at rear of 50 by 200 ft lot, giving privacy from street and scope for landscaping by florist owners. Turn-around and parking space for several cars is provided, shown in part at upper left of plan above. Right: entrance court seen from entry. Below: main entrance, bedroom wing at left. Opposite page: living room with view for which house was built

SITE CHOSEN FOR VIEW

Hedrich-Blessing

Left: entrance court with view through entry and living room to distant river and beyond. Kitchen at right. Trellis marks entrance walk and protects privacy of high bedroom windows from adjacent building. Below left: kitchen seen from dining room. Breakfast table folds up to close pass-through completely. Below right: dressing table in master bath

DESERT HOUSE WITH VIEW TO SOUTH

Residence of Dr. and Mrs. Paul Palmer

Phoenix, Arizona

A. Quincy Jones, Architect

Edgardo Contini, Engineer

THE DESERT SITE slopes down from Camelback Mountain on the north. To the south there is a pleasant view of the valley and the distant city. The approach is from the north. which makes it difficult to take advantage of the view of the mountain without sacrificing privacy.

The house was designed for a doctor and his wife and their two sons and three daughters. Facilities are provided for full family life, or complete separation of the two generations. A huge living-dining-playroom is the center of family life. However, if this room has been taken over by the teen-agers, the parents can entertain their friends comfortably in the study-sitting room adjacent to the master bedroom.

Alcove partitions in children's wing extend only to door-head height, facilitating future rearrangement as living needs change.

Each wing has its own outdoor living area.

Stuart A. Weiner

Stuart A. Weiner

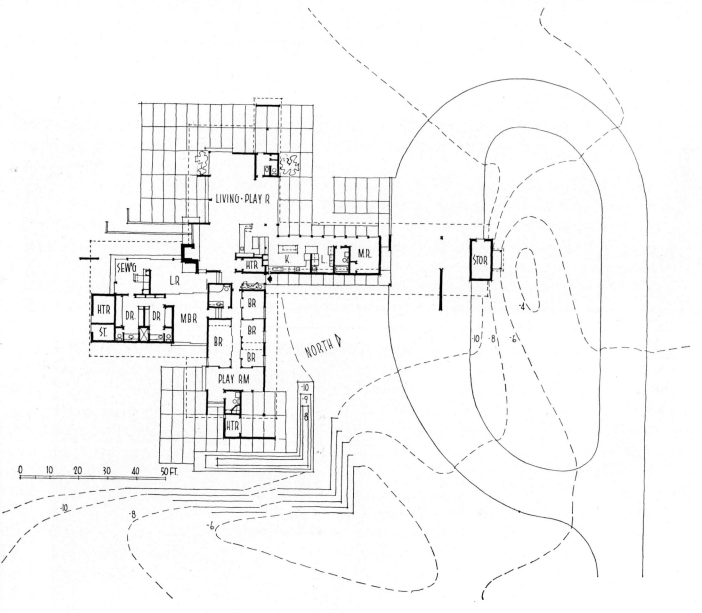

LIVING · PLAY R

SEW'G

LR

HTR

ST. DR. DR MBR

K. L. M.R.

HTR

BR

BR

BR

BR

PLAY RM

HTR

STOR

NORTH ▷

-4

-10 -8 -6

-10
-9
-8

0 10 20 30 40 50 FT.

-10

-8

-6

Opposite page: living room terrace, master wing on right. Outdoor dining is to north of living room where it is shaded from the afternoon sun and enjoys the view of Camelback Mountain. Above: children's wing and terrace. Below right: terrace outside master wing

On the plan (opposite page) separate functions are clearly expressed in the four distinct wings. The house is fully air conditioned by means of three separate package units. White gravel roofs, ceiling insulation, and large overhangs reduce the cooling load

Stuart A. Weiner

Floors are concrete, cork in the children's wing, asphalt tile in kitchen and baths. Interior finish is natural redwood or painted plywood. Behind curtains (right) sliding glass doors open to outdoor dining area. Handles in ceiling operate sliding clerestory windows

HOUSE TURNS INWARD ON PATIO FOR PRIVACY

Residence of Dr. and Mrs. William S. Beck

Los Angeles, California

Thornton M. Abell, Architect

Hillman & Nowell, Structural Engineers

THE HOUSE WAS DESIGNED for a young doctor, his wife and their two small children. The master bedroom is also a study, intended for serious work. This large, comfortable room with its own fireplace can readily be used as a second living room in the future when the children entertain their friends in the main living room. The children's bedrooms open onto their private play yard in front of the house, protected from the street by a high fence. Children can also play in the patio under supervision from the kitchen. A bedroom and bath near the entrance can be used either as a guest room or a servant's room.

Julius Shulman

With neighbors close by on each side, the house turns inward upon its patio and also opens out to the rear, which is entirely private. Seen from the street, the house is completely closed (right). In striking contrast is openness as seen from rear (above)

Julius Shulman

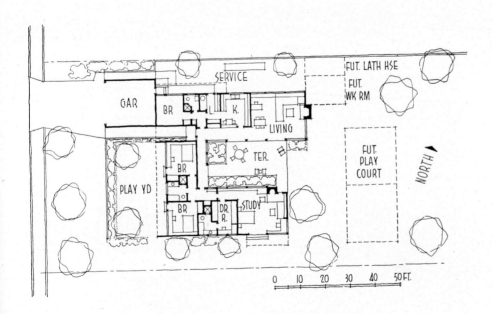

Locally popular patio plan is ideal solution for narrow lot between existing houses. U-shaped plan opens to rear (east) where property extends high up side of wooded canyon. Principal rooms open onto partially covered patio, used most of year as outdoor living room. Construction is plank and beam on exposed posts in 8 by 18-ft bays. Concrete slab floor with radiant heat

Above and opposite: three views of "outdoor living room." Absence of draperies brings indoor and outdoor rooms into closer relationship. Below: obscure glass provides privacy on other wall of living room

Above and below: master bedroom and study. Interior finish natural redwood or plywood stained yellow. Ceiling plank stained light turquoise. Structural frame, windows and doors, stained deep gray-green. Floors gray

PATIO HOUSE

HOUSE FOR SUBURBAN CORNER LOT

Residence of Miss Agnes Palley

Scarsdale, New York

Sanders—Malsin—Reiman, Architects

THE SITE is a corner lot in a highly conservative suburban community. With streets on the south and west sides of the property, the architect's problem was to provide favorable orientation along with a reasonable degree of privacy.

The house proper is a compact rectangle, 32 by 42 ft, with its shorter dimension facing the street. Needed length has been given to this elevation by means of a continuous roof across house and garage. This provides a covered walk between garage and service entrance, a convenient location for the basement stair, and on the rear a screened porch conveniently located for outdoor dining.

Concrete block walls are kept almost free of openings which is economical and also improves their appearance. Windows and doors are concentrated in wood walls, whose lightness is in pleasing contrast to the unbroken planes of masonry. The change of materials is emphasized by projecting the ends of the concrete walls beyond the plane of the wood and glass walls.

Gas-fired warm-air heater and domestic hot water heater are located in partial basement under front part of house, the remainder of the house being built over crawl space. Roof is topped with marble chips and edged with copper. Wood siding is stained fir.

Ben Schnall

View from southwest. Living room and terrace on right and service entrance on left are screened by planting

Above: view from southeast, showing rear elevation of wood and glass contrasted with almost unbroken masonry wall on south. Skylight and terrace sunshades add interest to exterior appearance and help to avoid boxy look often seen in small flat-roofed houses. Plot plan (below) shows house located near north property line in order to provide maximum privacy on south. Garage screens house on north. Bedrooms are on rear facing east. Living room is on south and opens onto terrace, screened from street by fence. Right: built-in seat utilizes structural column

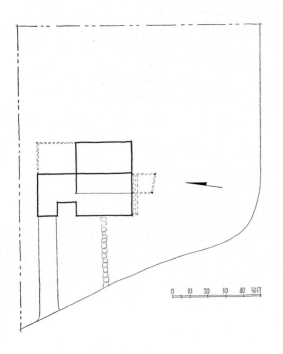

0 10 20 30 40 50 FT

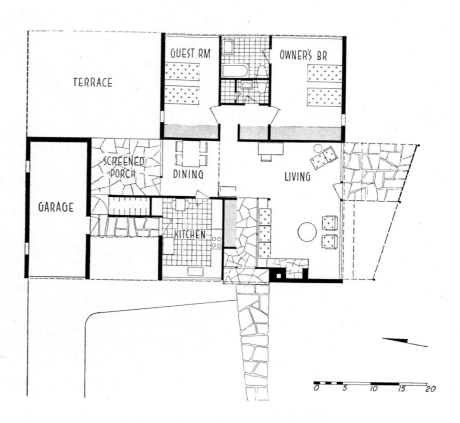

Privacy for terrace is provided by planting on west and fence on south. Fence and large trees provide afternoon shade. Louvered sunshades protect living room glass. Beams support sunshades, brace fence, furnish frame for future awnings, and tie whole together to form interesting spatial composition

SUBURBAN HOUSE

Continuous clerestory at rear of living-dining area provides extra light and ventilation, also adds interest and height to low-ceilinged room. Screened dining porch can be seen beyond dining room (right)

HOME FOR CARTOONISTS' FAMILY

Residence of Stanley and Janice Berenstain

Elkins Park, Pennsylvania

Norman N. Rice, Architect

THIS HOUSE for the well-known cartoonists and their young son, was built on a 75 ft suburban lot with existing houses close by. By setting the house well back and angling it in relation to the street, direct view of the neighboring houses was avoided and a pleasant southerly exposure provided for the living area. This also permitted the studio to face more nearly north.

At the 1951 Exhibit of the Philadelphia Chapter, A.I.A., the house received the Home Builders' Association award as "the most distinguished suburban house by a Philadelphia architect."

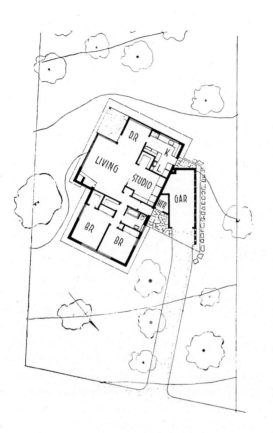

Dan Moerder

Exterior walls are waylite block or cedar siding. Interior mahogany plywood

Plan was kept compact by making studio inside room with skylight and window-type air-conditioner. Studio walls natural redwood. Below: studio can be opened to living room for spacious entertaining

CARTOONISTS' HOUSE

Dan Moerder

SUBURBAN SITES AND MODEST BUDGETS

INCREASE DESIGN RESTRICTIONS

The last four houses, all built on suburban lots and on modest budgets, have more restrictions to contend with than the first four. This may make them less interesting perhaps as architecture, but more interesting probably to architects, since they are nearer to the type of problem most often encountered by the residential designer. In these houses the emphasis shifts from exploiting a view to protecting privacy. While larger houses can rely upon remoteness for privacy, suburban houses must resort to such devices as high windows, obscure glass, planting and fences.

Of the suburban group, the Beck house is remarkably successful. It accepts its limitations gracefully, states its ideas clearly, and carries them out skilfully. The design is notable for its easy confidence and the absence of any straining for effect. There is no pioneering here, but instead the calm assurance that comes from working in a well-established tradition.

The house designed for sale has special limitations, in addition to having usually very stringent site and budget restrictions. Designing a house that will be suited to the needs of a large number of unknown families is more difficult than tailoring one to fit a single family. In this case the architect's client is an operative builder; he is not interested in living in the house, but in selling it. His first requirement from the architect is a house that will sell.

This is a field which architects have generally avoided in the past. But in recent years, with encouragement from Southwest Research Institute, the National Association of Home Builders, and the American Institute of Architects, many leading architects have entered this field. Another way of saying the same thing is that many operative builders are beginning to realize the value to them of good architectural services. In this connection it is interesting to note that while some builders are still avoiding architects entirely and others are shopping in the basement of the profession for the "cheapest" architect they can find, Eichler Homes is currently employing two of the West Coast's most distinguished architectural firms.

An unusual opportunity is presented in these pages to compare the work of one of these architects, A. Quincy Jones of Los Angeles, in two very different fields of residential design — a large custom-designed house for the Arizona desert and a small house designed (with Frederick E. Emmons) for a builder's development in northern California. Each of these houses is notably successful within its own field, and in spite of the great disparity between the two, there are perceptible similarities which mark their common origin.

DEVELOPMENT HOUSE OF HIGH QUALITY

Eichler Homes

Palo Alto, California

Frederick E. Emmons — A. Quincy Jones, Architects

Anshen and Allen, Architects: Site Planning

THIS is the model house for a 94-house development known as Fairmeadow. Four other models are offered, each with several variations. Prices for these three-bedroom, two-bath houses range from $14,750 for the model shown here to $15,750 for a model with an extra "all-purpose" room. Prices include the lot (6000 sq ft minimum), concrete terraces, redwood fences, electric range and refrigerator. Deducting $2500 for the lot, the cost of the house itself is less than $10 per square foot.

The circular site plan was an effort to give interest to a flat, treeless site. It resulted in 50 fewer lots than in the conventional grid scheme.

This development and three others by the same architects and builders were recently cited by the Housing Research Foundation of Southwest Research Institute as "the developments built during 1951 which best express the aims of the Quality House Program." These aims (see ARCHITECTURAL RECORD, May 1950, pp. 125–127) are briefly to improve the quality of the houses built by speculative builders. From the beginning the Institute has emphasized that this can come about only by getting good architects to work closely with good builders. Fairmeadow, already highly successful, is convincing proof that such collaboration is beneficial to architect, builder, and the public.

Randal Partridge

High bedroom windows face the street

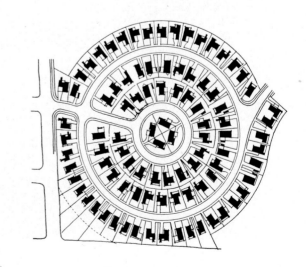

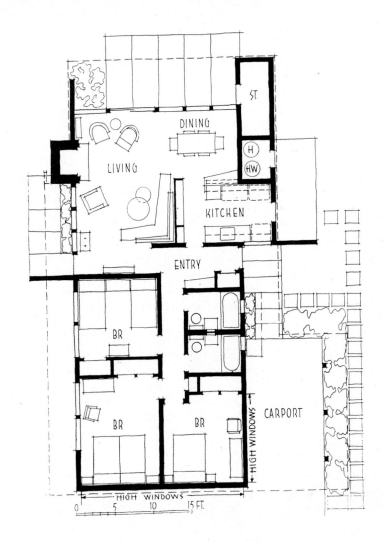

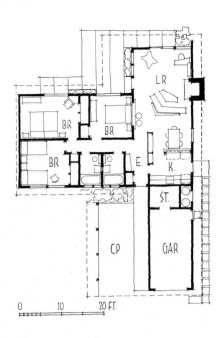

Rondal Partridge

Construction is plank and beam on radiant heated slab. Exterior finish stained redwood siding. Interior finish, redwood plywood, mahogany plywood (kitchen cabinets in view above), or redwood siding. Outlets provided for telephone and television. Roofs tar and gravel, built-in gutters. All models have fireplaces

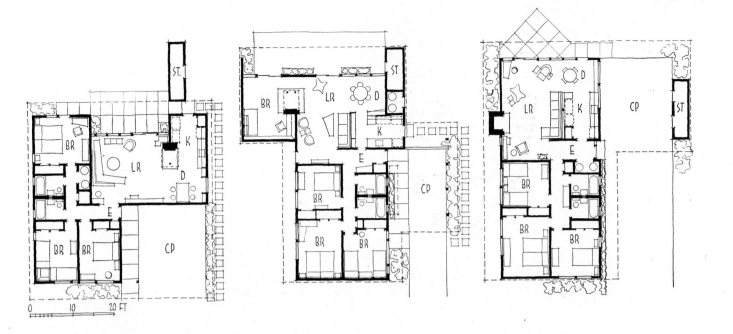

Plan of model house, opposite page, extreme left. Plans of the four other models above. All have bedrooms on street side, living areas at rear opening out to terraces, fenced for privacy

All models have entries, all but one have completely private internal circulation. Below: six-foot overhang makes terrace into porch. Glass wall at left of fireplace opens onto side terrace

Ezra Stoller

The exterior of the house combines vertical red cypress siding and roman brick. Above: side façade and dining terrace overlook garden and view. Top left: entrance drive at front. The two remaining photos show closeups of the studio and the rear façade

HOUSE FOR AN ACTIVE FAMILY

Sands Point, Long Island, New York

Albert Kennerly, Architect

THIS EXPANSIVE HOUSE was designed to provide for the somewhat formal way of life of a family with an amazing number of interests and activities. The architect was asked to include facilities for painting, sculpture, pottery work, piano playing, ballet practice, ping pong, photography, accommodations for extra guests, a wine and rare foods room, a dog room opening onto two dog runs, parking space for about 20 cars — plus the usual quarters for a family of four and a staff of servants. It was further specified that no family bedroom be on the ground floor level, yet a full stair was not acceptable.

These requirements have been skillfully worked into a very coherent, open plan which also provides a good degree of privacy and segregation for the various activities. The structural frame of the house is of Douglas Fir, with exterior walls of red cypress in a natural, lime-rubbed finish, and red roman brick. Roofing is built-up tar and gravel or white tile. Interior walls are finished in sand float plaster, oak paneling or figured gum. Floors in the main living areas are random-width teak doweled to the sub-floor; others are waxed common brick or asphalt tile. The clients worked very closely with the architect, especially in the design of the interiors and selection of furnishings, textures and colors.

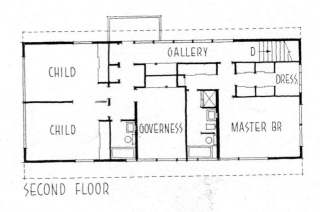

SECOND FLOOR

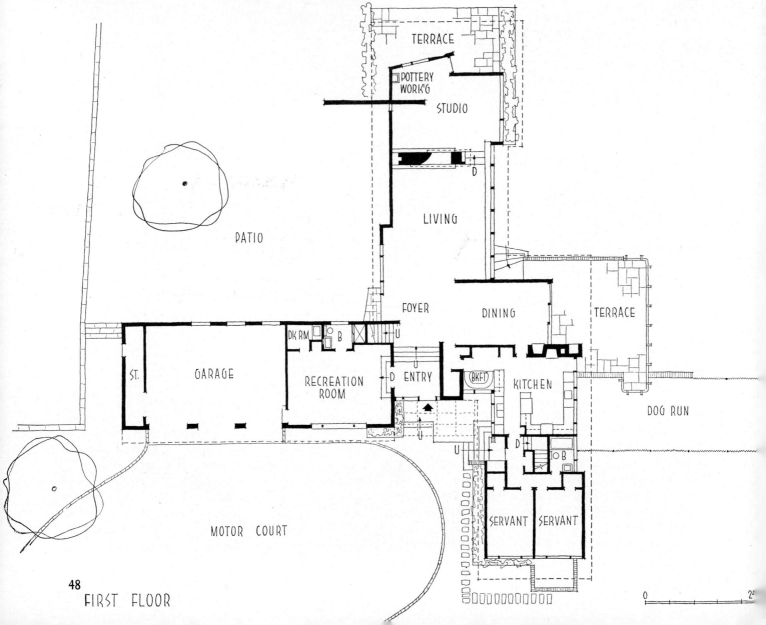

FIRST FLOOR

48

Ezra Stoller

Front entrance (photo far left) is sheltered by trellis; bay directly over door is glazed. Living room (above and right) has textured, warm colored finishes

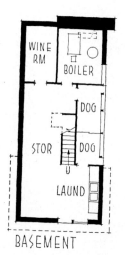

BASEMENT

Second floor bedrooms are only a half flight of stairs above living rooms, due to use of a small entry stair. The two children's rooms (right) are identical, separated by folding door. A governess' room is adjoining. Master bedroom suite is on same level

Ezra Stoller

Kitchen (above) is efficiently planned, has dining nook for 5

Richard Garrison

SIMPLE DESIGN FOR SOUTHERN LIVING

Residence for Dr. Ann Stuckey
Griffin, Georgia

Aeck Associates, Architects

THE QUIET, UNOBTRUSIVE CHARACTER of this house set
in a grove of pines somewhat belies a skillful handling
of its structural and design elements. Use was made of
the sloping site to divide the plan into three sections: on
the lower level are the utility areas — boiler room, storage, carport, entry — and a short flight of outside steps
to the kitchen; on the main level are the living areas,
flanked by kitchen and guest room; at the top level is a
suite for the owner which can be closed off for privacy
and a sense of security. All levels are connected by
ramps, frankly used to provide a gracious entrance, and
in this case fitted in without an extravagant waste of
space. The structure uses brick in all lower sections,
with lighter-weight pine boards on second floor exteriors
and above most of the window openings. The butterfly
roof with its wide overhangs permits larger, and protected, fenestration for major rooms.

DR. ANN STUCKEY RESIDENCE

*The property slopes up a half-story in the width
of the house, gives ground level entrance to all
rooms but owner's suite. Heating is by a hot
water radiant system in the ceilings*

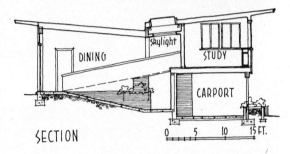

DINING   Skylight   STUDY

CARPORT

SECTION

0   5   10   15 FT.

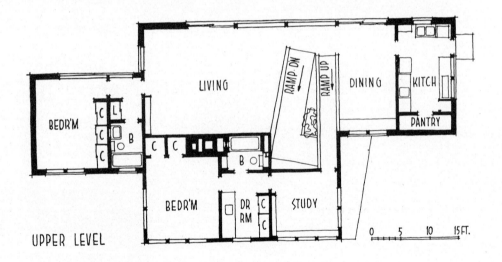

BEDR'M   C L   B
C   ○   B
C

LIVING   RAMP DN   RAMP UP   DINING   KITCH

C   C   ○ B   PANTRY

BEDR'M   DR RM   C C   STUDY

UPPER LEVEL

0   5   10   15 FT.

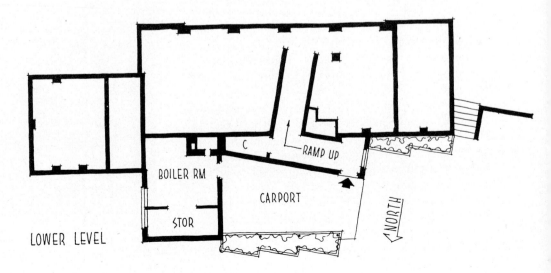

BOILER RM   C   RAMP UP

STOR   CARPORT

LOWER LEVEL

NORTH

Living area (below) has generous scale, great sense of spaciousness. Ramps have skylight above, serve to separate sitting and dining areas. Interior walls are painted plaster

Hedrich-Blessing

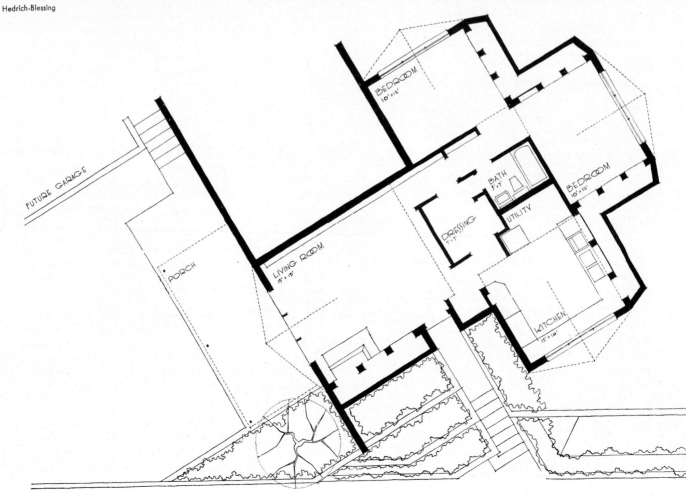

FUTURE GARAGE

PORCH

LIVING ROOM
15' x 19'

BEDROOM
10' x 12'

DRESSING
7' x 7'

BATH
5' x 7'

UTILITY

BEDROOM
10' x 12'

KITCHEN
12' x 16'

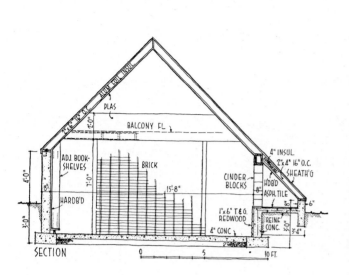

SECTION

UNIQUE CONCEPT PROVIDES LOW COST HOUSE

Residence of Henry C. Toll, Architect

Denver, Colorado

A minimum of walls—in the usual sense—characterizes this house both inside and out; less expensive roofing surfaces most of exterior, central utility core separates interior rooms. Floor slab rests on footing base 2 ft 4 in. below grade (see section above). Terraces are faced with brick and concrete because of water shortage, lack of grass

A NEW APPROACH to the problem of meeting Building Code requirements with low cost construction has been made by Architect Henry Toll in the design of his own house. Two major requirements of the Denver Code are masonry construction, and a footing depth of at least 3 ft below grade. Local investigation, however, proved that roofing was the cheapest exterior finish in that vicinity. These three items were combined to form an extremely interesting structural system for the house. Floor slabs were poured 2 ft 4 in. below grade, level with the top of minimum depth footings. To classify the house as masonry construction, 8 by 8 in. cinder block columns approximately 3 ft high are placed on top of the foundation, and carry a box girder on which the roof joists rest. A slab was poured on grade outside the wall line, and the edge of the slab tied to the back of the box girder. Thus masonry is reduced to about 1/10 of the usual amount, and the exterior is almost entirely roofing. No ceiling is required for a tension member, as the roof thrust goes directly to grade, so a saving was also made on lumber. Rooms are about 6 ft 3 in. high at plate line, 15 ft at center. Orientation and overhangs were carefully studied to reduce sun's heat and glare — a problem even in winter in the Denver area.

The four gable ends of the house are virtually all glass with ample overhangs for sun control, good provision for cross ventilation. The unique structural system provides much extra storage space at counter height without sacrificing floor space. Ceilings serve as radiant heat panels, have ¼-in. copper pipe embedded in plaster

Master bedroom on balcony, visible in photo above, is at roof intersection, overlooks all rooms of house. Walls are redwood, floors asphalt—or green ceramic—tile

Hedrich-Blessing

HOUSE ON A NEW ENGLAND HILLTOP

Residence for Mr. and Mrs. George W. Wilcox

Greenfield, Massachusetts

James A. Britton, Architect

Joseph W. Molitor

A hipped roof, wide overhangs and shaped cornices give a distinctive character to the otherwise simple design of this house. The east front (left) overlooks view; entrance is on west, has good sun protection

THE COMPACT, SIMPLE DESIGN of this house, with its natural finishes, reflects not only its setting, but also a tempered view towards contemporary design. Such details as shaped cornices and a hipped roof over the main portion of the house considerably soften the external appearance. The east elevation, which overlooks the view, has large windows opening off the major rooms, and a sheltered terrace. The entrance facade, on the other hand, is kept relatively closed and achieves a sense of solidity and privacy.

The house is wood frame, with foundation walls of cinder blocks. Siding is redwood, with a preservative stain finish; the roof is surfaced with asphalt shingles. Interiors are finished with plaster walls, either painted or papered, and oak floors. A full basement is under the main portion of the house, and contains the furnace for the warm air heating system, laundry, and provision for a future recreation room. The basement is lighted by steel areaways with iron grate covers. The large chimney wall is of fieldstone.

Joseph W. Molitor

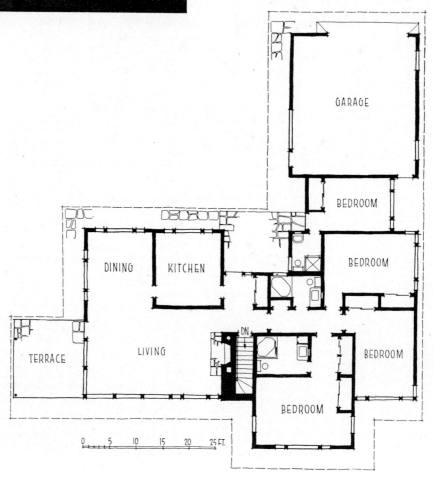

GARAGE

BEDROOM

BEDROOM

DINING KITCHEN

BEDROOM

DN

TERRACE LIVING

BEDROOM

0 5 10 15 20 25 FT.

Photo at far left shows garage wing from entrance porch. A 4-ft overhang shelters walk, continues around south and east sides of house for sun protection (smaller photo, left). Two views of living room are shown directly above. Kitchen (right) has all-electric equipment. Below: north elevation

HOUSE DESIGNED FO

Residence for Mr. and Mrs. Roland Phillips

Miami, Florida

Igor B. Polevitzky, Architect

HE SUB-TROPICS

THE unusual character of this Florida house is the result of the architect's great interest in developing large, but inexpensive, semi-protected living areas for houses in sub-tropical climates. In this example, a considerable amount of extra living space is provided by the use of an inexpensive wood frame, partial roofing, and baffle walls for privacy. This screened-in "atmospheric envelope" can reportedly be used for 95 per cent of the weather conditions. A minimum of completely closed-in areas is provided for use during the few really cold days in the area. These rooms are all interconnected, as the occasional cold weather makes it impractical to use only outdoor passageways.

The Douglas Fir frame was designed to withstand hurricane winds of 150 miles per hour, and is anchored in reinforced concrete footings. Exterior walls are concrete block and cement brick; the roof is 2-in. composition board.

SECOND FLOOR

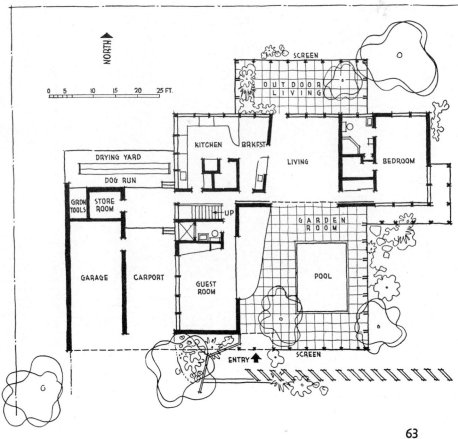

Rudi Rada

Privacy is gained for screened areas by use of low baffle wall on street side. All windows are fitted with glass or wood jalousies

Floors throughout the house are terrazzo; interior walls are plaster, plywood or cypress. Living room and guest room can be closed off with large sliding doors

Charles R. Pearson

ISLAND WEEK-END HOUSE FOR ALL-YEAR USE

Country House for Mr. Richard Lea

Lopez Island, San Juan Group, Washington

Lionel H. Pries, Architect

A DRAMATIC, isolated site which faces an often-stormy strait affords the owners of this house a retreat from the bustle of Seattle, 100 miles away. Designed for year-round week-end occupancy, the house is set off by half-mile stretches of beach on either side and by heavy woods behind. It is constructed of concrete block, clear-finished on the exterior, painted on the interior. Floors are tobacco-brown concrete and ceilings are clear-lacquered cedar. The sodded roof, which helps tie the low-spreading house to its setting, never needs trimming, since salt spray breaking over it stunts the native grasses and Japanese Iris with which it is planted.

Casual nature of house is pointed up by decorative effects, including painted motif on underside of entry and copper "thunderbird" sculpture atop chimney

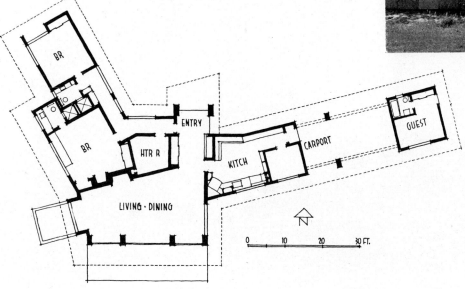

Charles R. Pearson

Simplicity of interior offers pleasant, effective contrast to the dramatic site, as in entry, above. Living room, above right and below, has glass doors leading to terrace, can be thrown open to breezes from the sound

RESIDENCE OF MR. AND MRS. E. J. GREANEY

Honolulu, T.H.

Vladimir Ossipoff, Architect

R. O. Thompson, Landscape Architect
Robert Ansteth's, Ltd., Interior Decorator

R. Wenkam Photos

IN PLAN, this house is characteristic of Hawaii, with sliding glass doors opening the main living area to surrounding lanais, or terraces. At first glance, however, it does not seem at all typical of the open architecture of the Islands. True, it has a balcony, but the high stone wall gives it a closed-in look which is surprising, particularly as the house faces the ocean. The reason is this: the house is situated on the slopes of the famous Diamond Head — slopes so steep that retaining walls were required along two sides of the property. (The stone used for the walls was excavated on the site, and the excavation in turn was used to form the lanai at the rear of the house.)

The architect obviously gave considerable thought to how the house would look against its background. As the photo shows, the horizontal emphasis, the varied levels, and the low hipped roof echo the contours of the mountain itself.

Exterior of the house is hollow cement block and rough Northwest pine which has been given a weathered finish; the tan of the pine blends with the warm dark brown of the stonework. The roof is cedar shakes, the foundation masonry and concrete. Ceilings are acoustic plaster and, upstairs, a local cane fiberboard with a pleasant texture and both thermal and acoustic insulating qualities.

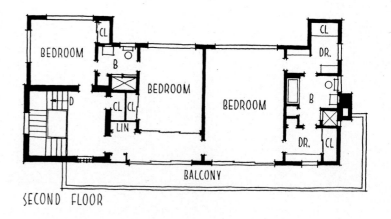

The site is both steep and irregular, sloping from 132 to 116 ft along northern edge and from 138 to 106 ft along southern. Elevation of the turn-around is 118 ft, that of the house and terraces 126. Garage is under the service wing

SECOND FLOOR

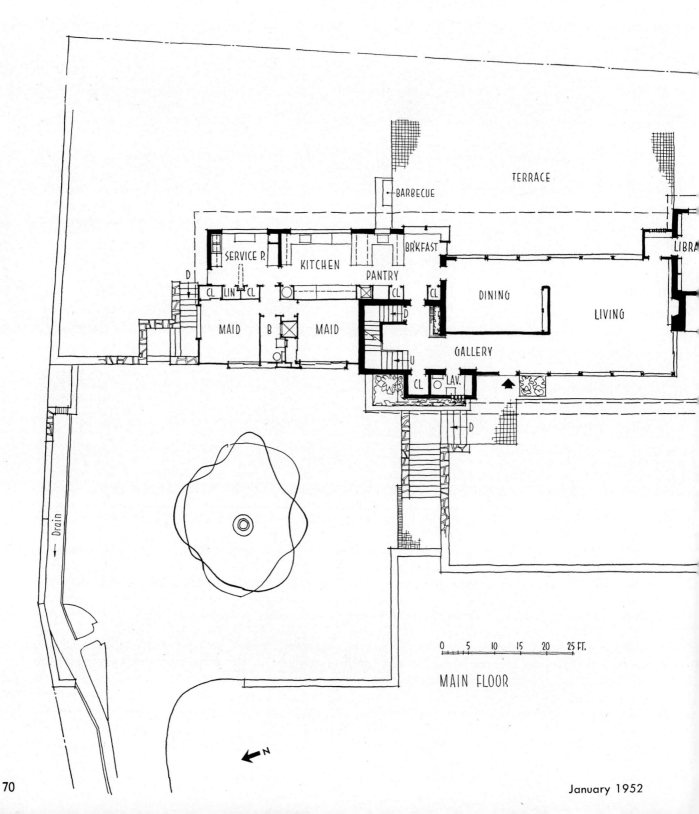

MAIN FLOOR

Right: barbecue is at one end of rear lanai, out of the way, but handy to kitchen. It serves effectively to terminate sitting area and shut off service wing from terrace

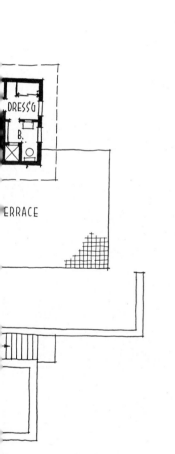

DRESS'G

B.

ERRACE

R. Wenkam Photos

Upper or rear lanai is paved with concrete blocks using a coral aggregate; joints are planted with a Japanese moss grass. Wires above are to carry vines to provide needed shade in middle of day

GREANEY HOUSE

Sliding glass doors in library (right) and elsewhere throughout house are hung with split Hong Kong reed. Floors are ohia, a Hawaiian hardwood. Below: another view of upper terrace, with living room at left and library at right

R. Wenkam Photos

Above, left: stairs to main entrance. Below, left: living room from entrance hall; floor here is black rubber tile, fireplace is gray marble. Above and below, second floor hall has sliding doors to balcony. Note louvered sliding doors of center bedroom, which has only one exposure

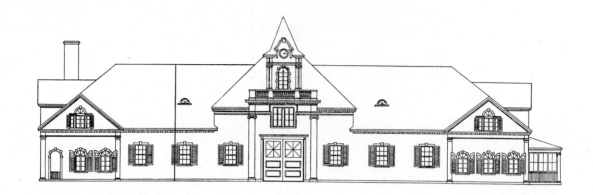

VICTORIAN STABLE BECOMES

Ben Schnall

House for Mrs. Alma Morgenthau

Lattingtown, Long Island, N. Y.

Herman Herrey, Architect

MODERN HOUSE

THIS STRIKING ADAPTATION of part of a Victorian stable for contemporary residence is the result of a series of carefully considered compromises between the qualities of the original building and those desired in the remodeled house. At the beginning of the project, the architect found himself confronted with sections of a dilapidated but still pretentious stable- and carriage-hall building, located in the midst of a lovely old park. The land had been divided through the center of the building, and the middle hall demolished. Both architect and client felt that the original structure had a pleasant mellowness, "a composite of age, weather, wear and patina that can go far in compensating for architectural deficiencies in an old house." It was reasoned that this quality "explains why sensitive people accept as greatly pleasing things that they might not tolerate in a fairly new building." Thus a conscious, deliberate effort was made to preserve this atmosphere — especially in the choice of materials and finishes — without any sacrifice of plan or design efficiency. The result is a fresh design that should not have to depend on a state of newness for effect.

Only the southern wing of the stable (portion to left of vertical line in sketch) was used in final house; photo at upper right is from same angle as the drawing

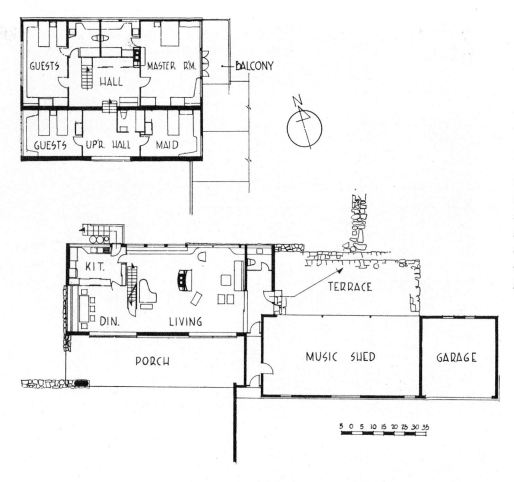

GUESTS MASTER R'M.

HALL — BALCONY

GUESTS UP'R. HALL MAID

KIT.

DIN. LIVING

TERRACE

PORCH

MUSIC SHED GARAGE

5 0 5 10 15 20 25 30 35

The main portion of the house was adapted from the carriage hall, retained only major parts of structure. Music shed and garage were transformed with only minor alterations from stable wing. House is site of annual Locust Valley Music Festival

Ben Schnall

It was desired to save as much as possible of the original structure for economy. The complicated roofs, however, were completely out of scale with the revised design, and were removed except for one large truss on the south. This was refashioned into a rectangular truss, and a simple built-up roof was sloped from it down to the north (see eave details at right — scale is in inches). Problems were also posed by the existence of four different floor levels. These were solved by converting the high-ceilinged, concrete-floored space to the south into an open porch, and by sloping the redwood siding of the upper story to conform with the 3 ft difference in floor level. The lower floor exterior was left stuccoed as it had been before. Interior partitions were rearranged to provide a convenient plan. All mechanical equipment is new, and is kept simple and unobtrusive.

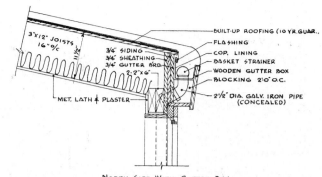

NORTH SIDE WITH GUTTER BOX

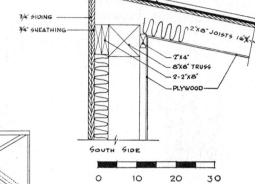

SOUTH SIDE

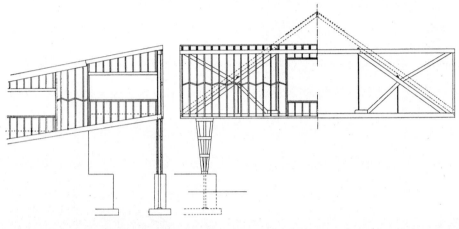

The original variations in floor levels were retained for economy. West elevation of upper floor was sloped to unify the two different levels. A rectangular truss, refashioned from an existing truss, spans new porch

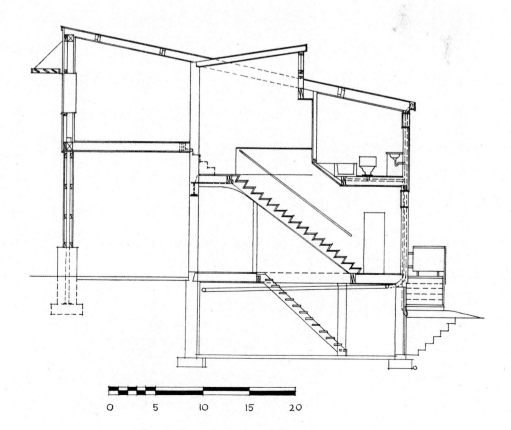

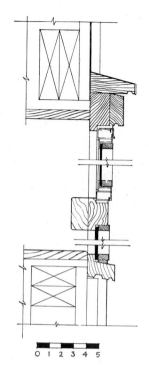

The living area (above and below) was planned to permit entertaining of large groups; broad windows open on park. Both fixed and metal casement windows have wood surrounds for uniformity, as in kitchen window detail above right (scale is in inches)

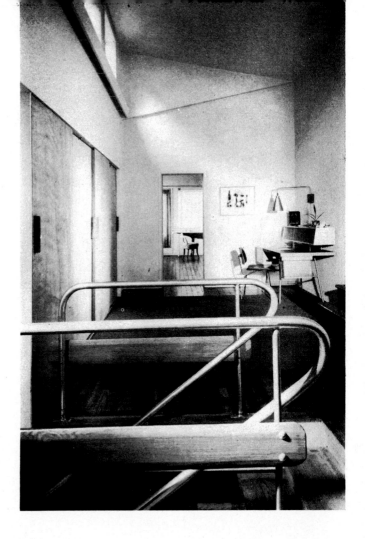

The existing stairs were opened up toward living and dining spaces, with a new railing planned to make rooms seem as open as possible. Large central hall on second floor (right) is lighted by dormer windows, has bank of storage closets. Interior walls are plaster, floors maple

Ben Schnall

Maynard Parker

FOUR HOUSES WITH EXCELLENT SITES

1. CALIFORNIA: LANDSCAPED CANYON

Residence of Mrs. Zola Hall, Los Angeles   **Edla Muir, Architect**
Edward Huntsman, Landscape Architect

THIS CALIFORNIA HOUSE was designed not only around a lovely site, but around a natural landscaping plan as well. The canyon in which it is located was once used for a botanical project; much of the planting and the foundations of the pool were already in place when the owner bought the property.

The house was placed with its long side facing the pool; living room and master bedroom are on this side, opening to a terrace cantilevered over the pool. The children's rooms are close to the main entrance. Since the

children are still small, ease of maintenance was an important consideration in the design of the house, and especially in the selection of materials. The entrance hall, for instance, is floored with acid-stained concrete; rough troweled and waxed, to minimize the carrying of dirt into the main part of the house.

Construction is wood frame on concrete foundation. Exterior walls are random width, saw-surfaced redwood. The house won an Honor Award in the recent Southern California A.I.A. Honor Awards Program.

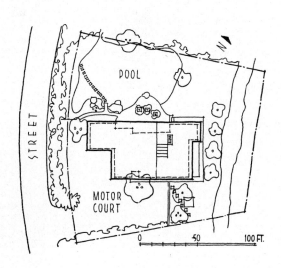

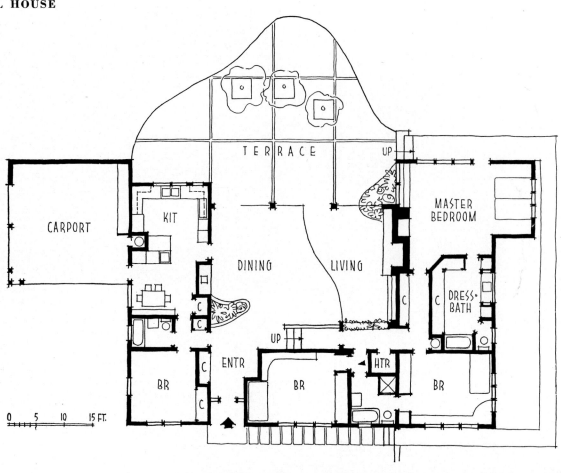

CARPORT

KIT

TERRACE

UP

MASTER
BEDROOM

DINING

LIVING

C

C

C

DRESS·
BATH

C

ENTR

UP

BR

BR

HTR

BR

0   5   10   15 FT.

Skylight in living room was an afterthought, the architect says. "During construction," she explains, "tops of eucalyptus trees were visible between rafters and were so effective that we installed clear, polished wire-glass instead of sheathing and roofing." Living room ceiling is Douglas fir, saw-surfaced and painted one coat, then wiped off to give a gray stained look; walls are redwood

One of owner's requirements was a housekeeper's room strategically located for supervision of the children, and suitable for future family use if desired; placement next to kitchen and across entrance hall from children's rooms was ideal solution. Bedroom hall was opened up with planting box and rail to add to apparent size of living room and at same time bring light to the hall. A motion picture screen on a roller is installed above the bar in dining area (see plan); projector is operated from closet in hall at opposite end of the room, with bookcase conceiling projector ports. Note excellent storage space all through the house, and convenient pass-through from kitchen to terrace

Maynard L. Parker

Residence of Mr. and Mrs. Albert Keep

Williamstown, Massachusetts

E. H. and M. K. Hunter, Architects

Looking at the sweep of rolling fields in the photo above, it is not hard to imagine why the owner laid down as his chief requirement a house with an open feeling.

The architects used the sloping site for a living room wing of one and a half stories and a two-story kitchen-bedroom wing. The desired openness was achieved mainly in the intermediate-level, high-ceilinged and spacious living room which has one wall entirely of glass; at one end of the room stairs lead up to the balcony connecting the second-floor bedrooms and study, and down to the first-floor library-dining room

Joseph Molitor

and kitchen. This upward and downward view adds materially to the open feeling of the living room. Built-in cabinets were used instead of railings on the balcony. A felicitous touch was the use of color on the balcony: a bright yellow curtain to cut off the upper story entirely; a bright red curtain to close off, either partially or wholly, the upstairs study; and bright blue burlap walls in the study, clearly visible from the living room. These pure-color curtains and burlap can be used in various combinations to give color to what is, in effect, one wall of the living room; the rest of the room is in quiet grays and whites.

A tremendous amount of book storage space was one of the owner's principal requirements. The architects supplied floor-to-ceiling shelves on two sides of the living room, and additional shelves in the library. Then they made a bet with the owner that he couldn't fill so much space. They lost the bet!

Foundation of the house is poured concrete, framing is wood. Exterior walls are rift-sawn fir, stained. The house is fully insulated and has radiant panel heating — in floors on lower level and ceilings on upper. The living room has ventilating louvers under the large south windows.

*One-and-a-half story living room wing opens to south terrace;
slatted roof overhang protects glass wall on this side from
too much sun. Below windows are ventilating louvers*

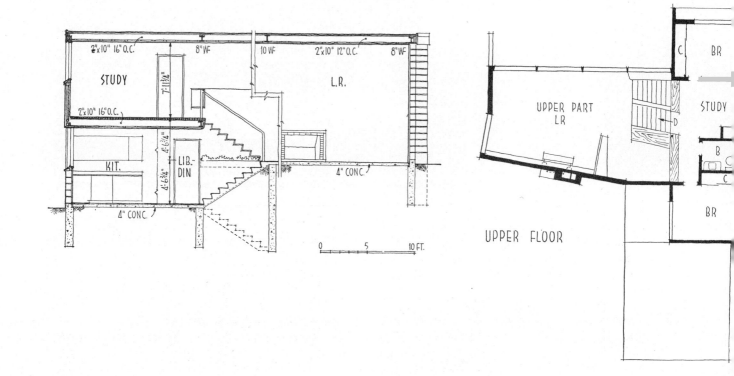

Joseph Molitor

Above left: on north side, house slopes steeply down toward garage on lowest level; living room wall here is windowless brick, with floor-to-ceiling bookshelves on interior. Above: at southwest corner of house, one bedroom projects over lower-level library-dining room (below)

KEEP HOUSE

Interior of the house is much con-
cerned with books, as these
photos show. Right: looking from
living room up toward balcony
study and bedrooms, and down
to library-dining room. Below, and
below right: living room has floor-
to-ceiling book-shelves on two
walls, completely filled

Joseph Molitor

3. ALABAMA: ROCKY LEDGE

Residence of Dr. and Mrs. W. C. Kennedy

Florence, Alabama

Turner & Northington, Architects

Jack Holmes

THIS SMALL ALABAMA HOUSE was planned as a lakeside retreat for its owners — and a retreat it certainly is. It is situated on an almost inaccessible rocky ledge jutting out into Lake Wilson; a private drive, some two miles long, terminates in a turnaround and parking area 25 ft above the house itself. From there, limestone steps wind down the side of the rock to the entrance terrace.

As originally planned, the house was to be built in two stages and used only for weekends until the bedroom wing was added. Actually, however, it is already being used as a year-round residence. When the new wing is added, it will be an entirely separate structure occupying an adjacent ledge; a glazed bridge spanning the deep crevasse between ledges will connect it with the living room wing.

The house is of wood construction with timber connectors used in all connections between beams, columns and rafters. The exterior is cypress, oiled and bleached. Interior walls are cypress and plywood, both natural and wiped. Floors are white concrete with terrazzo strips. The roof is covered with white marble chips — partly to provide a heat reflecting surface, and partly because the first view of the house (from the parking area) is of the roof.

KENNEDY HOUSE

The house is surrounded on three sides by terraces, each of which serves a different need. Eventually there will also be a lower terrace at water's edge, where a boathouse is to be constructed (see plan)

Living room has three 8- by 8-ft sliding glass doors along one side. Fireplace wall is stone, with copper trim; ceiling is of 2- by 2-ft striated plywood squares, laid opposing. Opposite: piano is recessed into the wall, with keyboard exposed and louvers above to direct sound into the room

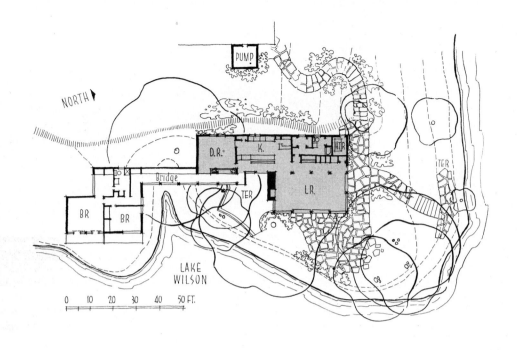

PUMP

NORTH▶

D.R.   K.

LR.

Bridge   TER

BR   BR

LAKE
WILSON

0   10   20   30   40   50 FT.

Jack Holmes

4. NEW YORK: RESERVOIR VIEW

House in Westchester County

Edelbaum & Webster,
Architects

Landscape Architect: Entourage Inc.
James C. Rose, Consultant

Contractor: Joseph Moje

LIKE MANY CITY DWELLERS who move to the country, the owners of this house purchased a site with a pleasant view and instructed their architects to make the most of that view. The 12-acre property, within commuting distance of New York City, is in a rural area where good hunting and fishing abound; it consists of rolling fields fringed with trees, and overlooks a city reservoir and pine-covered hills.

The house was placed on the brow of a southern slope, 1500 ft back from the road and facing the reservoir. Its T-shaped plan not only gives all main rooms a share in the view, but also separates the service and approach areas from the living area. The bedroom wing, at the east end of the house, is two-storied, with the master suite half a story up from the living room, and the son's room and study-guest room a half story below the main level. The master suite has its own sun terrace, dressing room and spacious bath (with two wash basins — one at standing height, the other at sitting height). The lower-level study-guest room has a stone fireplace, built-in desk and files, right-angled daybeds with a corner blanket-storage unit, and built-in drawers. The son's room has its own entrance, and even has a cork wall for pin-ups.

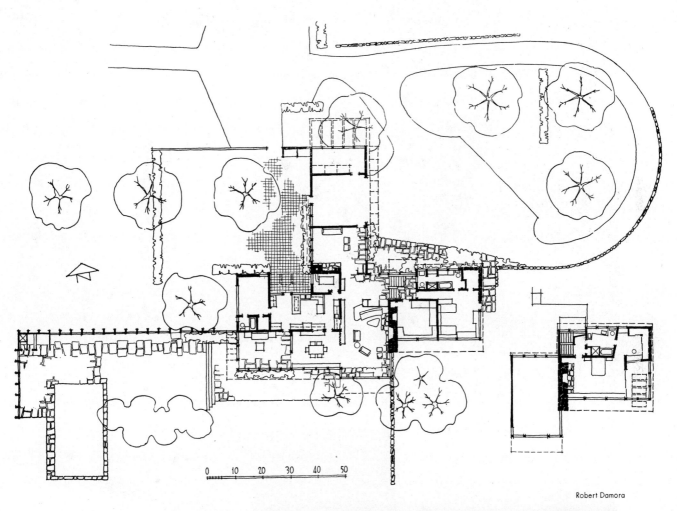

0 10 20 30 40 50

Robert Damora

Local rough stone and natural cypress boarding were chosen for the exterior to harmonize with the site. Foundations are stone and concrete block; framing is fir

Living room has three exposures, generous storage space for books and records, music controls at table height, and a bar with pantry access. Rough stone of fireplace wall was selected to contrast with smooth expanses of glass, and stone border of floor to emphasize texture of carpet and fabrics

Below: dining area can be curtained off when desired; change in ceiling height makes it almost separate room

Robert Damora

Below: left, the master bedroom, half a story above living room, has a stone fireplace and a private sun deck; right, kitchen cabinets are birch, made on job

Photos: Joseph Molitor

HOUSE MAKES THE MOST OF STOCK MATERIALS

Residence for Miss Veronica McCarthy

Fairport, N. Y.

Don Hershey, Architect

AN UNUSUAL AMOUNT of space and equipment at a cost of little more than half that of neighboring residences of similar size was provided in this simply designed house. Results of the architect's idea that construction costs could be lowered substantially by reducing the number of structural components involved are evident throughout the house. Only standard stock materials are employed, as in wall section, below right. The house is, in effect, designed to fully exploit these materials in the most straightforward and economical manner possible. The simplicity and logic with which the materials were treated made both for a low-cost, livable home and also for direct and uncomplex relations between architect and contractor. The ultimate benefactor of course was the client, who was afforded a maximum of space and conveniences for his expenditure. In addition to this, the direct expression of materials — cinder block, prefabricated concrete slabs, Vermont slate — without costly finishes results in a house as pleasingly simple as it is practical.

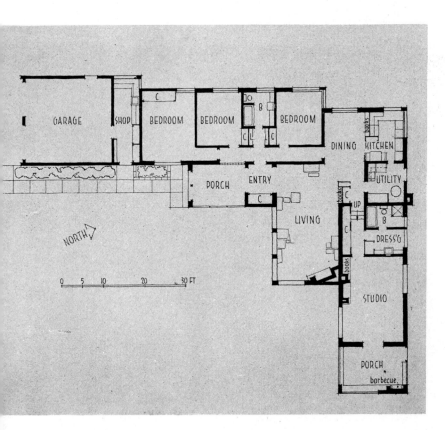

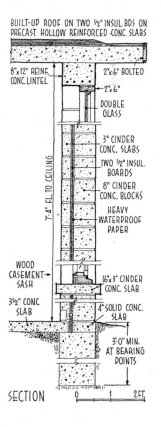

BUILT-UP ROOF ON TWO ½" INSUL. BDS ON
PRECAST HOLLOW REINFORCED CONC. SLABS

8"x12" REINF. CONC. LINTEL

2"x6" BOLTED

2"x6"

DOUBLE GLASS

3" CINDER CONC. SLABS

TWO ½" INSUL. BOARDS

8" CINDER CONC. BLOCKS

HEAVY WATERPROOF PAPER

7'-4" FL TO CEILING

WOOD CASEMENT SASH

16"x3" CINDER CONC. SLAB

3½" CONC. SLAB

4" SOLID CONC. SLAB

3'-0" MIN. AT BEARING POINTS

SECTION   0   1   2 FT.

Simplicity with which materials are combined is evident in entrance hall, above, and master bedroom, below. Prefabricated cabinets are used throughout

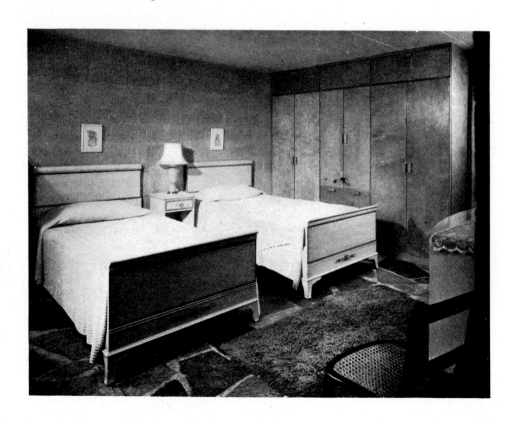

Living room, above center, and dining room, above right, are adjoining. Comfortable, uncluttered appearance of studio, below left and right, is effected by generous storage facilities

Photos: Joseph Molitor

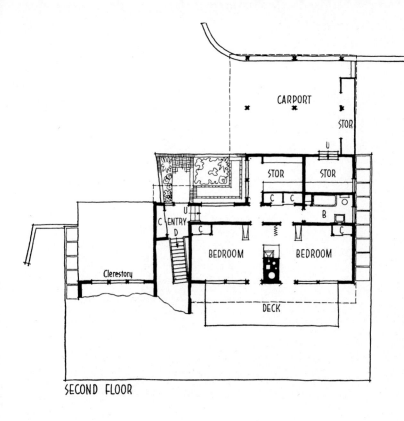

SECOND FLOOR

THE CASCADING FORMS and roof lines of this hillside house not only express the character of the setting, but also reflect skillful handling of the client's basic requirements. The owners desired an essentially one-floor house, secluded from the main road at the front, yet affording terraces for all rooms and good views of woods, creek and waterfall to the rear. The house was therefore kept low at the front, and placed where a knoll shields it from the road. Rooms were divided into three levels. Principal areas are on the lower floor to obtain the best views; entry and carport are on an intermediate level. The children's bedrooms are on the top floor, where they may be closed off when the children are away at camps and schools. The variety of roof levels provides a series of open decks, a clerestory for the master bedroom, a skylight for the open stairs, and overhangs for all windows. The site was landscaped by Henry Fletcher Kenney, with the idea of blending together the house and the woods.

SPLIT-LEVEL HOUSE FOR CINCINNATI, OHIO

Residence for Mr. & Mrs. J. Ralph Corbett   *Carl A. Strauss, Architect*

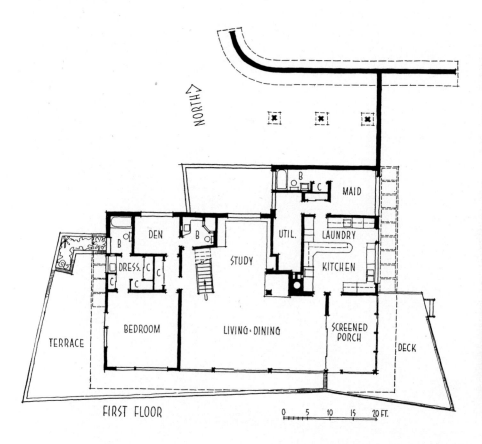

FIRST FLOOR

0   5   10   15   20 FT.

Photos: George Stille

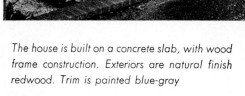

The house is built on a concrete slab, with wood frame construction. Exteriors are natural finish redwood. Trim is painted blue-gray

SPLIT-LEVEL HOUSE

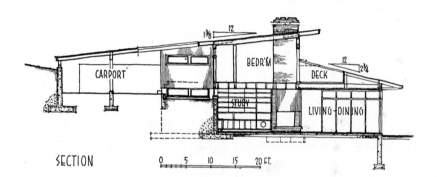

SECTION

CARPORT BEDR'M STUDY DECK LIVING-DINING

1⅜ 12 12 2¾

0 5 10 15 20 FT.

Principal living areas form single, open room with two walls of sliding sash. Corner fireplace is visible from all parts of room. A convertible screened and glazed porch beyond dining area has combination heating and lighting units in ceiling to permit year-round use. The rest of the house is heated by radiant ceiling panels. The furnace is oil fired. Study alcove and stair well are pine paneled, other walls plaster

Kitchen (right) is placed to serve both dining area and screened porch. A service entrance in the laundry portion opens onto a drying yard with steps up to carport. A built-in charcoal grill in the kitchen uses central chimney. Concrete slab floors are carpeted in the main living area; other areas are covered with asphalt or plastic tile. Recessed ceiling fixtures, some with flexible swivel lights, are controlled by low voltage switches. Master control panels are in upper hall and in the master bedroom. Bedrooms have built-in air conditioners

John Hancock Callender and

Allen & Edwin Kramer

Associated Architects

HOUSE DESIGNED FOR

Upper Brookville, Long Island, N. Y.

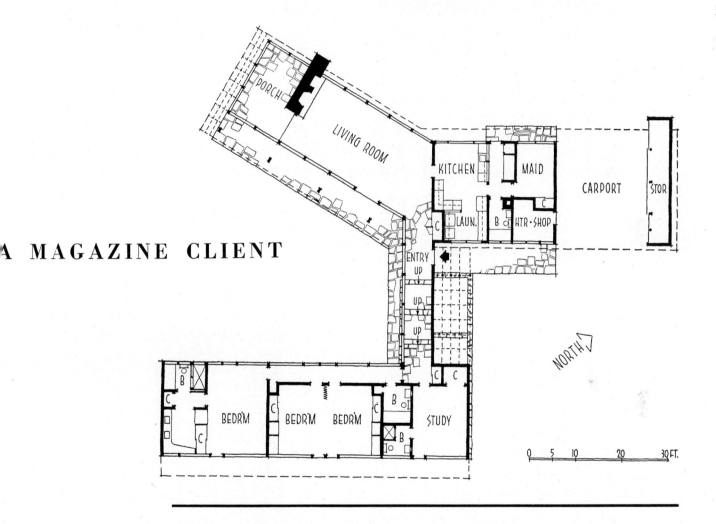

A MAGAZINE CLIENT

THIS EXTREMELY PLEASANT AND LIVABLE HOUSE, officially known as "House & Garden's House of Ideas," suggests one idea that is perhaps especially worthy of note. Its design seems to indicate a careful fusion of many better qualities of two widespread style influences — the crisp, clean lines of the International Style, and the rambling openness of the popularized Ranch House Style. Yet, it has eliminated the severity of the one, and the ungainliness and awkward combination of materials frequently found in the other. The house was conceived and sponsored by *House & Garden Magazine* in collaboration with John Hancock Callender and Allen & Edwin Kramer, Associated Architects, and constructed by Cy Williams, Inc. The landscape architects were Umberto Innocenti and Richard K. Webel.

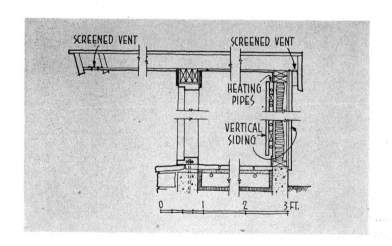

HOUSE FOR A MAGAZINE CLIENT

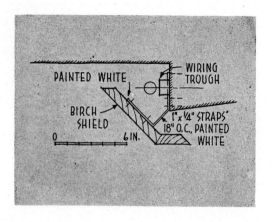

Photos: Tom Leonard

The entrance facade (left) has a closed-in look, was planned to give dramatic impact as front door opens on vista of outdoor court yard. Entrance corridor (below) connects bedroom and living room wings, serves as transition in grade levels. Difference in corridor and living room ceiling heights is concealed by light trough (detail above). Entire house is heated by radiant coils in floors, supplemented in corridor by coils behind wall panel (below left)

Careful, well studied planning and detailing are conspicuous throughout the house. Exterior walls are vertical cypress planks finished in clear creosote; trim is painted crisp black and white. The roof is of a special built-up type, consisting of aluminum foil, vegetable mastic and white marble chips. Rough stone is sparingly used to edge planting areas and for the chimney.

The house was planned for an "average family of four," and consists of three distinct wings for living, sleeping and service facilities, disposed around a central outdoor living area. A great sense of space and openness exists in each of the rooms, brought about chiefly by use of half partitions, glass panels, and window walls. Each room also has its own outdoor terrace.

Interior walls and ceilings are finished with painted gypsum board; floors are concrete slab, finished with flagstone or one of a variety of tiles. Interior furnishings were done separately by Macy's, New York. Heating is by copper tube radiant floor panels, split into three zones with outdoor bulb and indoor thermostat controls. The boiler is oil fired. All walls, ceilings and slab edges are insulated. An intercommunication system is installed throughout the house. Flush downlights are used in most of the rooms.

Space is added to living areas by covered walk, porch and central courtyard. Panels at top and bottom of window walls open for ventilation. Photo below: side exterior view of carport, kitchen, living room

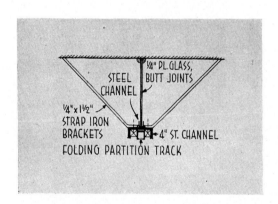

Children's bedroom (above) can be divided by folding partition; a glass panel (detail above) simplifies problem of joining track with sloping ceiling. Master bedroom is separated from dressing room by two-way closet (two photos right). Each bedroom has terrace

The sense of openness which carries through entire house is continued in kitchen by use of suspended cabinets, plate glass behind range and sink (right, top and bottom). A larder is provided adjacent to service entrance for storage of groceries. Exterior view (below) shows bedroom wing at left, service wing at right

Photos: Tom Leonard

RESIDENCE OF MR. AND MRS. FRANK McCAUL

House is set well back from street, with main entrance shielded by garage. Main entrance (right) is unusually effective with large side panels of diffusing glass

Bel Air, California

Arthur B. Gallion, Architect

*Calvin C. Straub in Charge
of Design and Construction*

Robert C. Cleveland Photos

THE OWNERS OF THIS HOUSE are a young couple with two small children and an awareness of the future needs of those children. Their principal requirements were ample space for informal entertaining, a protected play area for the children, and a large nursery which could be converted easily to two separate bedrooms when the youngsters pass the nursery age.

The house was planned to make the best of a difficult site — a flat bench of land bulldozed out of the foothills in western Los Angeles. A magnificent view of the mountains and the city, a strong prevailing west wind, and the problem of the area's occasional raw cold were

the main factors to be considered. Hence the almost solid expanse of glass at the rear, facing the view, and the more closed-in front.

Of particular interest is the remarkable amount of storage space provided in every part of the house (pp. 114-115). Also noteworthy are the interesting roof-line, the exposed rafters, and the use of cross-ribbed diffusing glass in ceilings. Both exterior and interior walls are vertical redwood siding, stained. Floors are concrete slab and gray slate.

Mr. McCauley, a contractor, personally selected all equipment for the house.

Living and dining areas are separated by a storage cabinet which is movable to allow for large-scale entertaining; dining area opens to a covered terrace and garden. Plan (below) shows care with which home was designed around family's changing needs: as children grow older, nursery can be divided into two bedrooms; meanwhile their play area can be supervised from guest room-den near front entrance

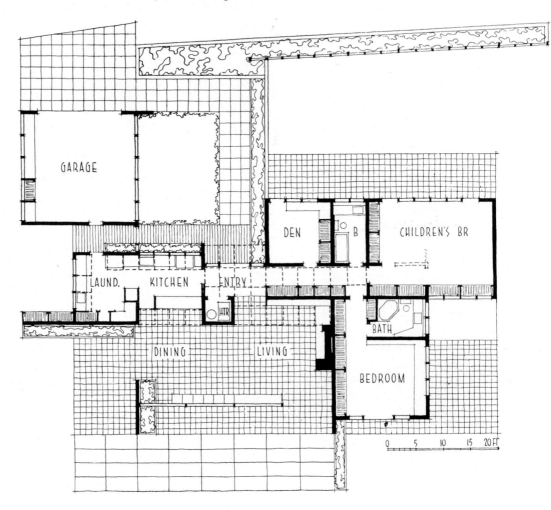

Living-dining area is one large open space, saved from being overwhelming by the introduction of a translucent plane beneath the clerestory windows. Clerestory lighting and glass ceilings and soffits, used here experimentally, have proved to be most satisfactory although quite expensive. Master bedroom (below) opens to northeast, will be more secluded when landscaping is complete.

MC CAULEY HOUSE

Storage Facilities
Unusually Generous

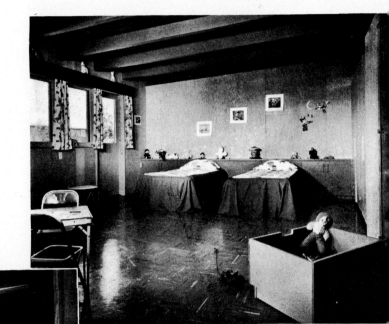

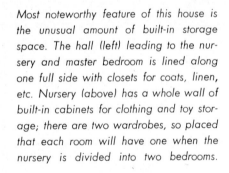

Most noteworthy feature of this house is the unusual amount of built-in storage space. The hall (left) leading to the nursery and master bedroom is lined along one full side with closets for coats, linen, etc. Nursery (above) has a whole wall of built-in cabinets for clothing and toy storage; there are two wardrobes, so placed that each room will have one when the nursery is divided into two bedrooms.

Robert C. Cleveland Photos

The master bedroom (above, right) has two cedar-lined wardrobes, meticulously planned to provide a space for everything. Kitchen (below and opposite) not only has innumerable built-in shelves and cabinets but boasts a highly unusual pantry shelf department adjacent to the ovens. (The ovens seem rather far from the nearest work surface, incidentally.) Even the garage has a storage room

SIX EAST AND WEST COAST HOUSES

A Presentation Prepared by John Hancock Callender, A.I.A.

WEST COAST — ATHERTON, CALIFORNIA

Residence of Mr. & Mrs. Kurt E. Appert
Joseph Allen Stein, Architect
Eckbo, Royston & Williams, Landscape Architects

Ernest Braun Photos

BEARING NO TRACES of "Bay Regionalism," this house nevertheless could hardly have been built anywhere else. The beneficent climate and a beautiful site were obviously basic conditions of the design.

To say merely that the location of the house on the site was determined by the existence of several splendid oaks, would be to miss the essential element in this design, which is the complete integration of building and site. In the illustration shown below it is apparent that house, tree, and terrace are esthetically and functionally integral parts of a single composition. The crisp lines of the house, its lightness and its geometrical precision, are beautifully contrasted with the magnificently rugged oak. Shade from the tree, in turn, softens

climate and the shaded site, these outdoor living areas are usable almost all of the time. The patio, protected on three sides by the house and on the fourth by a fence, can be used when the weather is too cool for outdoor comfort elsewhere.

The main entrance is from the motor court, through the patio (screened by planting from the private area) and into the loggia which gives access to all rooms. From the entrance there is a striking view through the living room to the terraces and gardens beyond. The loggia is nothing more than the conventional entry and bedroom corridor which have been skilfully combined and slightly expanded to form one of the principal features of the plan. In that portion of the loggia which

the severe lines of the house and makes the adjacent paved terrace one of the pleasantest "rooms" in the house.

The house proper — that is, the enclosed area — is not very large. Rooms are of modest size and the only small extravagance in the use of space is the pleasant entrance loggia. Yet this house provides a degree of luxurious living that is generally associated with much more elaborate establishments. The reason, of course, is that the usable space extends far beyond the walls of the house. Each room has its own terrace extension and the total paved outdoor area is actually greater than the floor area of the house. Because of the favorable

serves as entry, the privacy of the occupants is protected by means of a solid door and fixed obscure glass. Elsewhere the loggia opens freely to the patio and incidentally provides cross ventilation for the bedrooms and the living room.

The San Francisco area is justly famous for the quality of its residential architecture and the original work of its landscape architects. Less generally appreciated is the high degree of collaboration that has been attained between these two professions. The happy results of such a collaboration is exceptionally noticeable in this house, where it is difficult to find the line that separates the work of architect and landscapist.

Ernest Braun Photos

Left: main entrance. Above: looking from loggia into patio; entrance walk is behind plant screen at right. Below right: children's bedrooms face south and have their own terraces and playground. On the north side of the house, there is another play area which can be supervised from the kitchen. Note on plan opposite that all baths are windowless with vents

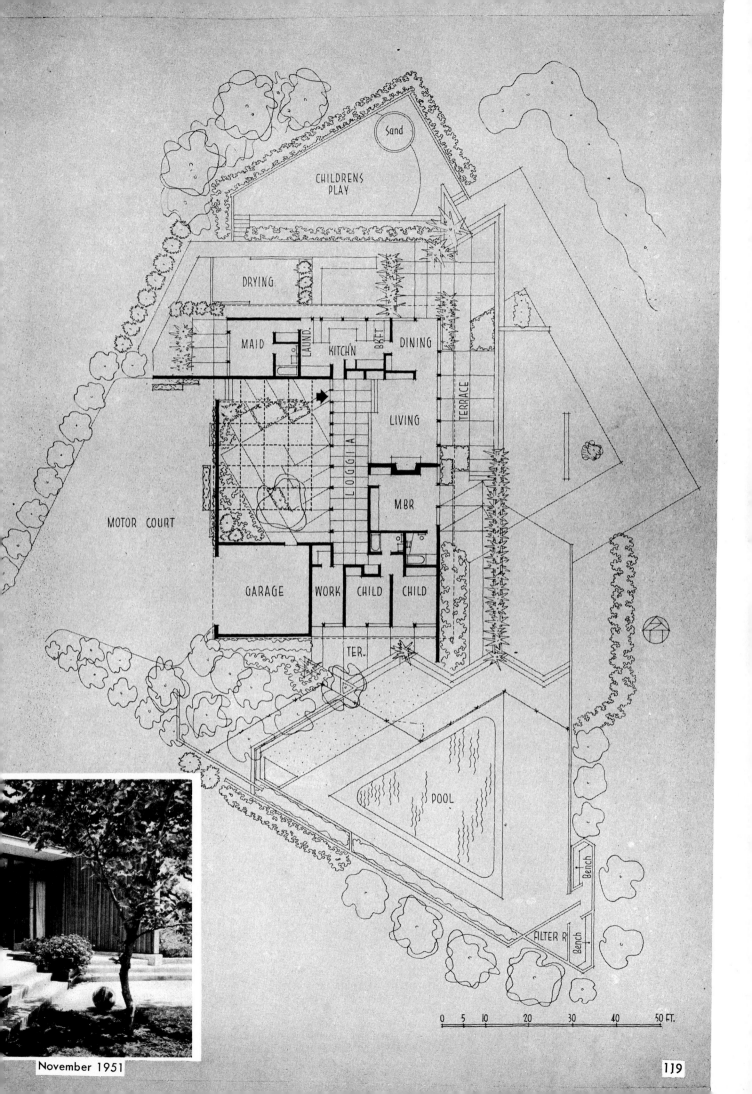

CHILDRENS
PLAY

Sand

DRYING

MAID   LAUND.   KITCHN   BKFT   DINING

TERRACE

LOGGIA

LIVING

MOTOR COURT

MBR

GARAGE   WORK   CHILD   CHILD

TER.

POOL

Bench

FILTER R.   Bench

0 5 10   20   30   40   50 FT.

November 1951

Ernest Braun Photos

Above left: effective contrast of masonry, glass, and plant materials. Note that the big oak is also an important element in the interior design. Masonry walls on two sides of the living room serve to anchor the airy structure to the ground and give a feeling of security. Left: looking from living room into dining room and beyond to dining terrace. Skilful use of the change in levels permits the living room to have a high ceiling and clerestory windows. Bookshelves form the only separation between living and dining rooms. Glass wall is continuous across dining room, living room and master bedroom. Large sliding glass doors open all of these rooms to the terraces

OLD GREENWICH, CONNECTICUT — | EAST COAST |

Residence of Mr. and Mrs. Walther Prokosch

Walther Prokosch, Architect

THE COMPLETE INFORMALITY of this house and the important place that children have in it are immediately apparent upon entering the large entrance hall. This room with its pleasant view through to the terrace and the small valley beyond, is also used for informal dining and as a children's playroom. A folding partition to cut off the playroom was originally intended but never installed. Both indoor and outdoor play areas are conveniently supervised from the kitchen.

The house stretches along the crown of a wooded knoll, with all rooms facing away from the road toward the south and the view. By fitting the car shelter inconspicuously into the hillside with informal stone steps leading up to the house, the natural beauty of the rugged site has been preserved.

To compensate for four very small bedrooms, the living room is huge, taking with ease a grand piano, dining table, sofa and several lounge chairs. Further spaciousness results from the high sloping ceiling and the two glass walls with their big sliding doors opening onto terraces.

Masonry walls are cavity type, 4 by 4 by 16 in. concrete block, plastered or painted inside. Pine siding is used on frame walls and also for ceilings of major rooms. Heating is by wrought iron pipe in 3-in. concrete slab over 3-in. vermiculite concrete on 10-in. gravel.

Above: glass doors to entry-playroom are behind the tree which helps the overhanging roof to shade the terrace in the summer. Kitchen windows overlook play terrace. Living room and terrace are at higher level. Plan: polite dining in the living room is facilitated by a serving hatch from the kitchen. Equipment includes electric water heater, dishwasher, laundry and dryer

Joseph Molitor Photos

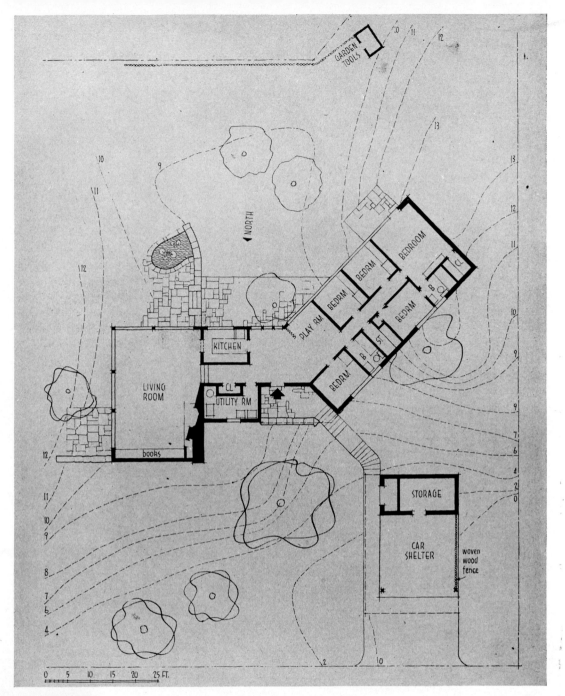

Beach Residence of Mr. & Mrs. Charles O. Martin

Hervey Parke Clark & John F. Beuttler, Architects

Thomas D. Church, Landscape Architect

MANY CONTEMPORARY HOUSES provide for outdoor living as an important auxiliary to the house. In a beach house the reverse is true, the house is merely an auxiliary to outdoor living. It is simply a cabana expanded to provide full facilities for comfortable outdoor life. The heart of the house, the real "living room," is not indoors but out. The design of this outdoor room lies in the province of the landscape architect.

The high quality of the landscaping and the sophisticated simplicity of the architecture mark the beach house shown here as a product of the San Francisco area. The most important element in the design is the patio, which is designed primarily for use, secondarily for appearance. The house serves the patio by providing privacy and protection from occasional cold winds as well as furnishing all practical facilities.

The site permits ideal orientation: the house faces the sun, the sea, and the summer breeze and is protected on the north by a cliff, which also makes a dramatic backdrop for the house as seen from the beach.

Roger Sturtevant Photos

Maximum privacy on the small lot has been achieved by means of the U-shaped plan with its enclosed patio. All rooms open on the patio which is used for circulation as well as for outdoor living. Provision has been made for the owners and their two grown daughters and several week-end guests. The west bedroom wing was an existing building which was adapted to the overall scheme

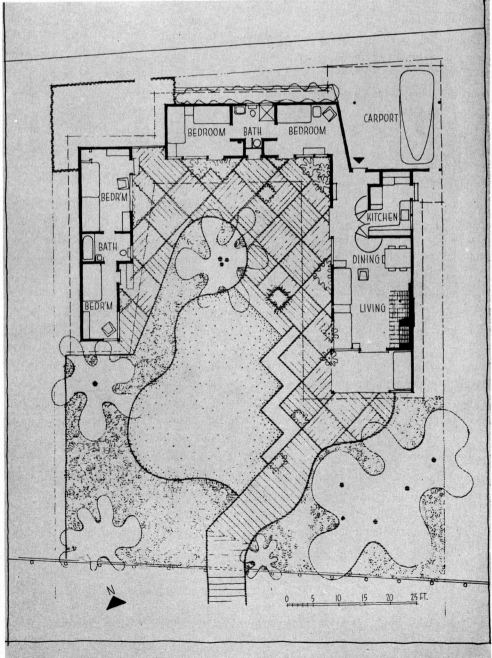

Roger Sturtevant Photos

Construction is of the simplest: exposed framing of 4 by 4 in. redwood posts 4 ft 0 in. o.c. and single wall of 1 by 12 in. redwood boards with 1 by 6 in. battens. Joists and roof sheathing are of fir, painted. Wiring is exposed. Concrete floor slab over membrane waterproofing forms the finished floor. Roof is topped with white marble chips for reflection of sun heat. Gutters and leaders are copper. Heat is furnished by fireplace and electric wall heaters

Residence of Harry N. Hirshberg, Jr.

Arthur H. Keyes & Basil Yurchenko, Architects

THE ARCHITECTS were presented with the always difficult problem of designing a house for a site on the north side of the street. Their solution was to place the main living areas as far from the street as possible. Planting protects the privacy of the dining terrace and the living room with its glass wall facing the street. Privacy from the approach side is provided by the projecting service wing. The dining room and kitchen face the side lot line and the master bedroom and study

are on the rear (north), where privacy is not a problem.

The house is designed for the future addition of two more bedrooms and a bath, which will be reached by a corridor through the present guest room.

The isolated garage and the covered walks add to the apparent size of the house and serve to make an interesting spatial composition. The relation of garage to house will be more apparent after the expansion of the bedroom wing.

Robert Lautman Photos

Clerestory windows give cross-ventilation to the master bedroom and also admit winter sunlight into that room and into the cabinet-lined corridor leading to the living room. All rooms have cross-ventilation and an attic fan removes excess heat from the kitchen, laundry, and heater room. Window shown on plan next to fireplace was omitted in actual construction (below)

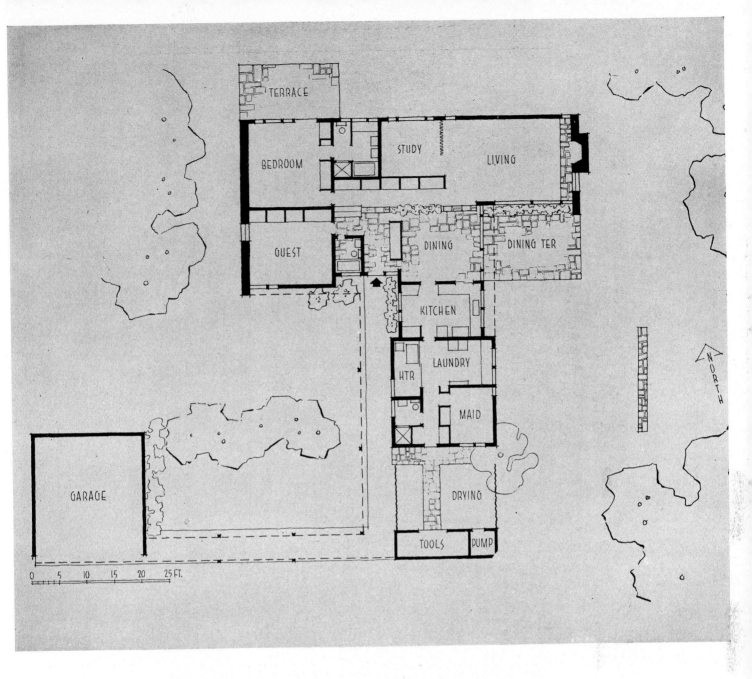

Residence of David M. Fisher

Paul Thiry, Architect

L. N. Roberson, Heating Engineer

THIS ALL-WOOD HOUSE for a lumberman is located in the heart of the Douglas fir country. The site is on a hill overlooking the town, the Willapa River, the harbor, and the lumber mills which, according to the architect, "add their smoke to the colorful haze at sundown." All major rooms face this view.

Southwest storms with abundant rain and overcast skies are frequent. These conditions are said to be ideal for growing Douglas fir, but they do not favor extensive outdoor living. However, terraces have been provided on the southeast adjacent to the dining room, and west of the master bedroom.

The owners are frequently visited by their children and grandchildren. Overflow guest accommodations are provided in the alcove off the bedroom corridor, which can be closed off when desired by a folding partition.

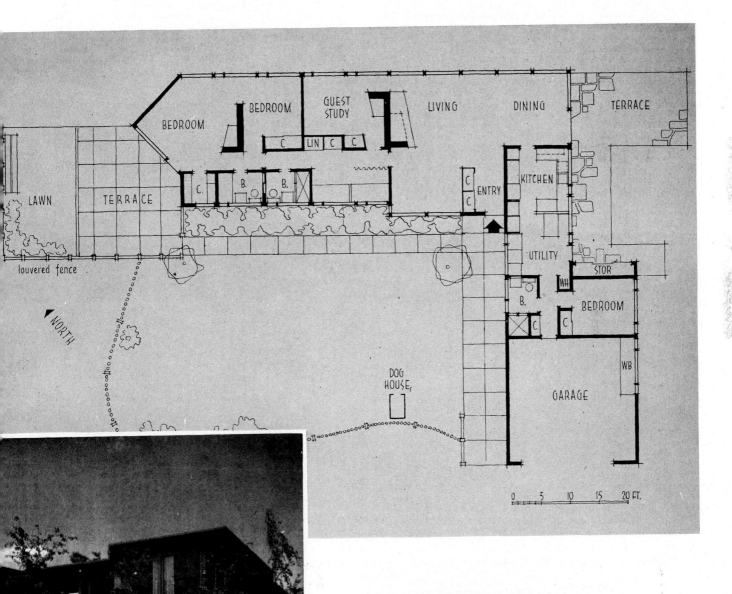

Master suite consists of two bedrooms separated by free-standing fireplace, dressing room, bath, and private terrace enclosed by louvered fence. There are also fireplaces in living room and study

Charles R. Pearson Photos

Living room, dining room, and entry are in effect one big room with a floor area of almost 600 sq ft. Higher ceiling over this portion of the house results in pleasing proportions and adds considerable interest to the elevations

Exterior finish is 1 by 10 in. bevel cedar siding, untreated. Interior walls and ceilings are 1 by 6 in. t. & g. spruce or cedar. Casement sash are Douglas fir. Roof is 5-ply with copper flashing and 3-in. rockwool insulation. Heating is by electric cable in concrete floor slab

Charles R. Pearson Photos

Residence of Mrs. Benjamin Halprin

Stanhope Blunt Ficke, Architect

THE PARTI FOR THIS PLAN was established by the owner's desire to have maximum sun in the bedrooms and morning sun in the kitchen, and her requirement that indoor and outdoor living areas should overlook the view to the west, over a small lake to distant hills. The owner does considerable informal entertaining and requested spacious living and dining areas, as well as direct access from the kitchen to the front door.

The original design included a drive-through carport along the east side of the entrance and bedroom, and a third bedroom and bath to the west of the present bedrooms. In the architect's opinion these additions, which were omitted for reasons of economy, would undoubtedly enhance the appearance of the house.

The steeply sloping site required a high stoop at the entrance, but had the advantage of permitting a partial basement to be placed under the kitchen. The basement, which has an outside door at grade level, provides space for the heater, laundry, shop, and storage for garden tools and terrace furniture.

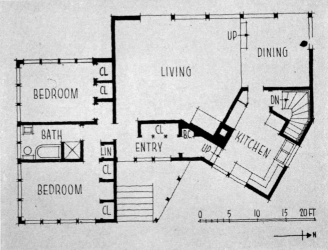

Bill Maris: **Pictor**

Kitchen and dining room are on a slightly higher level than the other rooms. All rooms have cross-ventilation. Corridor to future bedroom will utilize space now occupied by closets; new closets will be built between the two rooms. The view above gives an idea of the difficulties encountered because of the steep site

ARIZONA ARCHITECT DESIGNS

Residence of Mr. and Mrs. Edward L. Varney

Phoenix, Arizona

Edward L. Varney Associates

Architects and Engineers

WHEN THIS house was under construction a year ago, the architect-owner described it as an experiment in the application of light-steel welded rigid frames to residential use. "While this job is not strictly speaking a low-cost house," he said, "I have hopes of developing from it a structure suitable for low-cost mass housing. We have been using this type of structural system for several years in school buildings here in Arizona with some amazing cost results." (Steel was then available.)

Despite the fact that the house was built in the last quarter of 1950, when building costs in Arizona, as elsewhere, were zooming upward, the per square foot cost turned out to be only $10.18, excluding refrigerated air conditioning, but including $1.00 per sq ft for open terraces — considerably under the average for a house of comparable quality.

The house occupies a 2½-acre desert site just outside Phoenix, high enough to overlook the city to the south, and low enough for dramatic views of the mountains to northeast and east. Planned for a family of five (including two boys and a girl, at present all under ten), the house provides three separate outdoor living areas. One, to the east between living room and children's wing, is designed for sheltered dining and recreation in winter, when the prevailing wind is from the southwest. The second, to the south of the living room, is planned for enjoyment of the cool summer breezes. And the third, to the north, is the children's play area, visible only from their own rooms and (for supervision) the kitchen and maid's room. Every room in the house overlooks either mountains or city. Floor to ceiling glass areas are extensive throughout the house, but all are shielded from direct sunlight after 8:30 A.M. during the hot summer months.

HIS OWN HOME

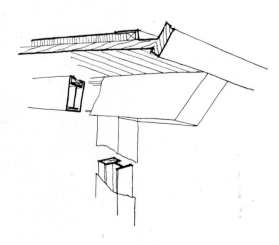

Foundations are poured concrete; floors are concrete on grade. Framing is steel, sheathed with 14-oz copper exposed on interior and exterior. Walls are 2- by 6-in. T & G hemlock, run horizontally and insulated with 2-in. glass fiber. Roof is 2 by 6 T & G, slate surfaced and coated with copper

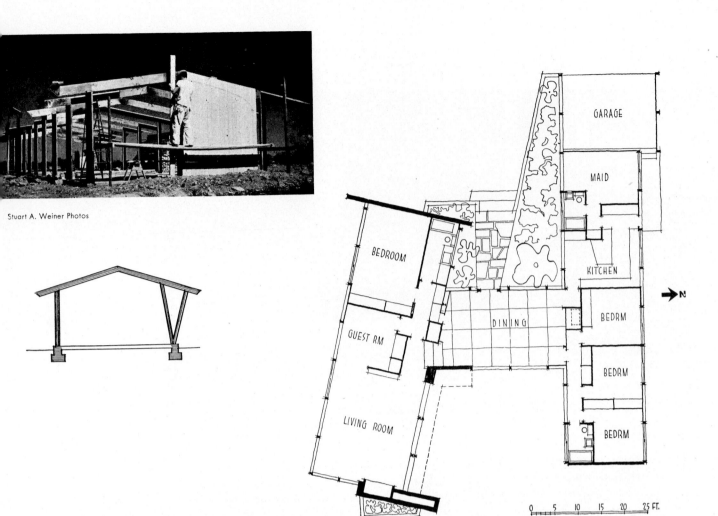

Stuart A. Weiner Photos

GARAGE

MAID

KITCHEN

BEDROOM

GUEST RM

DINING

BEDRM

BEDRM

BEDRM

LIVING ROOM

→ N

0   5   10   15   20   25 FT.

Method of construction is based on strength of welded-steel frame which eliminates necessity of cross-bracing. Diagonal strengthening at north side of south wing permits esthetically pleasing variation at reasonable cost. Above: section through south wing. Right: dining and recreation terrace between wings. Below: the dining room; kitchen door left background

Interior walls are random-width ash except for ceramic tile and walnut plywood in bathrooms. Floors are brown or gray rubber cut in 2-ft squares. Ceilings throughout are 2- by 6-in. V-joint hemlock painted a flat gray-green. Copper beams and columns are left unfinished to acquire a dull patina. All stone is native, laid in random rubble

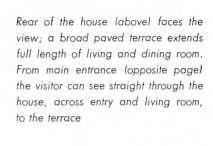

Rear of the house (above) faces the view; a broad paved terrace extends full length of living and dining room. From main entrance (opposite page) the visitor can see straight through the house, across entry and living room, to the terrace

HOUSE IN RALEIGH, NORTH CAROLINA

James W. Fitzgibbon, Architect

Joseph W. Molitor Photos

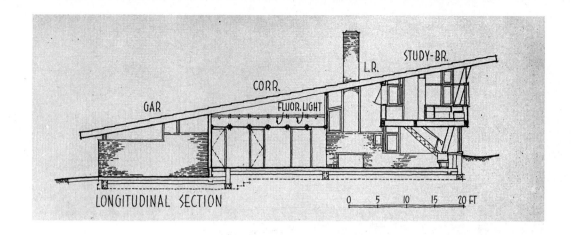

LONGITUDINAL SECTION

GAR   CORR.   FLUOR. LIGHT   L.R.   STUDY-BR.

0   5   10   15   20 FT

Materials and structure key this house to its site, echo natural surroundings. A sophisticated handling of the design preserves these qualities, yet lifts it above mere rusticity. The house slopes up from the low street front (below left) to encompass view at rear (above left). Main entrance is at side (above center)

An UNUSUALLY CLOSE RELATIONSHIP to its sloping, pine-dotted site characterizes this Raleigh, North Carolina residence of Mr. and Mrs. Ralph R. Fadum. From a low, unobtrusive street facade, the structure's roof slopes up, recalling the land contour, to afford two-story living areas at the rear which take full advantage of views across an adjoining golf course. The living room is half-sunken to avoid awkward changes of level within the house. The naturalness of the landscape is also reflected in the materials selected for the house — exterior walls are natural finish brick and cypress, interiors are cypress and douglas fir.

A light, suspended quality is given the design by the structural system used. The house is supported by a series of built-up wood columns, anchored by steel plates; roof girders fit between sections of the columns. Walls are mostly screen-like glazing, with much of the conventional sash eliminated. The suspended effect is greatly increased from the rear by slanting the columns to the interior, where they connect with built-in cabinets. Frank A. Walser was contractor.

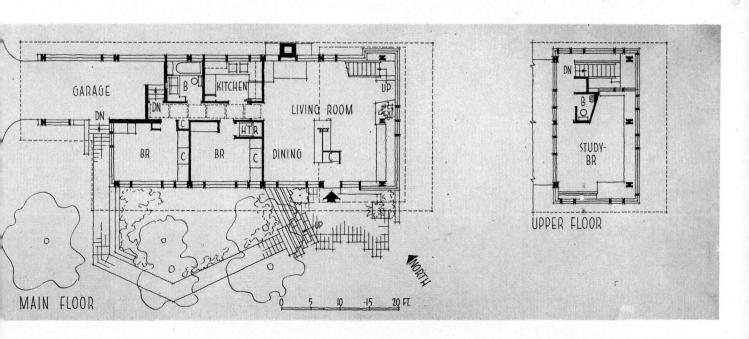

GARAGE   KITCHEN   B   LIVING ROOM   UP   DN   B   DN

BR   C   BR   C   HTR   DINING   C   STUDY-BR

MAIN FLOOR   UP   NORTH   UPPER FLOOR

0   5   10   15   20 FT.

The living room (below and left) focuses on view across golf course. The building was placed well back from the course for privacy and protection from golf ball hazards. A central built-in cabinet separates the living room from the dining area (far right), which runs full height of structure. Heating is by hot air, with an oil-fired furnace located in a central closet. Upper level study is heated by opening sash above dining area. The effect of lightness is carried through the design by such details as the elevation of stair and column bases on short metal brackets (see detail below center). Even the kitchen (right) shares view of woods

Joseph W. Molitor Photos

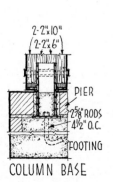

2-2"x10"
2-2"x6"

PIER

2-⅝" RODS
4½" O.C.

FOOTING

COLUMN BASE

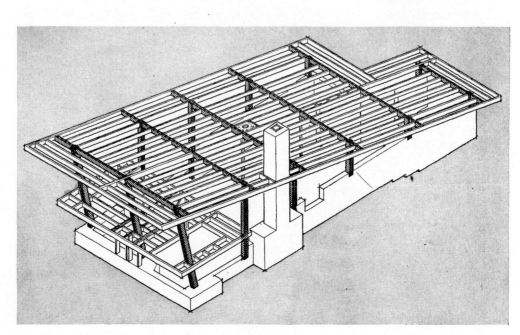

Joseph W. Molitor Photos

High windows give privacy to bedrooms (above left). Glazing is set between plywood ceiling panels, has no trim at corners. The upper level study-bedroom (above right, below) opens wide on view, can be closed by reed curtains

HILLTOP RESIDENCE OF JAMES DINWIDDIE

LAFAYETTE, CALIFORNIA

John Ekin Dinwiddie, Architect
and Richard Maxwell

Robert Royston of
Eckbo, Royston & Williams, Landscape Architect

LIKE MANY HOUSES in California, this one, designed for the architect's brother, occupies a hilltop site and boasts a broad view. To take advantage of this it is long and narrow, with the living-dining areas, den and master bedroom all at the "back" of the house, facing the view. Walls on this side are almost wholly of glass.

At first glance the plan (next page) seems simple. Further study, however, shows why the architect considers this house one of his best jobs to date: there is a general feeling of openness, yet each area has been given maximum privacy. The family wing is a unit quite by itself, with master bedroom and den completely shut off from the entrance court and foyer. Living and dining areas flow into each other along the terrace side, but are firmly separated for most of their width by the fireplace wall. The guest room, with its own bath, is adjacent to the main entrance. And the entire service wing is placed at a 45 deg angle to the rest of the house.

Of wood frame construction, on a reinforced concrete foundation, the house has exterior walls of redwood and a tar and gravel roof. Interior walls are gypsum board, floors are oak.

Morley Baer Photos

Above: the den is small, but handily situated between master bedroom and foyer; it opens directly to the terrace and receives light from both sides, thanks to the clerestory. Above, right: looking across living room and foyer to main entrance

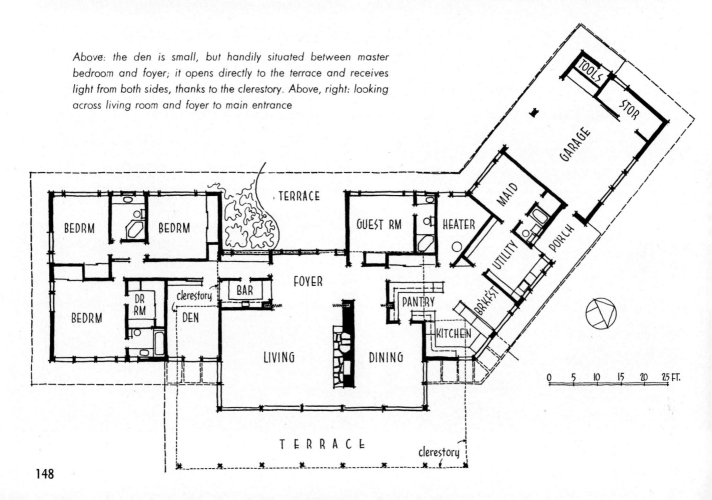

Above: living room looking toward dining room; fireplace wall effectively separates the two, but continuous glass wall and lack of doors give feeling of openness. Below, left: the dining room is wide open to the view. Below, right: kitchen, pantry and breakfast room are separated only by counters for an extremely compact, efficient unit; placement of kitchen at center of angle between wings gives maximum air, light and view

Morley Baer Photos

RESIDENCE OF MR. AND MRS. SAMUEL RUBINSTEIN

Seattle, Washington

J. Lister Holmes & Associates, Architects

Tucker, Shields and Terry, Interiors

Dearborn-Massar Photos

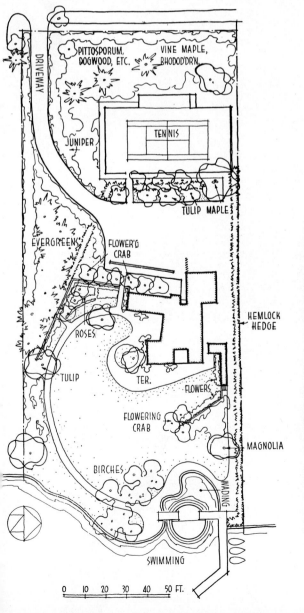

Although this house on the shore of Lake Washington is not exceptionally large, it makes more than the usual provision for family activities. It is built around a play-room opening to a sheltered terrace, and has a lanai as well as a large living room. Tennis courts, swimming and wading pools and a dock are also provided

Dearborn-Massar

Left: looking east past garage wall to windowed stair landing. Below: playroom opens along almost entire south wall to a sheltered terrace. Exterior walls are vertical cedar plank siding and a native Washington sandstone

Left: the built-in bar is handy not only to playroom and living room, but also to lanai and dining room. Bar is natural birch, with stainless steel counter and sink and a small refrigerator. Opposite page: terrace, with playroom in background and living room at right

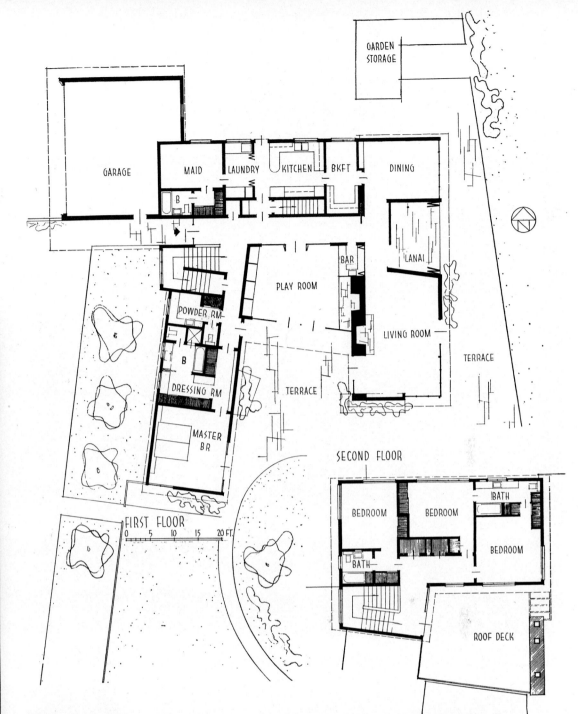

GARDEN
STORAGE

GARAGE · MAID · LAUNDRY · KITCHEN · BKFT · DINING

B

BAR

PLAY ROOM

LANAI

POWDER RM

LIVING ROOM

B

TERRACE

DRESSING RM

TERRACE

MASTER
BR

FIRST FLOOR

0 5 10 15 20 FT.

SECOND FLOOR

BEDROOM · BEDROOM · BATH

BATH · BEDROOM

ROOF DECK

RUBINSTEIN HOUSE

Dearborn-Massar·

Above: fireplace wall and bookcase in living room are walnut in natural finish. Fireplace frame is local sandstone and
salmon-colored natural brick; hearth is rust-mauve marble

Right: a corner of the dining room. Here one wall is of glass,
one of sandstone. Dining room has a set of three tables —
two square and one rectangular — which may be used
separately or together; they were custom designed, like much
of furniture in house, by the decorator

VACATION HOUSE IN OREGON

FOR MR. AND MRS. ROBERT WILSON, WARM SPRINGS, OREGON

Pietro Belluschi, Architect

Dearborn-Massar

Situated in excellent hunting, fishing and riding country, on the bank of the Deschutes River, this house is designed for comfortable summer occupancy, for entertaining guests, and for use by the owners a few days each week throughout the year. The family's children come often to ride; there is a separate wing for the owner's parents to use when they wish; overnight guests are frequent

Dearborn-Massar

Since there are usually many people around to enjoy the house, living room, dining space and kitchen are ample in size. The house is decidedly informal, but its informality has not been allowed to mean a rugged lack of comfort. Whatever is needed in the way of amenities is frankly included; for instance, there being no commercial laundry conveniently handy, the house has its own fully equipped laundry with enclosed drying yard. On the other hand, these mechanical aids to comfortable living—so often neglected in a vacation house—frankly and openly employed though they may be, are never unpleasantly obtrusive

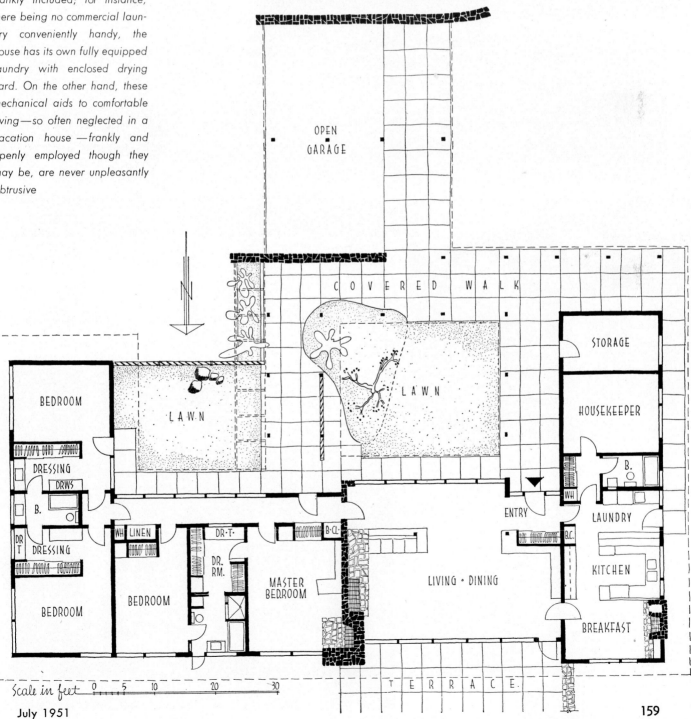

OPEN GARAGE

COVERED WALK

LAWN

LAWN

STORAGE

HOUSEKEEPER

B.

ENTRY

LAUNDRY

BEDROOM

DRESSING

DRWS

B.

DR T

DRESSING

WH LINEN

DR·T·

DR. RM.

B·CL

LIVING · DINING

KITCHEN

BEDROOM

BEDROOM

MASTER BEDROOM

BREAKFAST

TERRACE

Scale in feet 0 5 10 20 30

OREGON HOUSE

Dearborn-Massar

One arrives at this vacation house by automobile, so the carport is the obvious entrance. Here, as in the case of interior mechanisms, the mechanical means of transportation is judiciously separated from the house proper by the masonry and louvered wood walls which define the court

On facing page: three views of the central court; left, private court adjoining the grandparents room; above, living room. Local materials are extensively used: black and gray volcanic stone masonry and rough-sawed pine boards and battens stained a warm gray form the walls. Natural though these may be, there is no self-conscious striving for rusticity but rather a true naturalness. The curved sofa and leather fireside chair are green; the built-in sofa's cushions are coral; the coffee table is natural wood; and the natural cork surfaced concrete floor is radiantly heated by means of electric cable buried in it

From the more formal dining area (right) one door leads to the breakfast room and kitchen, another to the outdoor terrace where meals may also be eaten. The breakfast room-kitchen-laundry (below and facing page) are frankly combined, definitely utilitarian and unashamedly pleasant. These are no sanitary engineered work-areas; the cheerful fireplace wall, the wood cupboards and the rose-pink plastic which covers work-counter tops make this part of the house gay as well as useful

Dearborn-Massar

At the other end of the living room, shown
above, is a door leading to bedrooms

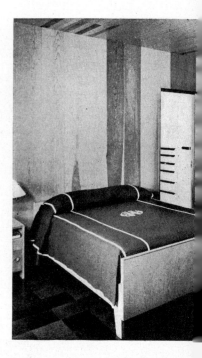

There you have the Wilsons' vacation house, built on the banks of the Deschutes River near Warm Springs in Oregon. It belongs in its wide-open setting. Yet curiously there is no insistent effort in its design to blend it into the landscape — none, at any rate, which forces itself upon the occupants. One cannot say of it that a pitched or hipped or gabled roof might have made its outline ape the profiles of the surrounding hills. Such a comment would verge on the silly, and so would any nonsense about its flat roof providing a welcome, relieving contrast to its rugged surroundings.

Neither is it a simple, unsophisticated cottage, nor does it possess any characteristics remotely cute. It is natural, as a place for relaxation should be natural; and how artfully has this human naturalness been achieved! It has its full share of glass walls and ventilating louvers, of contrastingly heavy piles of rough masonry and of unassuming wood, but not once is the contrast permitted to become a shock to the nervous system or does the common contemporary device become a cliché. The bedroom illustrated above is a comfortable bedroom, in which fragile glass butting into solid masonry takes its relative place just as satisfactorily as the plentiful built-ins and storage space do.

One more comment: to offset the possibility that the wide-open countryside might overawe the occupants, all the living areas focus inward on the series of courts.

Solidly built, with excellent craftsmanship, the house has a more or less conventional wood frame supporting a flat roof with built-up surface. Foundations and floor are concrete; in the slab are buried the electric radiant heating cables. Except for a few casements all glass is fixed, double-pane to provide insulating value. Rooms are ventilated by wood louvers with interior hinged panels. Interior walls and ceilings are pine boards; floors are covered with cork. The roof has 2 in. mineral wool insulation; the floor slab, vermiculite insulation. Sheet metal work is galvanized iron. All wood sills are treated to prevent decay. Kitchen and laundry are fully equipped with garbage disposer built into the kitchen sink, electric range, dishwasher, refrigerator, home freezer, automatic clothes washer, electric dryer, exhaust fan, incinerator built into breakfast room chimney, wood cabinets and laundry hampers, plastic counter tops. Domestic hot water is supplied by two electric heaters

Dearborn-Massar

RESIDENCE FOR MR. AND MRS.

HIGHLAND PARK, ILLINOIS

L. Morgan Yost, Architect

Nowell Ward

Situated on a bluff overlooking the broad Skokie Valley, this house obviously was designed to take full advantage of the view. Its plan, however, indicates that the view alone was not the major consideration. The owners — a couple with a grown son — stipulated that the bedrooms must face a small secluded glen to the south; they also required ample gardening areas around the house, and they insisted that the house be easy to maintain without servants.

The result was a T-shaped plan with living room, dining room and kitchen opened up to the valley view and accented by a projecting porch. The three bedrooms,

two baths, and utility room form a separate wing at right angles to the main wing, with all bedrooms facing south toward the glen as required. Prevailing winds plus differences in orientation made two heating systems — one for each wing — imperative, but a centrally located utility room accommodates both heaters.

Construction is brick masonry on concrete trench foundations and a slab floor. Walls are a pink buff, wood is natural cedar. The roof is built up with a light tan gravel topping. Interior walls are generally plastered, floors are oak parquet. Windows are fixed glass with ventilation louvers.

NORMAN C. DENO

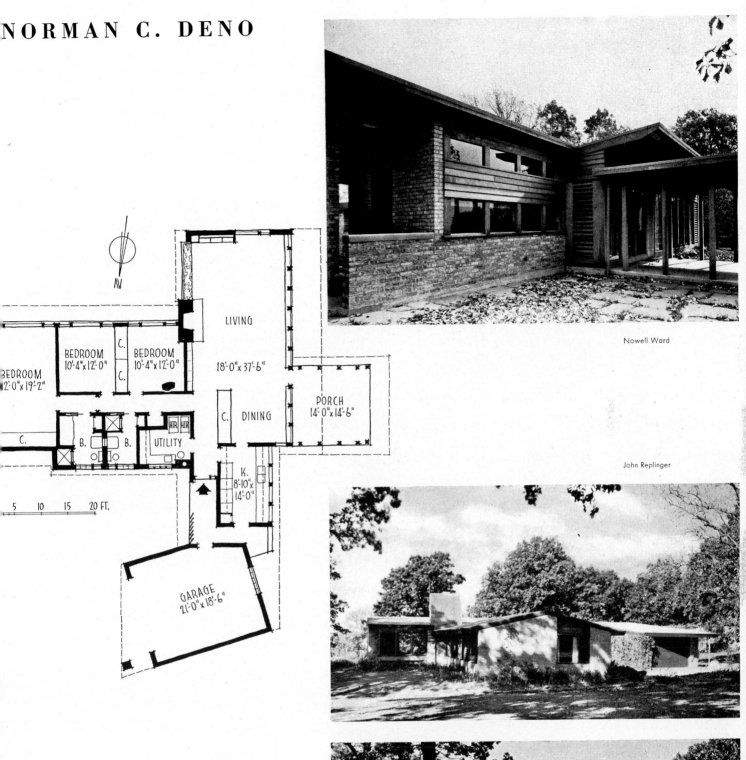

Nowell Ward

John Replinger

*Top, right: the kitchen is strategically located,
combining view with direct access to both front
door and garage. Garage is angled (two views,
right) to provide a small entrance court. Opposite:
living room faces west, overlooking the valley*

BEDROOM
10'-4"x12'-0"

BEDROOM
10'-4"x12'-0"

BEDROOM
12'-0"x19'-2"

LIVING
18'-0"x37'-6"

PORCH
14'-0"x14'-6"

DINING

UTILITY

K.
8'-10"x
14'-0"

GARAGE
21'-0"x18'-6"

C. C. B. B. C. HTR HTR

5   10   15   20 FT.

Living room looks toward glen (above) as well as toward main view over Skokie Valley (below, right). A slanting window and generous planting box give the owners a chance for winter gardening. Dining area (below, left) is separated from entrance hall by built-in closet

A HOUSE WITH "EMOTIONAL CONTENT"

Residence for Mr. and Mrs. Abel E. Fagen, Lake Forest, Ill.

George Fred Keck — William Keck, Architects

Marianne Willisch, Interiors

Hedrich-Blessing Photos

RECENTLY those once-heretical words "warmth" and "emotional content" have appeared more frequently in within-the-family discussions of architecture. Now the taboo has been shifted rather toward "functionalism," first because the word was so much over-used, also, probably, because of a growing sense of confusion about its application. In residential design particularly was it difficult to isolate the "function" to be expressed.

Here is a house in which there was no difficulty about words. Fred Keck's account of the planning assignment for the Fagen family speaks of family interests the house was to express, of development of the solar ideas, of spatial feeling to avoid the monotony of rectangular units, of colors and tones and sculptural forms "to enhance this feeling of relaxation." A considerable package of emotional content.

First in the list of family interests to be expressed was outdoor activities around the farm. The farm is of the suburban type, 80 acres, partially

wooded, just outside of Lake Forest, one of the beauty spots of the North Shore. Family comprises parents and three sons, two about ready for college. Mrs. Fagen is especially interested in sculpture and painting, and for the children, music. Entertaining was also mentioned, though the owners had already built a guest house and porch for summertime visitors.

The clients were also sympathetic to the architects' variations on the solar theme. "We made a point," said Keck, "of the angular placement of windows, not only for the view, but also for the feeling of space and for the reflective values of the glass, which add a note to the spatial feeling in the house, and rid it of the monotony of the rectangular unit." The architects also planned a sculptural quality in the spacing of forms and materials. "At the same time it is a comfortable and relaxing house . . . this feeling of relaxation is for me decidedly important, and is achieved by the sun when it is up, and the radiant heat when it is on during colder weather."

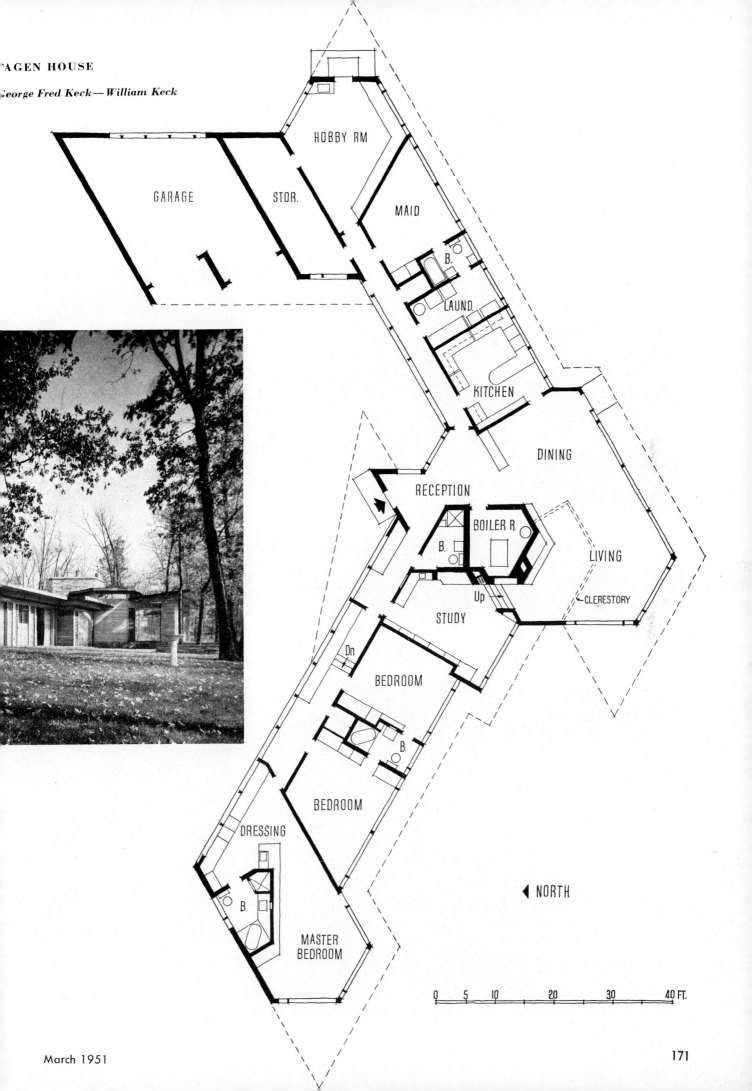

AGEN HOUSE

George Fred Keck — William Keck

GARAGE

STOR.

HOBBY RM

MAID

B.

LAUND.

KITCHEN

DINING

RECEPTION

BOILER R.

B.

LIVING

Up

CLERESTORY

STUDY

Dn

BEDROOM

B.

BEDROOM

DRESSING

B.

MASTER
BEDROOM

◀ NORTH

0 5 10   20   30   40 FT.

Hedrich-Blessing Photos

Scored plastic screen by Alexander Archipenko

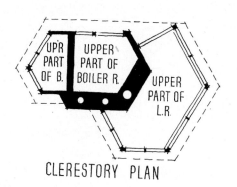

CLERESTORY PLAN

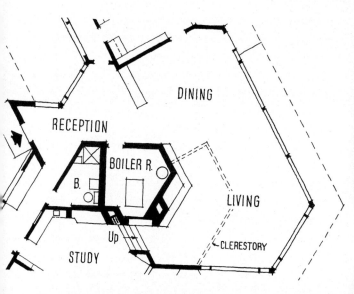

RECEPTION

DINING

BOILER R.

B.

LIVING

Up

CLERESTORY

STUDY

FAGEN HOUSE *George Fred Keck — William Keck*

Bedroom interiors of Fagen house have an intimate visual relationship
with the outdoors. All-glass walls are angled for views, also for a sense
of spaciousness. Rooms have a feeling of warmth not really seen in
photographs, compounded of colors and textures, also sunlight and
radiant heat. "It is remarkable how little need is found for an over-
supply of rugs on floors that are warm in cold weather"

Hedrich-Blessing Photos

March 1951

HOUSE IN A NEW YORK SUBURB

For Mr. and Mrs. Olindo Grossi

Olindo Grossi, Architect

WHEN an architect designs his own house, he's somewhat on the spot; when he is Head of the Department of Architecture (as Mr. Grossi is at Pratt Institute in Brooklyn), the spot becomes most definite. It behooves him to make judicious use of new ideas, techniques and equipment; and since his budget is just as limited as any of his clients' — how many architects or teachers are wealthy? — he must economize wherever possible. In his house his family must be able to live a normal life, and yet it must be available for demonstration. How well has this house succeeded?

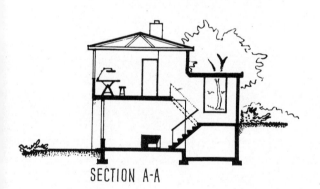

SECTION A-A

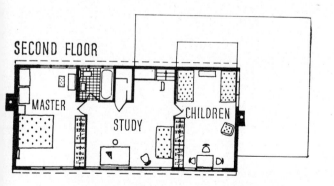

SECOND FLOOR

MASTER

STUDY

CHILDREN

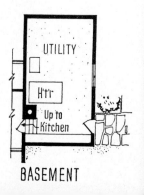

UTILITY

H'tr

Up to Kitchen

BASEMENT

Richard Garrison photos

Openness and flexibility characterize this house; there is not even a pretense of a partition between living and dining spaces. A radiant heating system, designed in accordance with average practice and with copper tubing in the plaster ceilings, also contributes to flexibility. Research showed that the two-zoned system functioned well. Served by an oil-fired boiler, each zone has its own indoor thermostat. Cost precluded installation of clock thermostats and outdoor controls; it was found, consequently, that manual operation of thermostats was necessary or else, in winter, the house became too warm in mid-morning, too cool in early evening. Two criticisms: Supplies and return to upstairs zone pass through the exterior three feet of the kitchen ceiling, and when heat is needed downstairs, this ceiling is cold unless upstairs zone is also heating; and the living room coil length, 500 linear feet, made for unequal flow and a large temperature drop in this circuit's water. Nevertheless, the system was found very economical — one year's fuel cost for heat and hot water was $186 — and quite appropriate for a basementless house with so much glass. Upstairs temperatures were consistently two to three degrees higher than downstairs, probably due to convection; average temperature differential, floor to ceiling, was four degrees; the living room's glass wall apparently induced mild air currents which were found very agreeable — and which reversed at night! — and as soon as the winter sun penetrated the interior the heating system did not need to function. From 10 to 4 the oil burner ran only for domestic hot water.

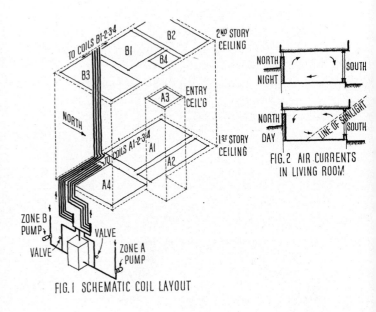

FIG. 1 SCHEMATIC COIL LAYOUT

FIG. 2 AIR CURRENTS IN LIVING ROOM

Careful study of the radiant heating system was made by six students in Pratt Institute's Mechanical Equipment courses: Giles Aureli, Howard Bonnington, Sven Gelin, Joseph Hnatov, William Johnke, and John Manley. Their findings are quoted at left

There are few interior doors; wall, floor and ceiling surfaces are natural and simple, and interest is obtained by the unobtrusive use of pleasantly light colors which are given substance by the contrasting solidity of natural masonry. Curiously, the family's three small children do not find it very satisfying to scribble on such natural surfaces, which simplifies one aspect of housekeeping. The kitchen has no doors, even on the passway to the living area. Mrs. Grossi finds that cooking on an electric range almost eliminates odors, and when something burns, the ventilating fan, installed so it really works, quickly expels smoke and smells

Richard Garrison photos

On a sloping site, one readily apparent economy is what we used to call "split-level" planning. The entry, halfway between main and second floors, is here kept quite open. In combination with the openness of the plan, and continuously glazed walls on the opposite—south—side, this provides perhaps the most striking first impression. Mrs. Grossi finds it a satisfying and permanent one, particularly in contrast to the confinement of the apartment in which the family previously lived. Though a more formal family might be disturbed by the fact that an entering visitor has an excellent view of the dinner table, this does not bother the Grossis

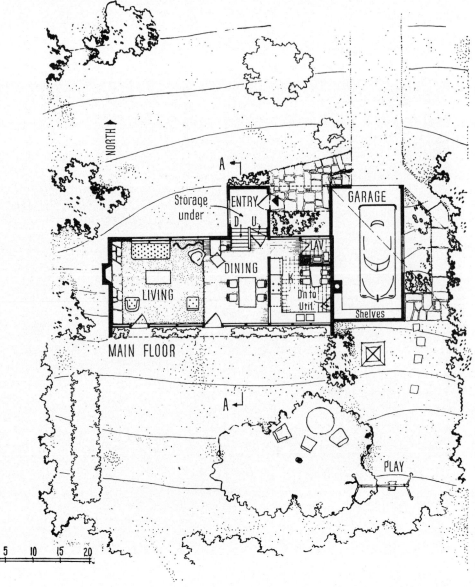

MAIN FLOOR

0 5 10 15 20

HEADMASTER'S HOUSE, COUNTRY DAY SCHOOL

Frederick Dunn, Architect   *St. Louis, Missouri*

John D. Falvey, Mechanical Engineer
William C. E. Becker, Structural Engineer

ITS plan worked out within the foundation limits of an old and very fancy Colonial house which burned down, this house sits on a knoll on the grounds of the St. Louis Country Day School. Using the old foundations and basement reduced construction costs but complicated planning; hence the north-facing bedrooms and certain other features.

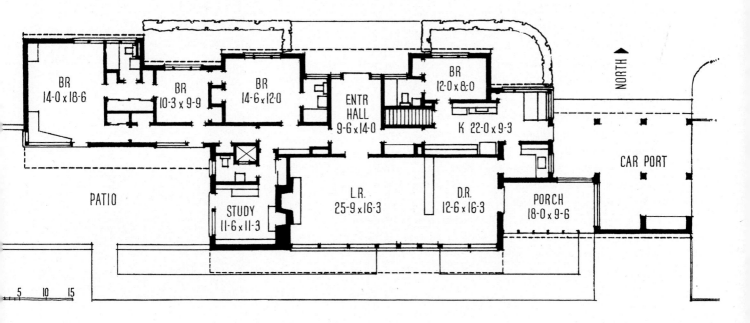

Center photo: large living room, from which the dining room is separated only by tall cabinets of curly birch plywood. Left, details of triple-hung sash and double glazing; right, details showing roof line following ceiling levels, which are lower in north rooms. At bottom: fireplace end of living room, and study

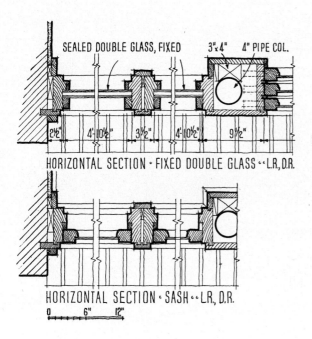

SEALED DOUBLE GLASS, FIXED   3"x4"   4" PIPE COL.

2½"   4'-10½"   3½"   4'-10½"   9½"

HORIZONTAL SECTION · FIXED DOUBLE GLASS · · L.R., D.R.

HORIZONTAL SECTION · SASH · · L.R., D.R.

0   6"   12"

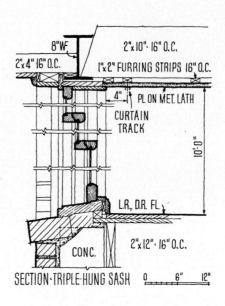

8"WF
2"x4" 16" O.C.
2"x10" · 16" O.C.
1"x2" FURRING STRIPS 16" O.C.
4"   PL ON MET. LATH
CURTAIN TRACK
10'-0"
L.R., D.R. FL.
CONC.   2"x12" · 16" O.C.

SECTION · TRIPLE-HUNG SASH   0   6"   12"

Of necessity, Headmaster and Mrs. Robert N. Cunningham's house is quite formal. In living and dining rooms the south wall is entirely glass; beneath the fixed glazing are hopper sash for ventilation, and set into the wall are three large triple-hung windows. These help maintain comfort in warm weather by providing a means for getting rid of warm air near the ceiling, which is ten feet high in these rooms for both proportion and comfort.

The house has brick bearing walls on concrete foundations. The exterior white lime facing brick is covered with cement paint, and the roof is built-up, surfaced with light-colored aggregate to reflect heat. Interior partitions are wood, with hard plaster finish throughout. Insulation is rock wool, 4 in. thick, and the house has an oil-fired air conditioner, rebuilt from the previous residence, which supplies a 4-zone duct system. Each zone has its independent controls. The house contains 3120 sq ft; total cost was approximately $42,000, or $1 per cu ft.

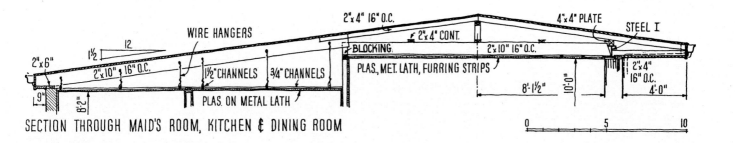

SECTION THROUGH MAID'S ROOM, KITCHEN & DINING ROOM

Labels within section:
WIRE HANGERS — 2"x 4" 16" O.C. — 4"x 4" PLATE — STEEL I — 2"x 4" CONT. — BLOCKING — 2"x10" 16" O.C. — 2"x6" — 1½ / 12 — 2"x10" 16" O.C. — 1½" CHANNELS — ¾" CHANNELS — PLAS., MET. LATH, FURRING STRIPS — PLAS. ON METAL LATH — 9" — 8'-2" — 8'-1½" — 10'-0" — 2"x 4" 16" O.C. — 4'-0"

0   5   10

Piaget Studio photos

Ben Schnall Photos

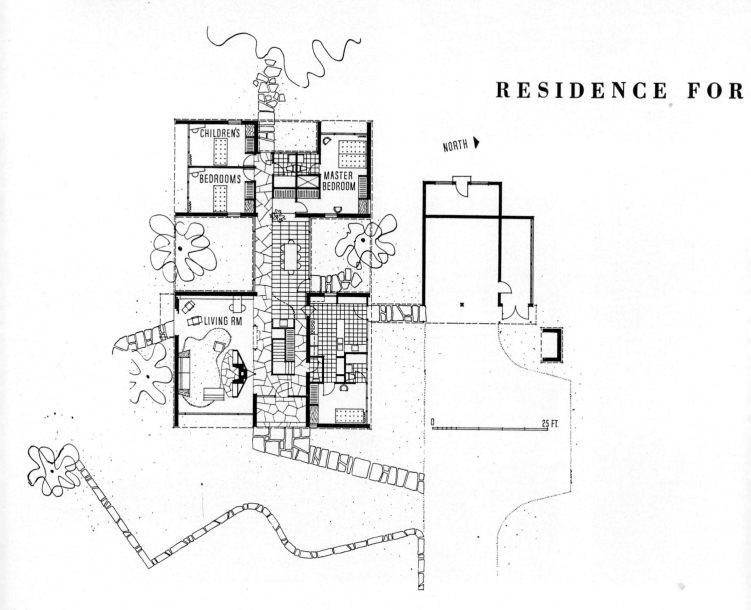

CHILDREN'S

BEDROOMS

MASTER
BEDROOM

LIVING RM

NORTH ▶

RESIDENCE FOR

0   25 FT.

MR. AND MRS. GEORGE PALLEY

Croton-on-Hudson, N. Y.

Sanders & Malsin, Architects

WHEN A HOUSE IS DESIGNED, as was this, chiefly for summer and weekend use, it should be as open and informal as possible. This one was planned as the successor to an earlier one on the same site which had burned to the ground except for the chimney. The first house had been two stories in height, and the chimney had been correspondingly tall; in this new version the chimney was left intact, and towers unexpectedly above the low roofline.

The bi-unit plan shown opposite was developed to meet the demands of a family which, entertaining a great deal and therefore needing a large dining room, nevertheless did not wish to waste space for dining facilities. By dividing the house into two wholly separate units — one for living and service, the other for bedrooms — and joining the two by a rather narrow passage containing the dining area, the architects not only solved the entertainment problem but also achieved an exceptionally open effect. And having achieved that effect they emphasized it by giving each wing a separate color for its below-window panel: yellow for the living room, bright red for the children's wing, gray for maid's room, blue-black for common areas, brown for owner's room. Other exterior walls are white-painted concrete block.

GEORGE PALLEY RESIDENCE

Ben Schnall Photos

Fireplace wall separating living room and entrance hall (above left and below) is duplicate of that in original house; owner is carving design in pine panel above mantel. Coat closet in entrance hall (above right) has no doors, an innovation which has proved popular with family

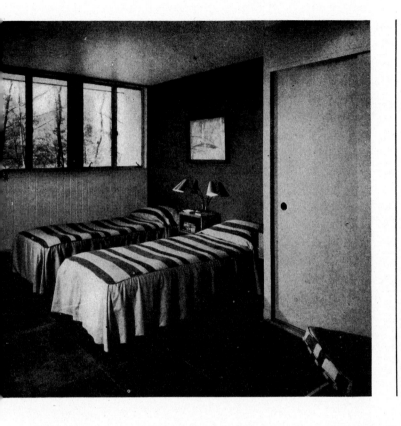

Bathhouse at end of swimming pool (above) was built by owner to architects' design; it is topped by a bright red tank in which water for the showers is heated by sun's rays

Interior walls are sheetrock covered with burlap and painted. Ceilings are plaster on wire lath, floors cork or rubber tile. Huge dining table is ash, was built by owner to architects' design as was much other furniture

HOUSE IN THE PACIFIC NORTHWEST

Residence of Mr. and Mrs. Trevor Roberts

Young & Richardson

Architects & Engineers

Blue Ridge, Washington

THE OWNERS OF THIS RESIDENCE facing Puget Sound had an unusually long list of special requirements: the house must be of straightforward contemporary design and must have an office-display room for Mr. Roberts, a salesman; it must have a shop for him, since his hobbies are woodworking, carpentry and landscaping; it must have four bedrooms (the family consists of three adults and two children), a playroom with outdoor terrace, and a dining patio. Since the site is a sloping wooded hill overlooking Puget Sound and the Olympic Mountains, the house obviously also had to be oriented toward the view.

The plan which resulted (page 185), and the way in which it was carried out, subsequently brought Architects Young & Richardson an award from the Washington Chapter, A.I.A. Living and dining rooms, three bedrooms and the kitchen all face the view; so does the large recreation room in the basement. A shop of generous proportions opens through the carport directly to the exterior. The office is strategically located just within the main entrance, virtually cut off from the rest of the house, and accessible from the shop, in effect giving Mr. Roberts a separate suite for his business and hobby requirements. The lower terrace has a built-in barbecue, and doubles as the play terrace and dining patio; the recreation room opens to it.

The house is of wood frame construction on a concrete foundation. Exterior walls are handsplit cedar siding, natural finish. The built-up roof is topped off with white marble chips to give overlooking residences a pleasant aspect — the first roof in the Northwest, the architects report, to be so treated for such a purpose. Heating is hot water panel in the concrete slab and hot water convectors in bedrooms and recreation room.

The sloping site permitted a basement recreation room over 30 ft long, opening to a paved terrace. The owner did much of the landscaping himself

Above: a brick walk curves under living room windows toward lower terrace

Above right: upper terrace can be reached directly from living room and breakfast alcove as well as from lower level, but is completely secluded

Right: main feature of living room is the glass-walled alcove cantilevered out to take full advantage of the view

Far right: dining area is tied to living room with one wall of vertical T & G fir, but is really a separate room; door at extreme left leads to upper terrace

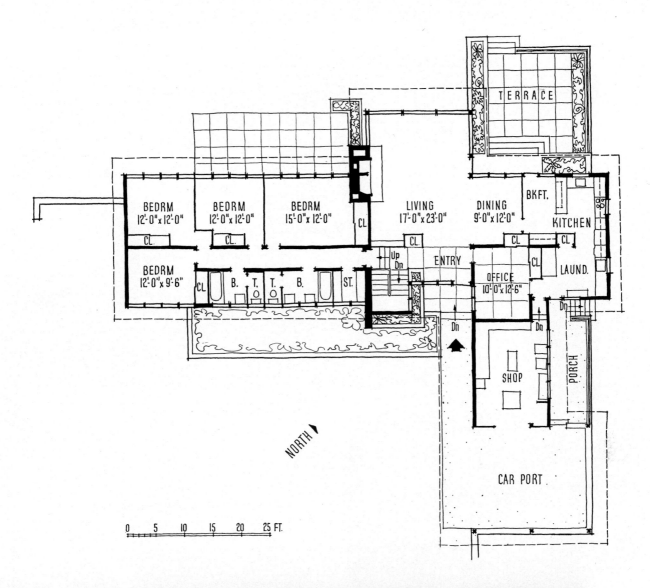

BEDRM
12'-0" x 12'-0"

BEDRM
12'-0" x 12'-0"

BEDRM
15'-0" x 12'-0"

LIVING
17'-0" x 23'-0"

DINING
9'-0" x 12'-0"

BKFT.

KITCHEN

CL.

CL.

CL

CL

CL

CL

CL

BEDRM
12'-0" x 9'-6"

CL

B.

T.

T.

B.

ST.

Up
Dn

ENTRY

LAUND.

OFFICE
10'-0" x 12'-6"

CL

Dn

TERRACE

Dn

Dn

SHOP

PORCH

NORTH

CAR PORT

0   5   10   15   20   25 FT.

Charles R. Pearson Photos

Above: even the kitchen looks out on the Sound. Left: larger of the two baths has well-lighted sloping mirror. Below: three of the four bedrooms face the view

ARCHITECT'S OWN HOUSE, CINCINNATI, OHIO

Carl A. Strauss, Architect   *John F. Kirkpatrick, Landscape Designer*

Full utilization of the fairly steep site overlooking the Ohio River and city beyond, and ease of maintenance and house-keeping for a family consisting of the architect, his wife and two sons, were the design criteria here. Access to the site is from the upper level, so carport, entry walk and principal entrance are on the upper level along with bedrooms; living room, etc., are below.

November 1950

Hedrich-Blessing Photos

Left, living-dining room, at ground level, has paving-brick floor extended outdoors. Though sliding walls are not screened, direction of prevailing breeze and an infrequent spraying with insecticide almost eliminate insects; the family's pleasure in easy outdoor-indoor access outweighs the nuisance of the occasional stray bug or dog. Above, second-floor entry

Like every detail of construction and finish of the house, planting is laid out for ease of upkeep

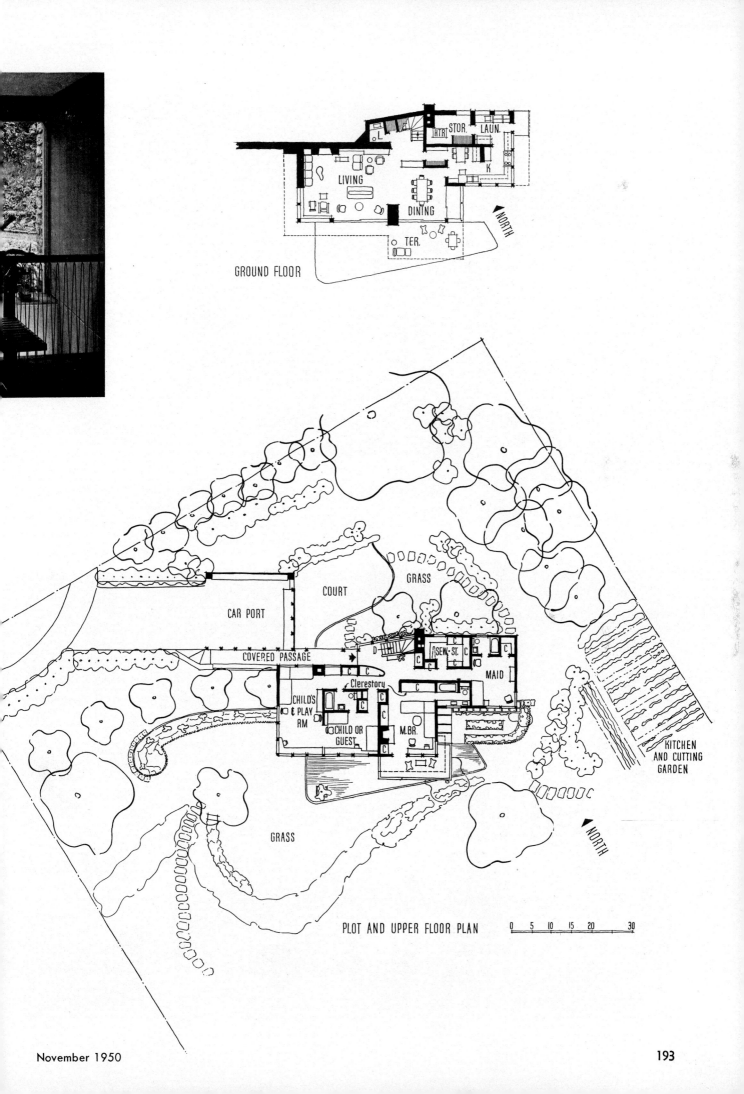

GROUND FLOOR

L.

HTR STOR. LAUN.

LIVING

K

DINING

NORTH

TER.

COURT

GRASS

CAR PORT

COVERED PASSAGE

D

SEW. ST.

C C C C

MAID

Clerestory

C

C C C

CHILD'S
PLAY
RM

CHILD OR
GUEST

M.BR.

C C C

C

KITCHEN
AND CUTTING
GARDEN

GRASS

NORTH

PLOT AND UPPER FLOOR PLAN

0 5 10 15 20   30

Boys have two bedrooms which can be separated by a folding wall or thrown together. On upper floor, walls are striated plywood; on lower floor some stone, obtained from excavation, is used

Far left, eyebrow to keep high sun off a glass wall which both admits a fine view and provides a hazard for junior on his tricycle; second, two-compartment bath; third, kitchen and dining space separated only by a cabinet (all three by The Architects Collaborative). Right, modern version of the hob seat plus masonry with scarcely visible support (V. K. Thompson, Designer).

HOUSE IN ANDOVER, MASSACHUSETTS

Bernard Kessler, Architect

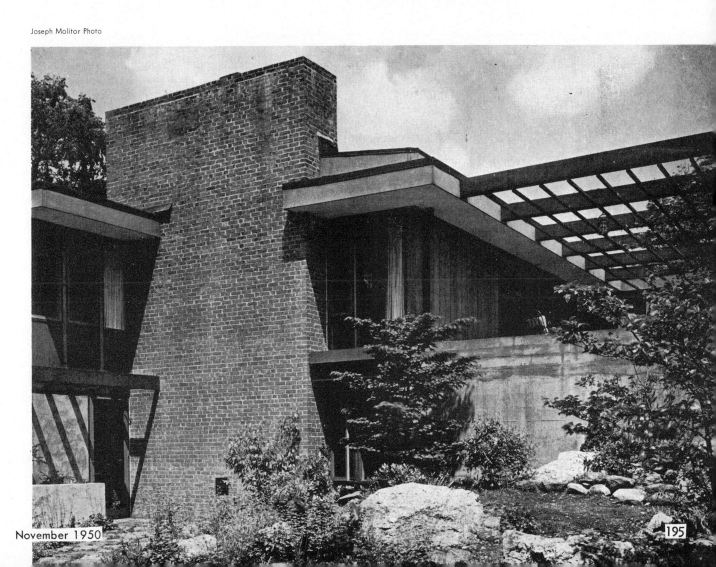

HOUSE IN ANDOVER, MASS.

THE owners, a couple in middle years, live alone and entertain informally and in small groups composed principally
of their children. They insisted on having their bedrooms off
the ground; hence the placement of the house on the sloping

Joseph Molitor Photos

site, with bedrooms five to eight feet above grade. The isolated
bedroom with its own interior bath (artificially ventilated) is
used for a servant or for guest quarters. The kitchen-dining
area, quite unusual and yet extremely sensible for this informal
household, is designed to permit husband and wife to share in
preparing and serving family meals; both are good cooks. At
the same time, a partial wall screens as much as possible of the
work area, with its stacked pots, pans, dishes, etc. The ease
with which after-meal mess can be closed off from the remainder
of the house, and the simplicity with which such a compact
space can be cleaned up, should be apparent. The same logic
has been applied to the entire house, together with a not inconsiderable talent for assembling the required elements pleasantly. In harmony with its natural setting and thoroughly
contemporary, this is a house in which it should be fun, not
work, to live.

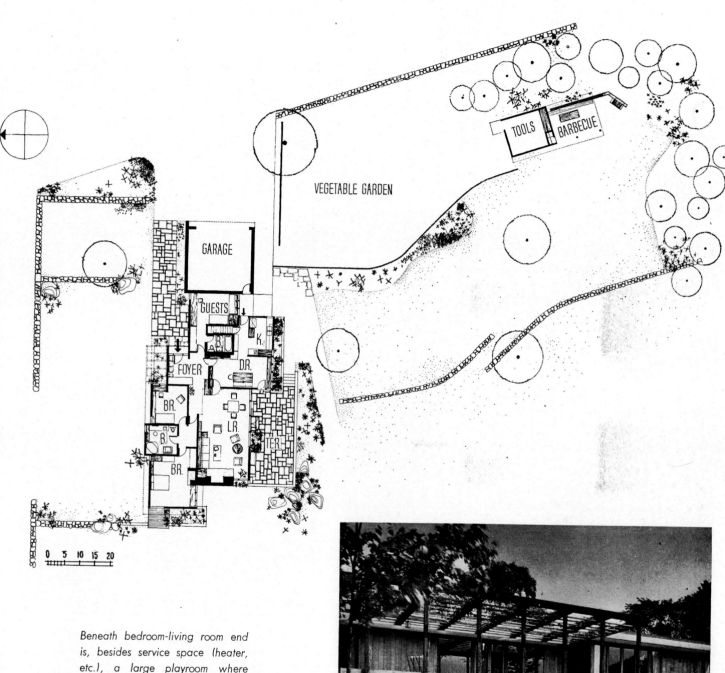

N

GARAGE

VEGETABLE GARDEN

TOOLS BARBECUE

GUESTS

K.

B.

FOYER DR.

BR.

B.

LR.

TER.

BR.

0 5 10 15 20

Beneath bedroom-living room end is, besides service space (heater, etc.), a large playroom where grandchildren can romp in poor weather while parents and grandparents visit on the first floor. Terrace, right, is shaded by a grape arbor which in winter, when leaves are fallen, admits plenty of sun to the living room. The deceptively simple landscaping both ties the house to its setting and opens to embrace a view, from the terrace, across a wooded valley

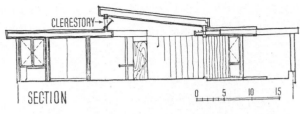

SECTION

Clerestory above interior corner of living room admits light, ventilates, forms a plant shelf which, continued around two sides of the room, becomes an indirect lighting trough. Ceiling is higher in living room than in other rooms

The same materials, common brick and vertical cedar siding, are used inside and out, with addition of some plaster on interior walls and ceilings. Everything is thoroughly up-to-date: heating is radiant panel with copper tubing in ceilings; most lighting fixtures are indirect or recessed; there is much built-in furniture; the flat portions of the roof are designed to be flooded for roof-cooling in hot summer weather. As in most outlying houses, entrance through the garage is at least as important as the formal ''front'' door (photo above), which is almost hidden. It is noteworthy that traditional furnishings fit into the house well

Despite the numerous refinements in this house, it is in spirit far from the modern showcase which so intrigues many architects. Rather, appropriate contemporary ideas and equipment have been adapted and blended in a way which neither denies that the oc-

Joseph Molitor Photos

cupants have roots, nor over-emphasizes them. The house, though it is no cottage, has domestic, human scale brought into sharp focus at the indoor barbecue (above) where the master can broil meat while his wife, with cooking muss out of sight around a corner, prepares the rest of the meal. That the house has also a friendly dignity is a compliment to both the owners and the architect

RESIDENCE FOR

MR. AND MRS. WILLARD C. MILLS

Near Danville, Calif.

Anshen & Allen, Architects

THIS HOUSE, planned for a family of four including two small boys, is situated on a level-topped spur projecting to the southeast from a higher hill. A fine view of the San Ramon Valley to the south and southwest prompted the placing of the house lengthwise along the spur, with the services and entrances on the northeast side, close to the access road. The living area, of course, faces the view.

The owners stipulated that the house must be built quickly and economically of readily available materials, and that it have a panel heating system. They required also a living-dining area opening to a porch and terrace; three bedrooms, two baths, a shop, and bulk storage facilities. The architects met the requirements with one-story wood frame construction on concrete floor slab. The top of the slab, which contains the heating pipes, is only a few inches above finished grade, but excellent natural drainage eliminates the risk of dampness.

A climate which is cool in winter and very hot in summer made the use of large glass areas something of a problem. To control heat and glare, the porch roof, 12 ft wide, was extended the full length of the living room and continued as a 4-ft overhang the length of the bedrooms. A ventilated attic air space with 2 in. of insulation at the ceilings gives still further control, and a sprinkler system, installed at the ridge of the roof, can be used for wetting down the roof in especially hot weather.

Exterior walls are redwood board and batten. Roofing is cedar shingles.

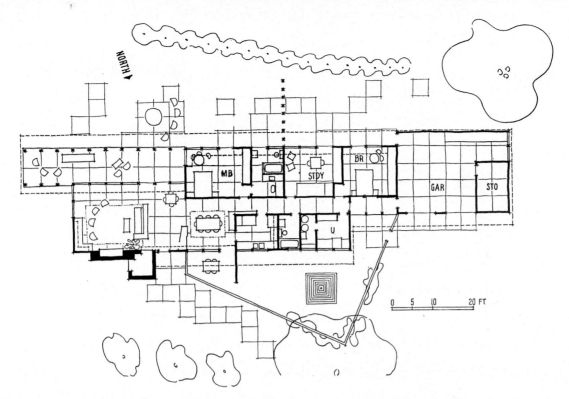

All entrances—main, service and garage—are on same side of the house.
Projecting dining terrace wall and drying yard fence on plan have not been built

RESIDENCE FOR MR. AND MRS. WILLARD C. MILLS

Huge mass of brick chimney provides convenient wood storage area opening both to exterior (opposite page) and to living room (below). Main entrance, immediately adjacent, leads directly into living room. Floors throughout are black asphalt tile, waxed. Interior walls are sheetrock, taped and painted, and stained redwood boards. Ceilings are sheetrock. Fluorescent lighting is used in living-dining area

Roger Sturtevant Photos

Living room makes the most of the view across the valley with large windows and doors opening directly to a covered porch and an open terrace beyond

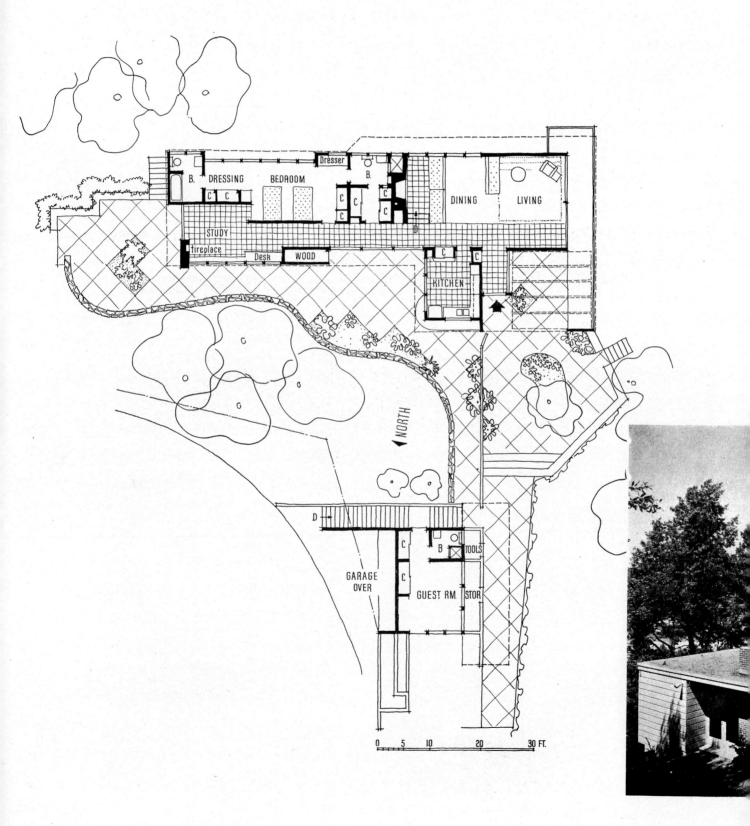

Residence for Mr. and Mrs. Clarence Bowman

San Rafael, California

Francis Joseph McCarthy, Architect

Thomas D. Church, Landscape Architect

HILLSIDE SITE

B. DRESSING BEDROOM Dresser B.

DINING LIVING

C C C C C C

STUDY

fireplace Desk WOOD

KITCHEN

C C

D

NORTH

D

GARAGE OVER

C

C

B TOOLS

GUEST RM STOR

0 5 10 20 30 FT.

USED TO OBTAIN MAXIMUM PRIVACY

WHEN this house was first planned it was intended solely as a weekend retreat, and only the living-dining-kitchen wing was built. Later its owners, a professional couple, decided to enlarge it to its present size to permit year-round occupancy after they retire. Their requirements included a large master bedroom with two separate baths and dressing areas and an adjacent study well isolated from the general living area.

The steepness of the wooded site (so steep that the actual building area had to be cut into the hill) was used to give the house unusual privacy and a secluded terrace facing the view. The garage was placed further up the hill, directly accessible from the main road.

Exterior of the house is redwood channel cut, rustic siding, stained gray. Framing is timber, foundations are concrete. The roof is tar and gravel.

Roger Sturtevant Photos

The steepness of the site permitted a 2½-story garage building, with the garage itself (two-car) on the upper level, a guest or maid's room and bath immediately below, and tool storage and laundry facilities half a story lower still. It also permitted a completely secluded terrace (top of page) facing the main view

RESIDENCE FOR MR. AND MRS. CLARENCE BOWMAN

Main entrance (above) opens to landscaped terrace, across which is garage and guest house. Living-dining area (right above and top opposite) has large fireplace with a sunken hearth accommodating a double sofa. Study (two lower photos opposite) is at quiet end of house, adjoining master bedroom (right). Floors are oak in living-dining room, carpet over pine in bedroom, terrazzo in bathrooms, hollow tile elsewhere. Interior walls are plywood, natural finish; ceilings are plasterboard, painted a golden yellow

Roger Sturtevant Photos

Damora

BARN REMODELED FOR RESIDENCE

Residence of Mr. and Mrs. David Plummer, Cohasset, Mass.

Hugh Stubbins, Jr., Architect

Surprisingly little construction work was required to transform a portion of this sturdy Cohasset barn into the delightful residence shown on these two pages. Exterior walls of stone and shingle, fir ceilings and fir walls were all perfectly suited to the purpose. Except for the great stone fireplace which adds so much to the character of the interior, the only major changes necessary for the transformation were the addition of several partitions (see plan opposite), new floors of hard pine, and new lighting fixtures.

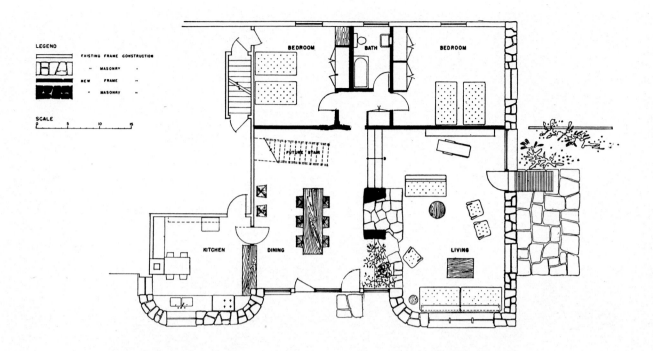

The converted barn overlooks the ocean from a high elevation, and has a distant view although somewhat limited in panorama. The interior is dominated by the huge stone fireplace which serves as an effective partition between living and dining rooms. The exterior was permitted to retain its original character in all essential respects, as indicated by the skillful modification of the main entrance shown opposite

Damora

Jean and Norman Fletcher

Walter Gropius

John and Sarah Harkness

Robert McMillan

Louis McMillen

Benjamin Thompson

HOUSE DESIGNED FOR

The Architects Collaborative, Architects

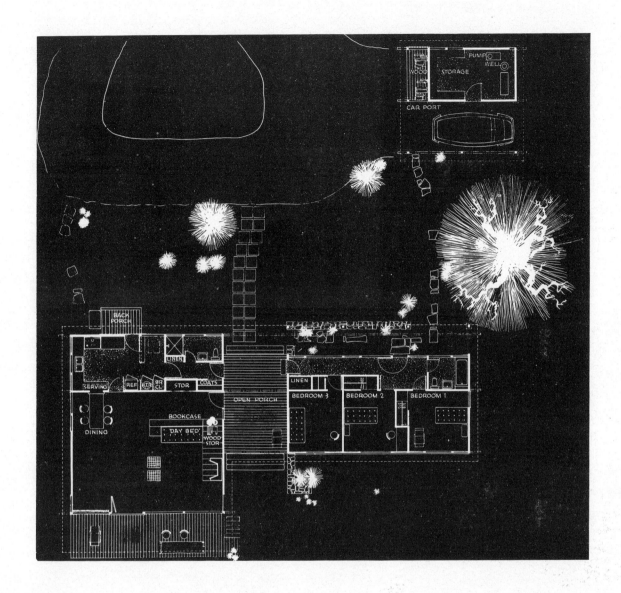

THE rugged north coast of Maine affords violent contrasts of weather, trees, rocks and sea. This vacation home, simple and direct in composition, has a strength which echoes its background. Its roof overhangs on all sides for protection from snow and driving rain. House and carport are built around a huge spruce which first attracts attention as you arrive; but then through the open porch separating the bedroom wing from the rest of the house you see the Atlantic Ocean.

THE MAINE COAST

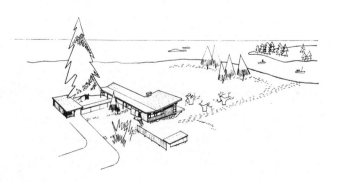

Of the two units of which the house is composed, the main portion, comprising living room, dining room, kitchen and utility space, may be used year 'round. This area has a heat-circulating fireplace and provision is made for a future heating plant. Living in a vacation house, particularly a small one, may become disagreeable in poor weather when there is no place to go; hence the wide open living room with its glass walls, and the sheltered porch adjoining. Construction is of simple wood frame with exterior finished in pine boarding and redwood siding. Roof and side walls are insulated; living-dining room has interior walls of figured red gum plywood. All doors are flush plywood. Floors are of beech and cork-and-rubber composition. Originally there was to be little if any interior trim; but local builders found it difficult to cut and fit rough framing members with sufficient accuracy

HOUSE IN MAINE

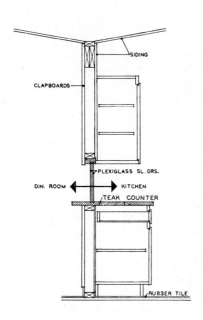

SIDING

CLAPBOARDS

PLEXIGLASS SL. DRS.

DIN. ROOM ← → KITCHEN

TEAK COUNTER

RUBBER TILE

Damora

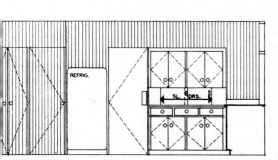

REFRIG.

SL. DRS.

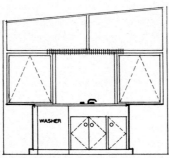

WASHER

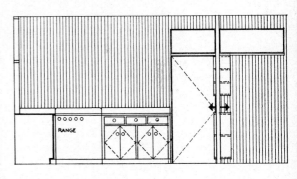

RANGE

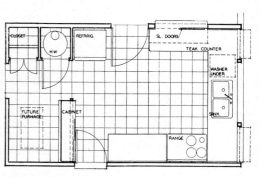

CLOSET
H W
REFRIG.
SL. DOORS
TEAK COUNTER
FUTURE FURNACE
CABINET
WASHER UNDER
SINK
RANGE

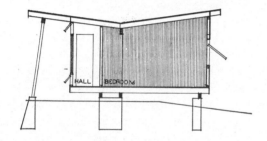

HALL BEDROOM

The bedroom wing of the house, unheated, is intended only for summer use and is built upon posts. Like the other wing it is fully insulated and the combination of verticals, horizontals, slanting columns as well as walls and openings is very carefully studied

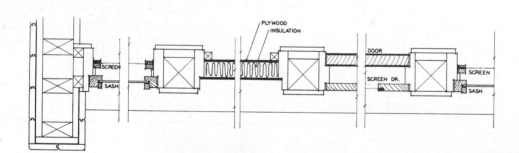

PLYWOOD
INSULATION
SCREEN
SASH
DOOR
SCREEN DR.
SCREEN
SASH

HOUSE

IN MAINE

Within the limits of this small house there is a variety of size, shape and finish. In the bedroom hall you can see outdoors constantly, and where the glass goes to the floor the foreground comes into view. Succeeding bedrooms each have two walls of plywood — the first in birch, the second in walnut and the third again in birch. The remaining two walls and ceilings of all bedrooms are white painted siding with window sills high enough to give a sense of enclosure and privacy

Damora

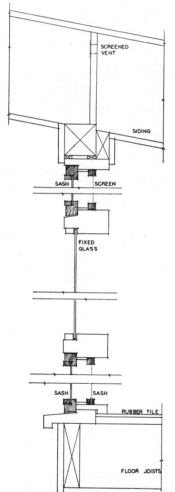

SCREENED VENT

SIDING

SASH | SCREEN

FIXED GLASS

SASH | SASH

RUBBER TILE

FLOOR JOISTS

Roger Sturtevant Photos

A LARGE SMALL HOUSE IN STOCKTON, CALIF.

Joseph Esherick, Architect

THE site of this house for Mr. and Mrs. Harry Holt is in the ranch country of the San Joaquin Valley where the climate and various factors incidental to it afford the architect some interesting problems. Summers are intensely hot, and winters cold and raw, especially when there is a fog. Prevailing summer winds are westerly, and there are occasional cold north winds in winter, but these usually blow on clear, sunny days and, if protection is provided, sitting outdoors is pleasant. The shallow, U-shaped plan, suggested by the clients, was adopted by the architect as desirable, since most rooms would get the advantage of the cool-

ing west wind on summer nights, and the house, facing southeast, would provide shelter on the garden side from both west and north winds.

In order to avoid movement of the foundation in a very unstable soil, concrete piers on 10-ft. centers were extended 6 ft. below grade to stable soil, and support a reinforced concrete beam at grade level.

Following a current trend to large houses of few rooms, reducing the help problem to a practical minimum, the Holt house is also, in this respect, a return to an early California tradition and a reminder that sound ideas are apt to reassert themselves.

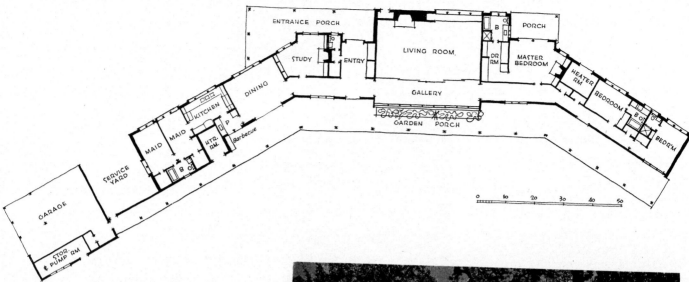

In plan above, note flexibility of heating
afforded by independent forced warm air
units in each wing, supplemented by fireplaces in three center rooms. At right,
the entrance porch; below, the garden
side, seen from the bedroom wing. Soffits
and roof beams are gray-green; redwood
siding, sash and trim are buff, to match brick

The garden porch, at right, is paralleled indoors by the gallery shown below; through the sliding glass partition is the living room. In order to admit the sun to this area, the porch roof is omitted. All porch floors are exposed-aggregate concrete with redwood division strips

Above: the upper chords of the trusses extend out to carry the overhangs and porch roofs. The roof is 2 by 6 plank laid over the trusses and covered with asphalted felt, over which was laid 1 by 4 stripping for the redwood shakes. Because of the low pitch of the roof, the shakes were interlaid with 15-lb. felt strips. No additional insulation was used, but hot-weather performance has been excellent. Right: living room, from the gallery

The dining room is designed as an inward extension of the dining porch. Because of the prevalence of warm weather, every effort was made to achieve a cool, fresh feeling; hence the generous proportions of the rooms, the relatively high ceilings, the occasional introduction of plan material, and the green tile floor which, extended into the gallery, entry and hall, also defines the circulation area. The dining table is composed of two independent units to facilitate moving indoors or out, as desired

Roger Sturtevant Photos

Above: the master bedroom opens on a small, private porch facing northwest, which, together with the polished oak floor and beige walls and ceiling, helps create an atmosphere of cool spaciousness. Below: the study houses a gun collection, a small bar, and, on the opposite wall, books. All interiors in the house are of oak or gypsum board, the oak sealed, glazed and lacquered, and the board either painted or enameled

A HOUSE WITH TWO WINGS AND RARE PRIVACY

Residence of Mr. and Mrs. Marshall Hale, Jr., Burlingame, Calif.

Clarence W. W. Mayhew, Architect

COMPLETE separation of all the varied activities of family living marks this unusual, distinguished California house, designed for a department store executive, his wife and three children. The house is located in a large terraced garden, and follows the natural slope of the land. It is divided, as the plan on page 225 shows, into two wings, one containing the living and dining rooms, servants' room and kitchen, the other containing the bedrooms. Each wing, however, is subdivided by the entrance hall and gallery, so that the effect is really one of four wings, with each "department" of the house completely segregated. This arrangement, furthermore, provides two secluded courts, one for the family and the other, below the kitchen and laundry, forming a screened service yard. The servants' room, large enough to be a combination bed- and sitting room for a couple, turns its back on the rest of the house, and the guest room, with its own bath, is likewise secluded.

Exterior finish of the house is light buff cement stucco accented by the burnt orange interior seen frequently through the large glass areas of the walls. Heating is by forced warm air, with filters and humidity control. Three gas furnaces are required: one for the bedroom wing and guest room, one for the living room, dining room and kitchen, and a third for the servants' wing. Lighting throughout is indirect and flush.

Roger Sturtevant Photos

The bedroom wing stretches across the front of the house, but the master bedroom (right in photo above and extreme left on opposite page) faces the garden court separating the two wings, and has its own balcony. Room beneath the balcony is combination tool room and hot house. Veneer walls in living room (below) are bleached Philippine mahogany

A magnificent oak tree, shown in both photos on this page and also on pages 226 and 228, grows up through roof treillage outside the glass walls of living and dining rooms, and is visible from the main entrance through the gallery. Above: the living room looking across the gallery toward dining room. Below: the living room terrace is shielded by wall of servants' wing at left. Opposite page: the connecting gallery, seen from garden court; living room is at left, children's bedrooms are at right

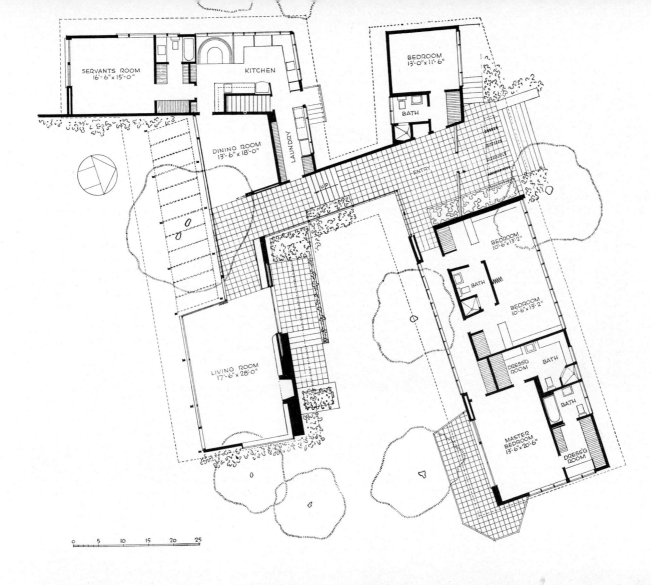

SERVANTS ROOM
16'-6" x 15'-0"

KITCHEN

BEDROOM
13'-0" x 11'-6"

BATH

DINING ROOM
13'-6" x 18'-0"

LAUNDRY

ENTRY

UP

BEDROOM
10'-6" x 13'-2"

BATH

BEDROOM
10'-6" x 13'-2"

LIVING ROOM
17'-6" x 28'-0"

DRESS'G
ROOM

BATH

BATH

MASTER
BEDROOM
13'-6" x 20'-6"

DRESS'G
ROOM

0   5   10   15   20   25

Roger Sturtevant Photos

Left: main entrance, with living room windows visible through glass wall of entry. *Below:* another view of living room terrace and the fine old oak. *Opposite page:* the gallery, looking past garden court toward living room wing (above) and down the steps toward main entrance (below); floors here are 12-in. square red quarry tile

The master bedroom, above and opposite, is generously proportioned, has two baths and two dressing rooms. Below: a corner of the dining room, looking across gallery to living room. Floors are overall-carpeted except in kitchen, laundry and bathrooms, where linoleum is used. Interior walls are hard plaster, canvased and painted. Lighting throughout is indirect and flush

Because the house follows the natural slope of the site, the master bedroom is virtually at second floor level and its private balcony (see also page 223) is hidden in the branches of the trees. The kitchen, below, has a comfortable dining corner for the servants, and, like most rooms in the house, has two exposures. Window at right overlooks service court

Roger Sturtevant Photos

Roger Sturtevant Photos

DESIGNING WHAT COMES NATURALLY

"Tamalpais House," North of San Francisco

Henry Hill, Architect; Eckbo, Royston and Williams, Landscape Architects

IF this house, by virtue of being published in the magazine, advances the "cause" of architecture, it will probably be because it obviously was not designed to be published in the magazines. It does not bundle up the clichés; it does not flaunt its inventions. Its claim to distinction is the modest naturalness with which it wraps up a pretty expensive package of space. Included in this package is a lush treatment of the outdoors, what with swimming pool, bath house, stone walls and terraces, not to mention the direct floral treatment or the fence to give it all privacy. This naturalness, while readily seen in the photographs, tends to grow

more impressive as one begins to appreciate the scale of the house and its glass areas and views.

It was designed for a man and wife, without children, who specified a one-level house with complete privacy for outdoor living and room for extensive but informal entertaining. The site, overlooking the ubiquitous Mt. Tamalpais, is a pointed corner of hillside leveled down to a convenient driveway level, and well fenced in — for privacy, yes, but also to prevent falling into the valley; it simply wasn't possible for the landscaping to flow gently into the countryside. In fact the fence acts as barrier against the closing in of the wilderness.

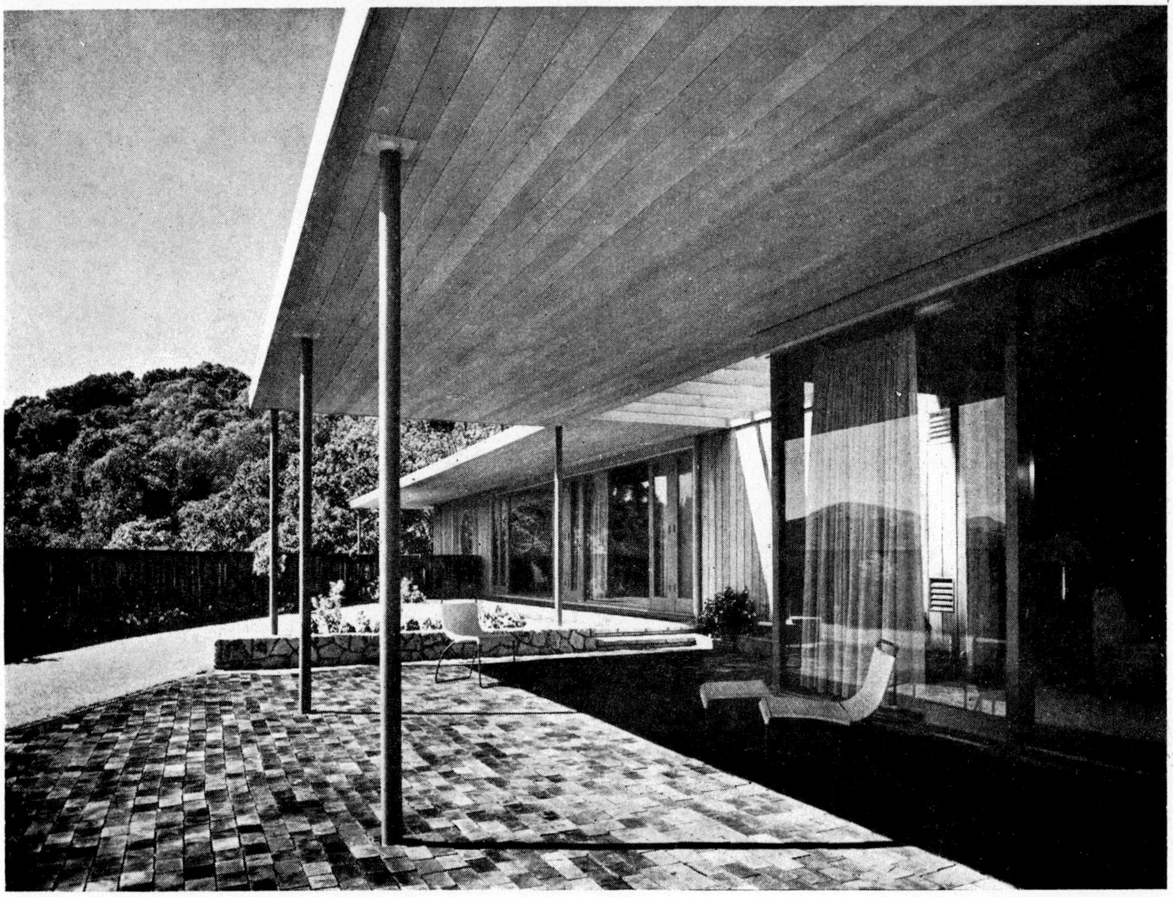

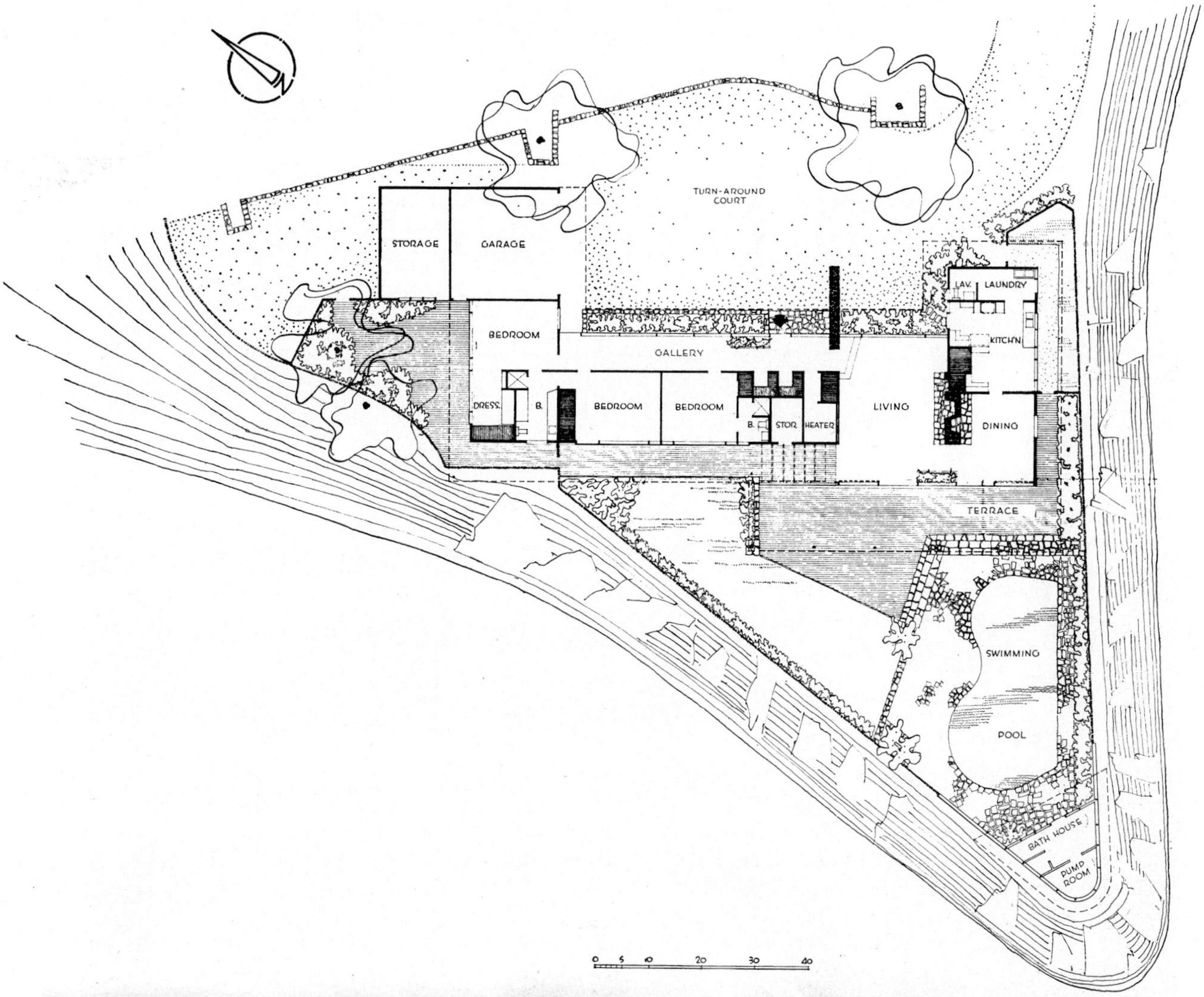

TURN-AROUND COURT
STORAGE
GARAGE
BEDROOM
GALLERY
LAV.
LAUNDRY
KITCH'N
DRESS.
B.
BEDROOM
BEDROOM
B.
STOR
HEATER
LIVING
DINING
TERRACE
SWIMMING
POOL
BATH HOUSE
PUMP ROOM
0 5 10 20 30 40

The glazed gallery (above and below) is the only area opening directly to the approach side of the house, facing the turn-around court. The heavy masonry wall serves to shield the living room from direct gaze of visitors at the entrance door, and the planting strip can be arranged to provide further screening if desirable. Exterior siding is all natural redwood, unfinished and left to weather. The continuous facia board is painted gold; the front door is painted inside and out a dubonnet wine red

Eaves at the bedrooms (foreground) are 7 ft. wide; at the living room, 12 ft.; they protect the windows against the western summer sun, but admit the winter sunlight. Terraces under the eaves are paved with redwood blocks, with end grain exposed. The long wall in each bedroom is of pine, stained a gray gold; ceiling is surface pine

The upper view of the living room gives some idea of the scale of the house and its vistas. It easily accommodates the massive furniture (by Frank DeWitt), indeed the heavy furniture is really necessary to the room. The heavy masonry at the fireplace also is in scale, as is the huge painting on the opposite wall. Living-dining room walls are natural redwood

Roger Sturtevant Photos

The principal bedroom has its glass wall opening into a private garden formed by the outside storage room, the house itself and the last section of the fence. With this assurance of privacy, even the dressing room can have a full glass wall (dressing room and bath at lower right)

Above: this side of the house faces a broad panorama of hills. Below: identifiable by roofs are carport, studio, bedroom, entry and living areas

April 1949

Clarence W. W. Mayhew, Architect

ONE of the owners of this house, a well-known portrait photographer, required that her studio and related workrooms comprise an integral part of the design — yet furnished with a separate entrance, and isolated from the indoor and outdoor living areas. The studio, which has its own southeasterly terrace for outdoor work, also doubles as a bedroom with bed and closets concealed by sliding Japanese paper screens. The other bedroom and bath provide the buffer between this section and the main entry and living room. Servant's wing is at the extreme opposite end. Exterior is flush redwood siding; roof, tar and gravel. The heating system is forced warm air.

RESIDENCE IN CONTRA COSTA COUNTY, CALIFORNIA

The plan arranges itself around a large private terrace at the rear, affording a pleasant contrast to the expansive view on the opposite side

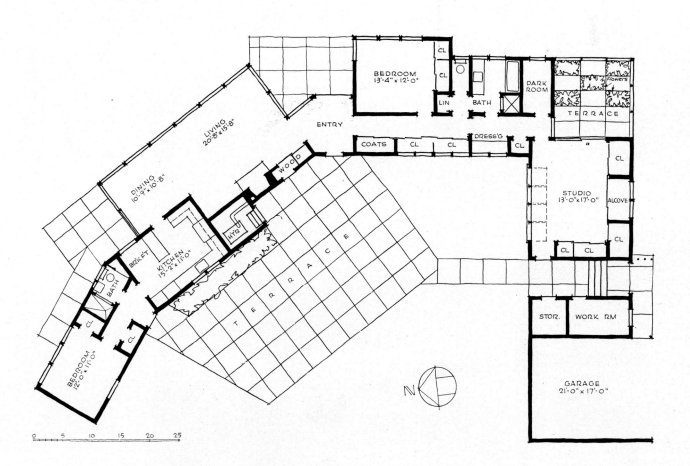

Above: a small terrace faces the sweeping view of the Contra Costa Hills and Mt. Diablo. Beyond, a wooded hill screens the larger terrace at rear. The studio, right, opens on an outdoor work space and has north skylight, also seen in terrace view below

Three views of the living-dining room.
Right: detail of sliding glass doors opening
on terrace shown at top of opposite page.
At other end of room similar doors give
access to dining terrace near kitchen

Roger Sturtevant Photos

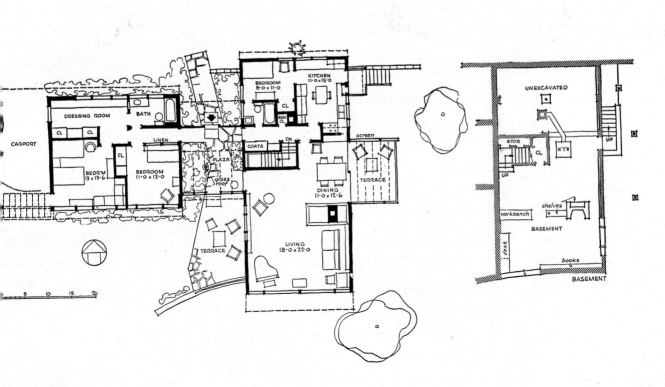

Ezra Stoller Photos

PLANNED FOR A PLEASANTER LIFE

House for Mr. and Mrs. Francis Bitter near Cambridge, Mass.

Carl Koch, Architect, Frederic L. Day, Associate

IF proof were needed that ways of both living and architecture have changed vastly — and for the better — in two generations, this new house and the formal, three-story Georgian mansion that stands hard by on the estate of Edward W. Forbes would provide beautiful and typical examples of the contrasts between 1908 and the present.

Social convention only forty years ago dictated many a whopping and elaborate (albeit elegant and suave) "manor house" designed with all the architectural mannerisms of other bygone golden eras. Today the set-

pattern and the servants and the lavish hand have perforce largely vanished, and in their stead we have the freedom to design the environment and facilities for the particular way of life of the individual family. So in this house we have the straightforward, thoughtful planning that reflects and serves the owners' individual needs and desires — convenient, cheerful, efficient, informal — but with its own welcome dignity. The understanding logic of its planning and design becomes more and more evident as one analyzes its many interesting and unusual features, for it will bear the closest scrutiny.

Instead of entering a dark cramped hall or foyer, one is welcomed to the Bitter house through its sunny garden "Plaza" which both joins and separates the living and sleeping areas of the house. A glance at the page opposite will show why the Bitters refer to it as the "Plaza," for the sculptured figure is a small-scale study of the one that graces New York's Plaza; both figures are by Karl Bitter, sculptor, Mr. Bitter's father. Flooded with sunshine which pours through the south wall and the wire-glass skylight, this indoor garden will soon be verdant with flourishing olive and lemon trees, and eventually with camellias. Its flagstone walk is integral with the entrance path and the open terrace beyond to the south (shown below).

Ezra Stoller Photos

When the door is open one can see that the entrance plaza is really an enclosed continuation of the sunny south terrace. From this bright center, one can enter directly the living room or the service hall (with the coat closet and the stair down to Mr. Bitter's study), or the quiet bedroom wing. In too many houses all-on-one-floor, the living room is actually a big and busy corridor. Not so here. The vertical tongue and groove fir wall of the living room is stained with linseed oil and pigment

The dining end of the living room opens wide on a shielded terrace to the east. The counter of the cabinet at the left is level with the counter and range in the kitchen and the sliding panel (shown partially open) is a time-and-step-saving convenience. Plates of black and gold Burmese lacquer from Mrs. Bitter's collection are displayed on the shelves above

Central feature of the living room is the unusual fireplace open on three sides instead of the usual one; in fact, it was originally planned to be open on all sides with just a suspended hood to control smoke and draft. The hood is constructed on a 1⅛-in. pipe frame with metal lath covered with an insulating cement; the throat is equipped with a rotary-type damper. The chimney carries the flue from the fireplace in the study below

The living room is readily adaptable to entertaining and to intimate musicals, for Mrs. Bitter, author of the book *Thirty Indian Songs*, is an authority on Indian folk music and used to sing under the name of Ratan Davi. The room has remarkably good acoustics and the grand piano is strategically placed at the southwest corner of the room. The land slopes sufficiently to the south to permit large windows in the study-workroom, under the living room, where Mr. Bitter can be in quiet seclusion or enjoy informal discussions with fellow physicists. Here are his workbench and bookshelves.

The bedroom wing is designed for quiet privacy and comfort; both bedrooms open to the south, looking out across the grass terrace toward the Charles River. The spacious and conveniently equipped dressing room, complete with wardrobes, shelves, dressing table, drawers and pressing board, is *en suite* with the master bedroom and the bath. The master bedroom, thus unencumbered, is arranged and furnished for rest and relaxation by day or night, as will be seen in the plan.

Ezra Stoller Photos

Looking east along the bedroom window-wall toward the paved end of the terrace and the west wall of the living room. The roof extends to form the projection which shields the windows from both rain and summer sun; note similar protecting eyebrow over the south living room window at the far right. The door from the bedroom (extreme left) gives access to the carport via a trellised walk which will someday be an attractive greenhouse

A fine wire mesh screen shields the dining terrace from the service steps and entrance. At the left of the kitchen door is a slotted panel which opens to permit packages to be delivered into a large kitchen cabinet whether anyone is at home or not. The cabinet is seen in the photograph on the opposite page, center, above the counter and at the left of the sink. The main roof slopes down from south to north, one inch to the foot. The kitchen entrance roof is of corrugated transite. Outside entrance to the heater room in the basement is down a flight of steps at the left of the kitchen porch. Exterior concrete blocks are coated with cement paint

An ingenious linen closet is provided opening from the hall and forming the backrest for the bed-couch in the guest room. The bed is pulled out from the wall when its full width is needed. Note the borrowed light over the linen cabinets and door. The bedroom wing is built of 8-in. concrete block furred with 2 by 3's laid flat, then rock lath and plaster

Ezra Stoller Photos

Above, looking west across the north front, service wing in foreground, bedroom wing beyond. Right, east side of the kitchen, package delivery cabinet between door and window, sliding pass door in corner opens to counter in dining area. Below, looking toward the north window of the kitchen. The incinerator door is in the southwest corner (left, not visible). Kitchen floor is linoleum; bedroom floors, rubber tile; living room, oak. Radiant heating is employed throughout the house, the pipes imbedded in the concrete floor of the bedroom wing, and in the ceiling of the living and service wing. Both walls and roof are insulated

SPACIOUSNESS VIA THE THIRD DIMENSION

Residence in Concord, Massachusetts

Hugh Stubbins, Jr.

Architect

THE owner of this house, a musician and music teacher, required a living room large enough for piano lessons and group singing. As the building budget was extremely limited, the dining and hall areas are made small additional parts of the living room and the architect has cleverly acquired space vertically, as seen above, and has opened the entire long side of the room with glass — all of which makes the 18 by 20 ft. area seem more spacious.

At right: view from the southwest. Projecting above the roof line, the bathroom window, cocked up at a saucy angle, gives an unexpected lift to the design. Walls, oil-finished redwood; roof, asphalt shingle. Above: the living room

The chimney, except for the fireplace and flue, is concrete brick with a plaster hood supported on metal rods. Walls are rock lath, ceilings metal lath, with a single coat of plaster. Floor is painted concrete

As shown in the plan and pictured at left, the entry serves multiple purposes, acting as front door, kitchen entrance (via the utility room) as well as giving access to the storage room through the door at right. The larger bedroom, occupied by the two children, can be divided by a curtain. Plans for future additions to the house include a large family sitting room, and a garage connected to the entrance by a covered way. Steel pipes laid in concrete supply radiant heat. All fixed glass is wood framed, opening vents are projected metal sash

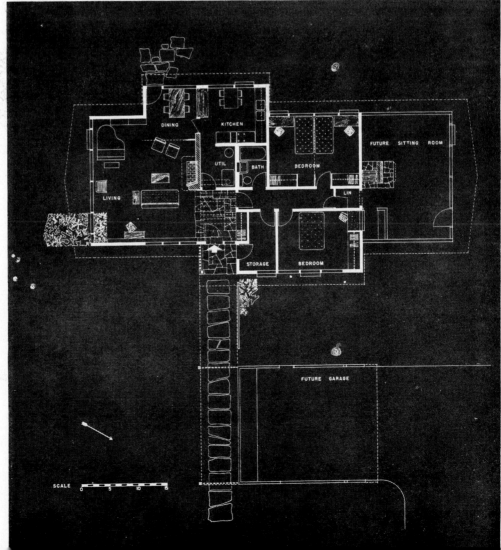

DINING KITCHEN

FUTURE SITTING ROOM

UTIL BATH BEDROOM

LIVING LIN

STORAGE BEDROOM

FUTURE GARAGE

SCALE 0 5 10

Piaget Studio Photos

PLANNED FOR THE SERVANTLESS WAY OF LIFE

Residence in Ladue, Missouri

Robert Elkington, Architect

April 1949

Two factors, actually, were dominant in developing this design: the owners do their own work, and Missouri summers are hot. As a result of the first we find such features as the location of the kitchen near the bedrooms for early morning convenience, the laundry placed near the entry and telephone-equipped to minimize effect of interruptions. There is provision for small dinner parties only (the accent is on after-dinner entertaining). In consideration of the summer heat clerestory windows are provided in the living room to exhaust the pocket of hot air, and sliding doors enable porch and living room to merge into a single, cross-ventilated "breezeway" for summer use.

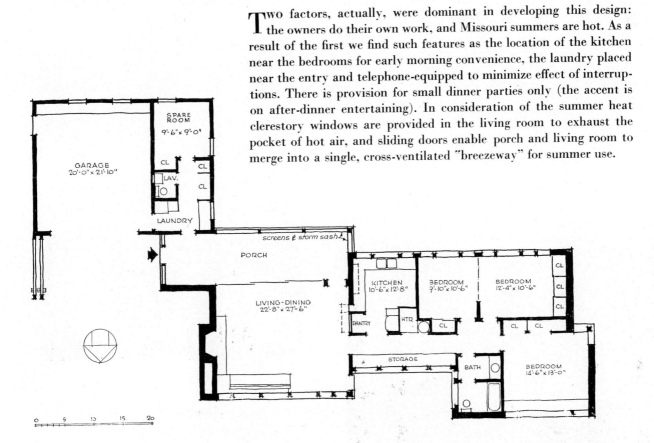

Piaget Studio Photos

The living room is bright and spacious. Screened in summer, glazed in winter, the porch is here shown opened to the living room. Below, detail of bracket for sliding door track. Floors are asphalt tile on concrete base. The ceiling is of fibreboard. Cabinets flank hall opposite kitchen

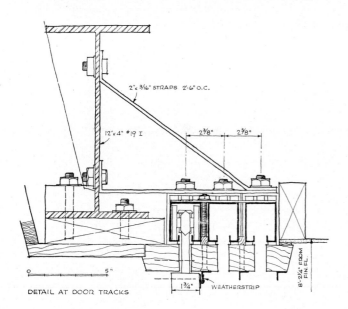

2"x 3/16" STRAPS 2'-6" O.C.

12"x 4" #19 I

2 3/8"   2 3/8"

8'-2 1/4" FROM FIN. FL.

0   5"

DETAIL AT DOOR TRACKS

1 3/4"   WEATHERSTRIP

Left: folding partition opens children's room for daytime use. Guest room can be "isolation ward" in case of sickness

April 1949

BUDGET HOUSE NEAR PITTSBURGH

Residence of Mr. and Mrs. Robert Kirkpatrick, Bradfordwoods, Pa.

Mitchell & Ritchey, Architects

A TIGHT budget and an urgent housing problem were prime factors in the design of this small Pennsylvania house. The owner, an Army pilot during the war, had just been released from service when he contacted the architects; his wife and two children were living separately with relatives, and the family could not be united until the house was finished. For this reason, in view of the limited budget, the house was designed for two-phase construction, with one bedroom to be built immediately and the other two to be added later. Bunks were added temporarily in the utility area to take care of the children in the interim.

Native stone was used for the rubblestone walls. The fir siding is in natural finish.

Single plate glass was used in the living areas, with the details developed so as to provide for future double glazing if desired, but the radiant heating has proved very satisfactory with the single glass even in the coldest weather. Interior walls are stone and birch plywood; floors are concrete and flagstone; ceilings are plywood, painted a chartreuse yellow; trim is ivory white

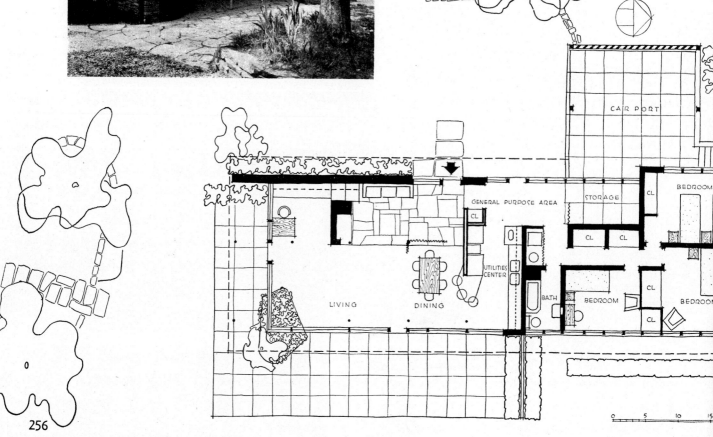

CAR PORT

GENERAL PURPOSE AREA

STORAGE

CL

BEDROOM

CL

CL

CL

UTILITIES
CENTER

LIVING

DINING

BATH

BEDROOM

CL

BEDROOM

CL

0   5   10   15

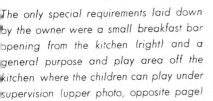

The only special requirements laid down by the owner were a small breakfast bar opening from the kitchen (right) and a general purpose and play area off the kitchen where the children can play under supervision (upper photo, opposite page)

Newman-Schmidt Studios

Ives & Hogan, Architects

Like most of the houses in the Islands, this one in Manoa Valley is simple in plan and designed to make the most of climate and view. Its steep site was used to good advantage in the placing of bedroom wing on a lower level to bring the view to every room in the house. Foundation is timber and hollow tile; framing is 2 by 4 studs; exterior walls are fir.

RESIDENCE OF

MILDON A. PIETSCHMAN ▶

Richard N. Dennis, Architect

The Pietschman residence, right, is one of the buildings to be presented in detail in a later issue of Architectural Record. It is of single-wall construction, on cement block foundation.

November 1950

HONOLULU

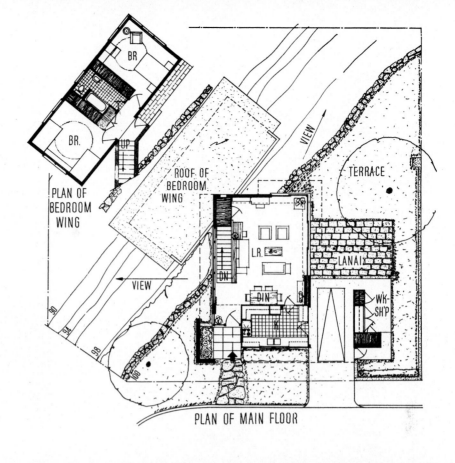

PLAN OF BEDROOM WING

BR

BR.

UP

ROOF OF BEDROOM WING

VIEW

VIEW

TERRACE

LANAI

L.R.

DN

DIN

K.

WK-SH'P

PLAN OF MAIN FLOOR

R. Wenkam Photos

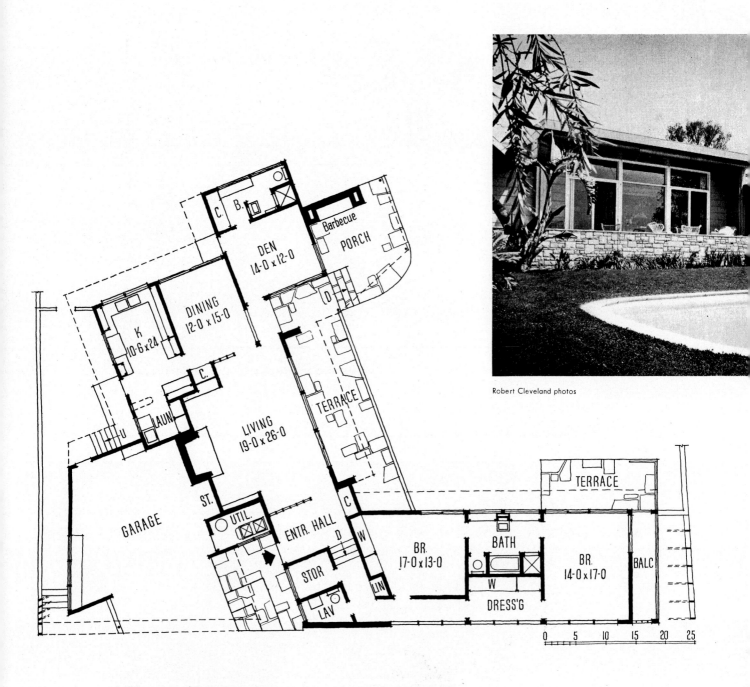

DEN
14-0 x 12-0

Barbecue PORCH

DINING
12-0 x 15-0

K
10-6 x 24

C.

LAUN

LIVING
19-0 x 26-0

TERRACE

ST.

GARAGE

UTIL.

ENTR. HALL

D

C

W

BR.
17-0 x 13-0

STOR

LAV

LIN

DRESS'G

W

BATH

TERRACE

BR.
14-0 x 17-0

BALC

0 5 10 15 20 25

Robert Cleveland photos

The California climate practically dictates design for outdoor living, the architect tells us, and consequently the house turns its back on the street and its neighbors, facing toward an outdoor living area which it surrounds on three sides. Beyond, across the pool seen above, is an excellent view extending to the ocean

HOUSE IN BEVERLY HILLS, CALIF.

Residence of Mr. and Mrs. Axel Zacho

Paul Laszlo, Architect

THE owner's family consists of husband and wife and a son of high-school age. They do not employ a resident maid and do not do their own laundry; so there is no maid's room and the laundry is small. Husband and wife have separate bedrooms. The son's room can be converted into a den or guest room. Since the family does not entertain elaborately the dining room was kept a nominal size. Mr. Zacho, an importer, required space for storing and displaying objets d'art; and space was provided in the garage for the son's hobbies.

The lot is large, but part of it is very steep and even the restricted usable building area, far from level, needed retaining walls at either side. This necessitated very economical planning. Fortunately the fine view of Los Angeles, beach towns, and ocean lay directly south. In this direction the house opens, away from the street, with floor-to-ceiling sliding doors. Deep overhangs here keep out the high, hot sun, but admit it early and late.

Construction is reasonably conventional, with 2 by 4 in. studs, fieldstone, redwood, and cement plaster on the exterior. Interiors are finished with plaster and striated plywood. Floors are oak, carpeted, with cork tile in Mr. Zacho's and his son's rooms.

Above, left, boy's room or den; floor here is cork tile. Right, Mrs. Zacho's bedroom has mirror wall with built-in dressing counter. Below, entry hall, with living room beyond

Robert Cleveland photos

A SITE FULLY EXPLOITED

House for H. W. Eldredge, Norwich, Vt.

Ezra Stoller: Pictor

E. H. & M. K. Hunter, Architects

M R. ELDREDGE, a Dartmouth professor of sociology and
planning — at Hanover, N. H., just across the Connecticut River — chose this site during his student days. Mrs.
Eldredge, an Englishwoman, saw the house plans in England
prior to their marriage. The architects, whose office is in
Hanover, knew the 8-acre hill-top site and were able to exploit
fully its extensive view of river valley to the south, and the
mountains of New Hampshire and Vermont to east and west.

March 1950

Eldredge House

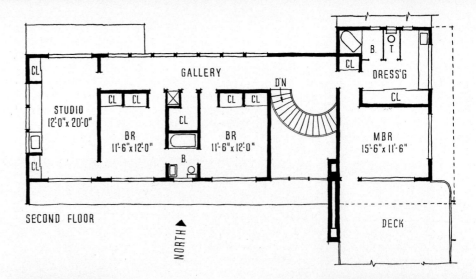

SECOND FLOOR

STUDIO
12'-0" x 20'-0"

GALLERY

DRESS'G

BR
11'-6" x 12'-0"

BR
11'-6" x 12'-0"

MBR
15'-6" x 11'-6"

D'N

CL

B.

DECK

NORTH

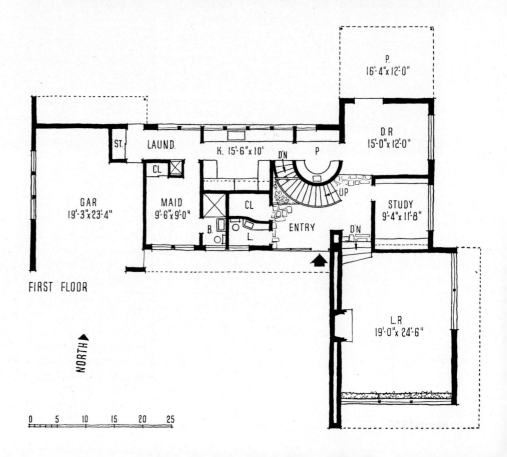

FIRST FLOOR

P.
16'-4" x 12'-0"

D.R
15'-0" x 12'-0"

ST.

LAUND.

K. 15'-6" x 10'

D'N

P

STUDY
9'-4" x 11'-8"

GAR
19'-3" x 23'-4"

MAID
9'-6" x 9'-0"

CL

B.

L.

ENTRY

UP

D'N

LR
19'-0" x 24'-6"

NORTH

0 5 10 15 20 25

Sitting in a 5-acre open field — the rest of the site is wooded—the house is reached by two dirt roads leading up from the valley; a Jeep negotiates the climb in snowy weather. The menage is planned for a pair of servants whose first-floor quarters together with kitchen and laundry are completely separated from family living areas, a requirement expressed visually by the heavy masonry chimney-wall which, on the exterior, is the dominant vertical. To it the horizontal of roof and sunshade projections are deliberately, strongly opposed. This is a conscious composition; it has a definite idea to convey: the house is a setting for urbane people who entertain handsomely, on a rural site but with no hint of rusticity even in the cypress siding

Ezra Stoller: **Pictor**

Mrs. Eldredge has a great interest in painting; hence the studio and wide, northlighted corridor for exhibiting pictures. At right, master bedroom, bath-dressing-room and deck. Below, right, living room; imagine the reaction of a guest standing in the entrance hall, four steps above the living room, seeing through the opposite glass wall fifty miles or more of the Connecticut valley

Ezra Stoller: Pictor

Kitchen: full electrical equipment, including garbage disposer. Visible beyond is pantry, constantly used in preparing refreshments

*Steps lead up from street to
the paved entrance terrace
overlooking Lake Washington*

Kenneth S. Brown Photos

*From front door one can see
right through the house to
rear terrace and garden area*

September 1950

RESIDENCE OF DR. AND MRS. R. L. GLASE

Seattle, Washington

Bain, Overturf, Turner & Associates, Architects

To look at the photo above is to guess immediately that the house faces a fine view. And it does — of Lake Washington and the Cascade Mountains. The site is in a restricted residential district about 20 minutes from the center of Seattle; the view is to the east, along the 100-ft-wide front of the lot. Lake and mountains were brought into every room by stretching the house across all but 20 ft of the frontage. In addition, master bedroom and breakfast alcoves were given bay win-

dows, and the living room was projected some 9 ft out from the rest of the house, with windows on three sides. A paved terrace was added to the front, and the rear half of the lot was converted into a sheltered garden area.

Exterior of the house is white painted brick and handsplit cedar siding, done, say the architects, "in a manner reminiscent of some of our pioneer western homes." The roof is handsplit cedar shakes.

Richard Garrison Photos

Dining end of living room (background, left, and small photo opposite) gains a feeling of separateness by lowered ceiling and stub partition which hides kitchen door from living room. All rooms are amply proportioned, closet and storage space is unusually good. Arrangement of bedroom wing gives both parents and daughter maximum privacy, but at the cost of an inside bathroom for the parents. Storage room in service wing is intended to be used as a maid's room, in which case the lack of direct passage from kitchen to front door might prove to be inconvenient

NORTH ▶

GARAGE
21'-0" x 22'-0"

CL. CL. CL. WOOD

STOR.

DN
LAUNDRY
CL
B. CL CL

PORCH

Piano Alcove

CL. CL. CL. DRESSING CL. CL.

CL.

B.

B.

BEDROOM
12'-0" x 20'-4"

BEDROOM
17'-0" x 12'-3"

ENTRY

W'D

LIVING RM
15'-8" x 31'-2"

D.R.
8'-6" x 16'-8"

K.
8'-6" x
16'-8"

0   5   10   15   20   25

Front end of living room has windows on three sides to make the most of the view. Bay window in kitchen makes a pleasant and sun-filled breakfast alcove

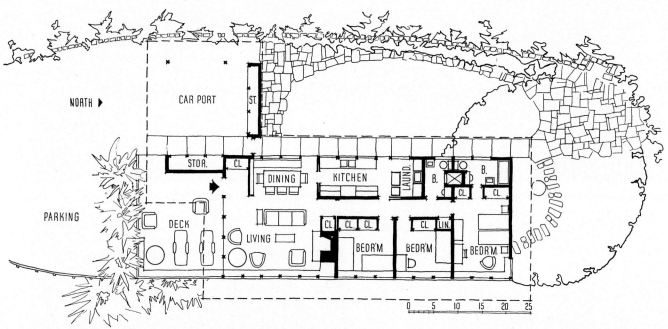

NORTH ▶

CAR PORT

ST.

PARKING

STOR.   CL

DECK

DINING   KITCHEN   LAUND.   B.   B.

CL.   CL.   CL.   CL.   CL.

LIVING   BEDR'M   CL.   LIN.   BEDR'M   BEDR'M

0   5   10   15   20   25

Rondal Partridge Photo

July 1950

BUILT OUT FROM A HILL

Residence of Mr. and Mrs. Gaston J. Ley

Lafayette, Calif.

Fred Langhorst, Architect

THE SITE which in a sense this house does *not* occupy (it is built out from the hill, on posts) centers on a long, level graded area cut from the hill. Location of the entrance drive and carport at the south end of this plateau permitted the utilization of the entire level area for a sheltered garden, not yet planted in the photo opposite. The carport itself is used to shield the garden both from arriving guests and from summer and winter winds. An open deck at the southeast corner of the house serves as an entrance porch and flows visually into the open living room. Kitchen and bath are on the west side of the house; living room and all three bedrooms face the view.

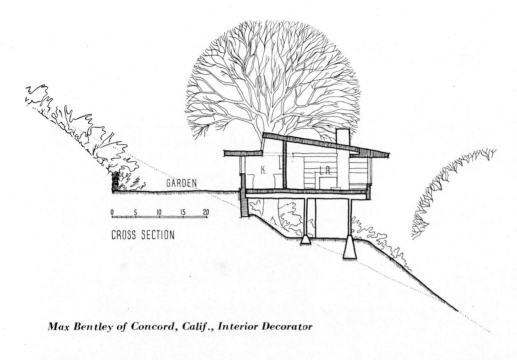

GARDEN

0 5 10 15 20

CROSS SECTION

Max Bentley of Concord, Calif., Interior Decorator

The house, built on posts, seems to reach out from the steep hillside toward the dramatic view of valley and mountains. Diagonal bracing required for earthquake resistance is incorporated into the horizontal plane of the floor and transmitted to west retaining wall. This leaves under-house area free and open for use; bedrooms may be added here in the future. Two-element roof adds interest to house profile, permits contrast of scale in interior between low-ceilinged entry and dining area, lifted ceiling of living room

The random-width horizontal cedar siding of the exterior carries inside throughout the dining and living areas, where it contrasts with the brick fireplace and plastered ceilings. High dish shelves separate the entrance hall from the dining alcove on the west side of the living room. Lighting is indirect, from light shelves; at night, says the architect, it "creates a lifted ceiling effect, or vertical space-extension, and compensates for the horizontal space-extension which is lost when the window drapes are drawn." Radiant heating coils are in the ceiling.

With these two basically dissimilar houses, Architect Paul Thiry has met the common problem of the narrow lot in two uncommon ways. One of the two he spread lengthwise, all but covering the site; the other he stretched across the width of the lot, leaving most of the length for terraces and landscaping.

Residence of

Mr. and Mrs. Charles D. Alhadeff, Seattle, Wash.

THE ALHADEFF RESIDENCE occupies a lot only 40 ft wide — exceptionally narrow for so large a house. It is within Seattle's city limits, fronting on Lake Washington, one block north of the Floating Bridge and only six minutes via traffic tunnel from the owner's downtown office. Since Mrs. Alhadeff wanted all principal rooms on one floor, the zigzag design resulted, the architect explains, from "the effort to obtain the maximum use of the land, to provide outlook plus privacy. . . . Each room looks out at the view or into the sheltered garden and has a seeming independence from the others."

TWO SEATTLE HOUSES BY PAUL THIRY SOLVE

Residence of

Mr. and Mrs. Roy Halsey, Hunt's Point, Wash.

THE HALSEY HOUSE, across the lake at Hunt's Point, has a wider lot — almost 80 ft — across which the house is stretched, cutting off road from waterfront. Mr. Halsey spends long periods in Alaska supervising his business interests there, living then aboard his boat. When at home on Lake Washington he uses his boat for getting about almost as frequently as he does his car, so access to the dock is vitally important. Because he and his family do a lot of large-scale entertaining, the carport was planned as an adjunct to the paved yard onto which the combination living-dining room opens: for large parties the whole area can be thrown into one by opening the gates (not shown on plan, page 280) between yard and carport. A large workshop next to the carport and a workroom beneath the bedrooms are provided for care of boats and gear.

Richard Garrison

NARROW-LOT PROBLEM IN TWO DIFFERENT WAYS

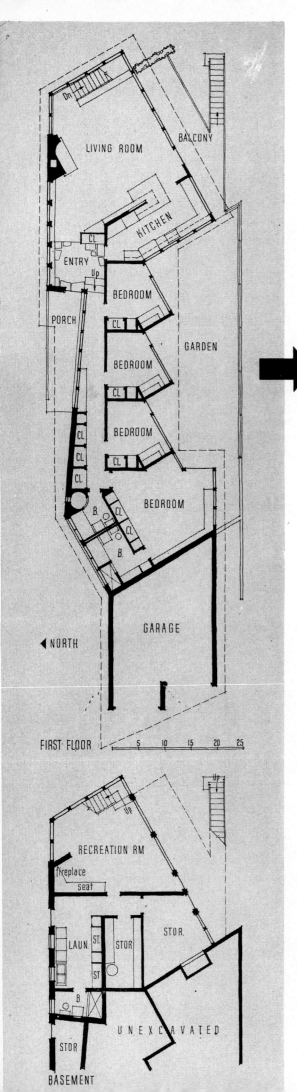

LIVING ROOM

BALCONY

KITCHEN

CL

ENTRY

Up

PORCH

BEDROOM

CL

GARDEN

BEDROOM

CL

BEDROOM

CL

CL

CL

CL

B.

CL

CL

BEDROOM

B.

NORTH

GARAGE

FIRST FLOOR   5   10   15   20   25

Up

Up

RECREATION RM

fireplace

seat

LAUN.   ST.   STOR

ST.

STOR.

B.

UNEXCAVATED

STOR

BASEMENT

Concrete-paved terrace accessible to all four bedrooms is major feature of Alhadeff house. Louvered screen (both photos across page) is so constructed as to give a view of lake from court and still maintain privacy. Strip windows in background (opposite page, left) are over working area in kitchen. South facade (far right) shows how completely the house is shielded from neighbors

Alhadeff Residence

Halsey Residence

The Halseys have flagstone-paved courtyard, separated from carport and entrance by fence and planting beds. Exterior walls are Douglas fir plywood. Bedrooms and living room (opposite page) face the lake; below them is workroom used to supplement workshop next to carport (next page). Wider margin to property line at south was allowed for carrying boats and gear to shop

Richard Garrison

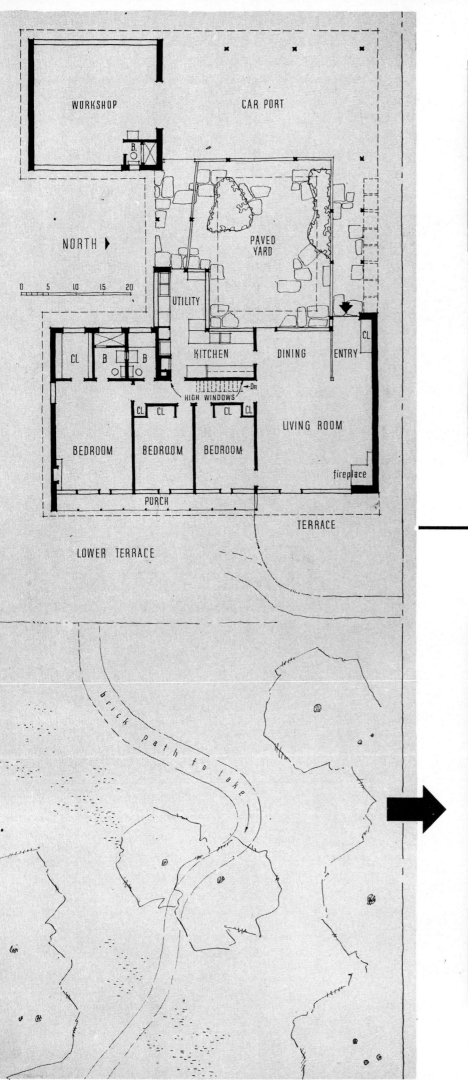

WORKSHOP

CAR PORT

B.

NORTH ▶

0 5 10 15 20

PAVED YARD

UTILITY

CL B B

KITCHEN

DINING

ENTRY

CL

HIGH WINDOWS → Dn

CL CL CL CL

LIVING ROOM

BEDROOM BEDROOM BEDROOM

fireplace

PORCH

TERRACE

LOWER TERRACE

brick path to lake

Alhadeff Residence

Halsey Residence

Richard Garrison

Alhadeff living room is paneled in birch plywood; fireplace is Roman brick. Random marble floor in kitchen (above) and hall (next page) is relic of fish pool in the retail market originally maintained by Mr. Alhadeff's father. The family-owned market, now grown into a wholesale business national in scope, was in past years one of the show places of Seattle

North wall and corner fireplace of Halsey living room are of reclaimed brick; remaining walls are of African mahogany veneer; floor is asphalt tile. Combined kitchen-utility room has charcoal grill built into chimney from basement furnace

Alhadeff Residence

Richard Garrison

Chief difference in the two houses is best shown in the two large photos on this page: the verticality of the Alhadeff residence, marked by the steps leading from street to entrance past the garage; and the horizontality of the Halsey home, characterized by the broad sweep of lawn from lake to terrace.

Halsey Residence

A HOUSE FITTED TO THE BERKSHIRE HILLS

Marcel Breuer

ARCHITECT

IT IS by the resolution of strong opposites that this house gains its character. Breuer as architect avoids easy rustic "blending"; on a magnificent site outside Williamstown, Mass., he has pitted strong geometry against the big Berkshire hills. Yet the butterfly roof-lines echo the hills; and by means of long stone fences or parapets the architect has "run the building out" and tied it in with the ground.

A sports-loving, skiing family asked to have virtually no barriers between itself and the great out-of-doors. Quartz-stone parapets are intended to act as psychological retainers *outside* the big glass walls, and keep

the space from "floating away." Despite the simplicity of the large house forms, and the unity of the work, the space cadences are highly multiplex.

The plan is an H-shaped, or "bi-nuclear" one, with the living room to the north and east (for view) instead of south (for sun); but the dining room is virtually a southern extension.

Materials are boldly contrasted: multi-hued tapestries of rusty-toned field stone against smooth, natural golden cypress, against subtly painted sheets and lines of trim, in light grays, blues, greens, yellows — and even an off-white pink — playing with the polished glass.

N

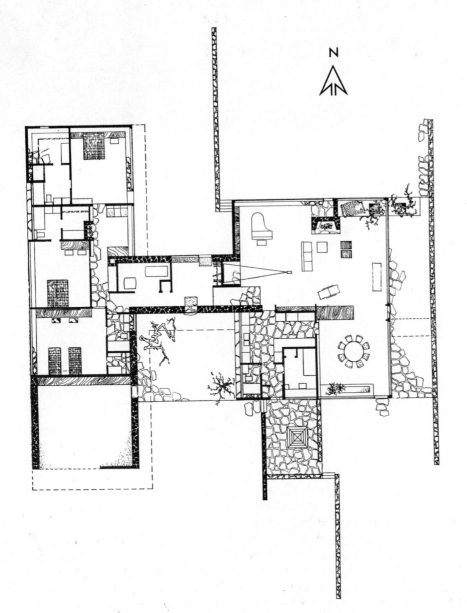

Here's a "bi-nuclear" H-plan turned ninety degrees for views north, east, west. The patio entrance arrangement, to the south, is worth special study. Garage, main entrance, kitchen entrance are closely grouped but service areas segregated nonetheless. The living room, to the right of the entrance, turns a corner around a head-high bar and china closet, to become the dining room. "Pass-through" arrangements between dining space and kitchen have been strictly avoided. The north suite of the bedroom wing, to the left in the plan, is the master bedroom, with dressing room and bath to the west, and to the south a miniature sitting room and study with fireplace. The next suite is the daughter's and the bottom suite the guest's. From the entrance court to the garden court there is a glimpse right through the connecting corridor into the garden court off the master bedroom

Visitors have found the entrance patio one of the most successful features of the house. From the garage (seen across-page) the way leads through a blue-stoned paved court (glimpsed at the left in the view above) to the entrance door (again at the left, in the view below). To the west the court is firmly defined and held by the garage stone wall and roof overhang; to the east it drops gradually away past the glazed kitchen wall (below) and successive stone walls, ever widening the area. As the entrance door is opened, there is suddenly another big vista, across the corridor and through the garden court to the north

285

Damora

The big visor facing the east originated in the owners' desire for a generous "unscreened porch." It admits cheerful sun, mornings; shades the terrace, afternoons. Breuer explains the sharp cleft, or well, near the middle of the overhang, as a device of multiple service: it carries a sense of the sky into the room; it encourages convection currents on still days, and funnels out storm winds which might otherwise threaten both the roof and the glass. In the larger horizontal view above may be glimpsed one of the clerestories (one for each wing) which admit more sky and light, and add another dimension of freedom in space

The little postage stamp view (left) repeats the color illustration on the Record cover, showing the north end of the living room. (At the extreme left on this small picture is the piano.) The fireplace capitalizes the rusty local quartz. Ceiling is polished birch plywood. Floor is carpeted with Haitian rush matting. Glass wall is full curtained with fiberglas fabric, and cove light (detailed overleaf) is reflected from plywood covering the truss. Desk is situated in the sitting-room study off the master bedroom

The little pantry leading into the dining room is also a compact office. The owner's wife enjoys the magnificent view as she sits at her linoleum-topped work desk with telephone (top view). Through the kitchen (top right) she can observe the entrance. The kitchen has built-in cabinet work aligned to the electric stove under metal casement windows (used throughout the house). Above is an acoustic-tiled ceiling and glass clerestory. Like all fixed-glass openings, this is double plate glass (Twindow). The floor, like all floors except living room and bedrooms, is hot-waxed flagstone (in this instance, blue-stone). Breuer believes this is the floor easiest to maintain; with radiant heating by copper coils under the floor (all through the house) it is warm in winter, cool underfoot in summer; and it carries right on through into the out-of-doors in places such as the forecourt, establishing space interpenetrations.

As a final view, the stone-wall sculpture seen below is the humble laundry and drying yard, with a drain at the center of its stone pavement; it lies adjacent to the kitchen, and the flagstones lead to the entrance patio or forecourt

Damora

David Fried, Architect

CAPE COD COTTAGE STYLED FOR SUMMER

Cottage for Mrs. Ruth Boardman, "Saltboxes," South Yarmouth, Massachusetts

CAPE Cod in summer is as mild and delightful as it is blustery and cold in winter. So a house designed primarily for a sunny summer vacation can and should be quite different from the traditional snug, tight and tidy cottage. This house therefore makes the most of sun, breeze and view, opening the main rooms to the south, the services to the north. The clerestory invites a pine-scented air flow through the rooms, as well as added light. The kitchen, or galley, is small and doubles as a passage for economy's sake — not an objectionable feature where informal living is the rule. A forced warm air heating system is provided for, with a duct along the ceiling of the corridor serving all rooms.

Haskell Photos

The east terrace-porch is frequently used for dining, served through the utility room. Below, a broad roof overhang on the south side shields the living and bed rooms from too much sun or rain and the pines provide shade for outdoor living. Exterior, vertical T & G local pine, painted white

The plan is simple and direct, permitting easy, economical construction and straight-line mechanical equipment. Storage is both ample and strategically placed, even ''functionally segregated.'' The living room day-beds can serve overnight guests, but if an additional room is ever needed the carport could be converted. The separate shower room and lavatory are convenient and desirable

PLAN OF SASH ABOVE ROOF

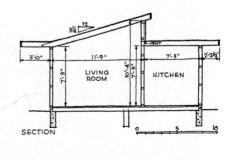

SECTION

Natural-finish local pine boards form attractive living room walls. The ceiling is painted a soft yellow-green and the upholstery is sienna, chartreuse and brick red. Window drapery has a yellow and tan leaf pattern on a gray-green background. The plaid wallpaper of the bedroom is a Dorothy Liebes design in sand and green, bedspread a deep green, rug sand-color, and drapery off-white. The yacht-chair adds a note of coral

The kitchen ceiling and one wall are of sheetrock painted a persimmon color which is found also in the plaid of the white and yellow curtains. Other walls are finished in natural pine. Lilian E. Kenrick was the interior decorator

the Tompkins house

HEWLETT HARBOR, LONG ISLAND

Marcel Breuer

ARCHITECT

Because everything about this house is so logical, so straightforward, so ingeniously simple and so all-of-a-piece, a casual beholder might miss the imaginative thoughtfulness that went into its design and construction. From orientation and plan down to the last detail, its purposes are achieved directly, simply, efficiently — with a skillful choice and use of materials and a deft sureness in scale and proportion.

The house is spacious without being large because of the openness of its plan and its extension into the out-of-doors. By cleverly cantilevering the second story, a gracious outdoor living terrace is obtained on the upper level and at the same time a necessary car shelter is provided below.

Color is used daringly and successfully to make the house blend with the sky and the landscape — cobalt blue, bright yellow, white, coffee brown, and shades of gray.

A careful analytical scrutiny of the design in detail will be rewarding in revealing both the forthright logic and the sensitive handling of "the simplest means to the desired ends."

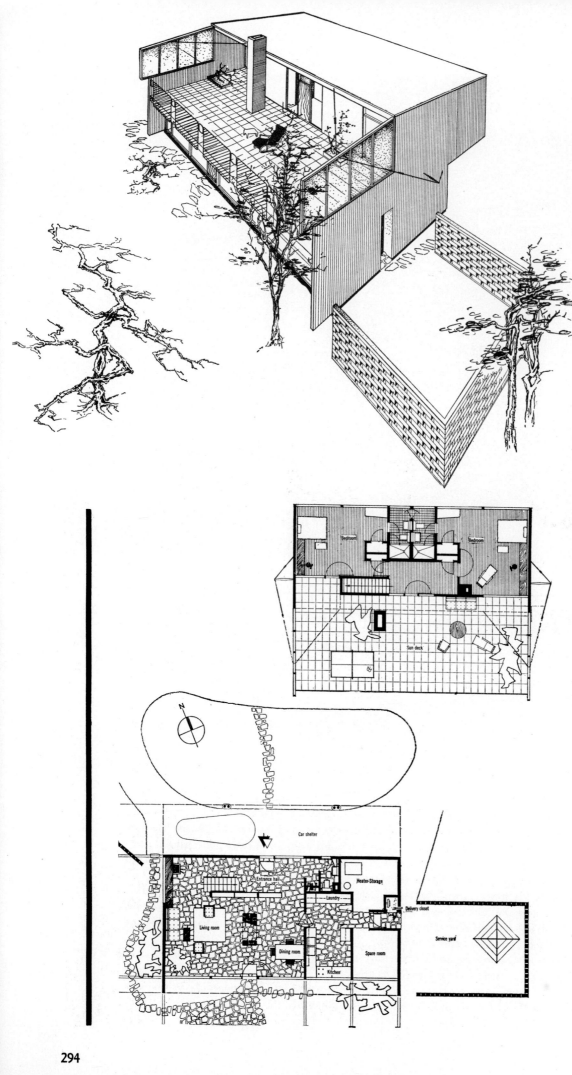

In supporting the cantilevered second story, the walls are developed as trusses by utilizing the ⅝-in. plywood sheathing as an integral ''stressed skin'' element of the structure.

Perspective and planning show auxiliary glazed shields (with their tension braces) for additional protection and privacy

The two-way fireplace separates the living and the dining areas so that the cheer of a single fire can be enjoyed from either or both sides. The bookcase wall divides the living-dining area from the entrance hall and stair. The open planning provides for a maximum expanse of view to the south

Looking through the double-duty fire-place from the dining to the living area. Winter heating is provided by a split system which supplies hotter water to the coils of the convector system of the second floor than is needed for the concrete-embedded coils of the radiant system of the ground floor. Temperature controls are automatic and thermostatic. Advantage is also taken in living and dining area of solar radiation through the large windows to the south

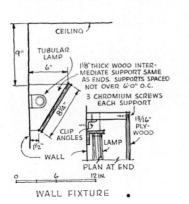

WALL FIXTURE

CEILING

TUBULAR LAMP

9"

6"

1⅛"THICK WOOD INTER-
MEDIATE SUPPORT SAME
AS ENDS. SUPPORTS SPACED
NOT OVER 6'-0" O.C.

3 CHROMIUM SCREWS
EACH SUPPORT

8¼"

13/16"
PLY-
WOOD

CLIP
ANGLES

LAMP

1½"

WALL

PLAN AT END

0   6   12 IN.

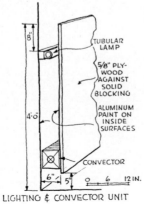

LIGHTING & CONVECTOR UNIT

8"

TUBULAR
LAMP

5/8" PLY-
WOOD
AGAINST
SOLID
BLOCKING

ALUMINUM
PAINT ON
INSIDE
SURFACES

4'-0"

CONVECTOR

6"   5"

0   6   12 IN.

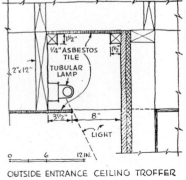

OUTSIDE ENTRANCE CEILING TROFFER

1½"

¼" ASBESTOS
TILE

2"x12"

1½"

TUBULAR
LAMP

3½"   8"

LIGHT

0   6   12 IN.

The open tread stair is supported on one side by the back of the bookcase and on the other side by the paneling suspended from above. . . The detailed drawings show simple but most effective details of the indirect lighting. The lighting-and-convector unit is shown also in the illustration (right) . . : The service entrance has an outside delivery closet from which meters can be read without entering the house

CALIFORNIA HOUSE WITH AND WITHOUT A VIEW

Residence for Mr. and Mrs. William Davey, Monterey Peninsula, California

Richard J. Neutra, Architect

TOPPING a site of several pine-studded acres on the Monterey peninsula, this house embraces, and at the same time rejects, one of California's supercolossal views. Living and sleeping areas have the Neutra full-glass walls oriented to view and winter sunshine, but work rooms, the studio and writing study, resolutely turn their backs to this distracting enchantment.

The exterior is of naturally treated redwood with steel sash, metal gutters and downspouts in dark red oil paint. The patio wall and paving are of random-size Monterey flagstone. All interiors are finished in enamel-coated wall fabric, and floored with eggplant colored battleship linoleum, except for the living room, which is carpeted.

Panoramic view includes Point Lobos, west, fishing harbor of Monterey Bay, north, a wooded ridge, south.

Bedrooms and bathrooms (second floor plan omitted) are arranged in two suites, which include dressing facilities. An open deck, accessible to both, has been placed on the upper level, behind a wind screen. The gallery connecting separate units has soffit lighting

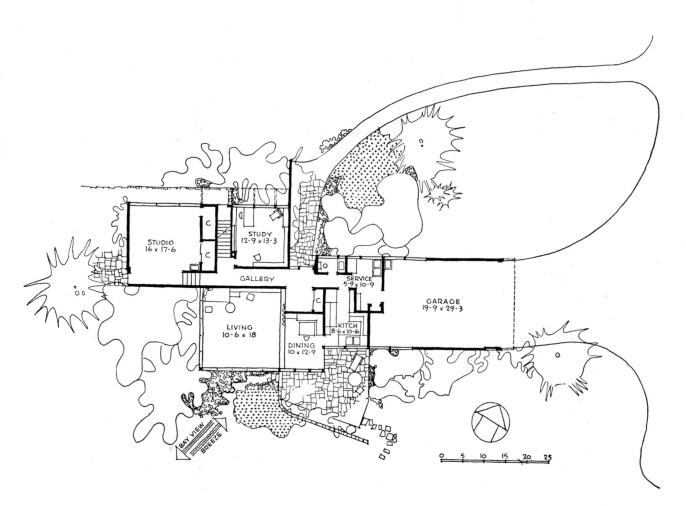

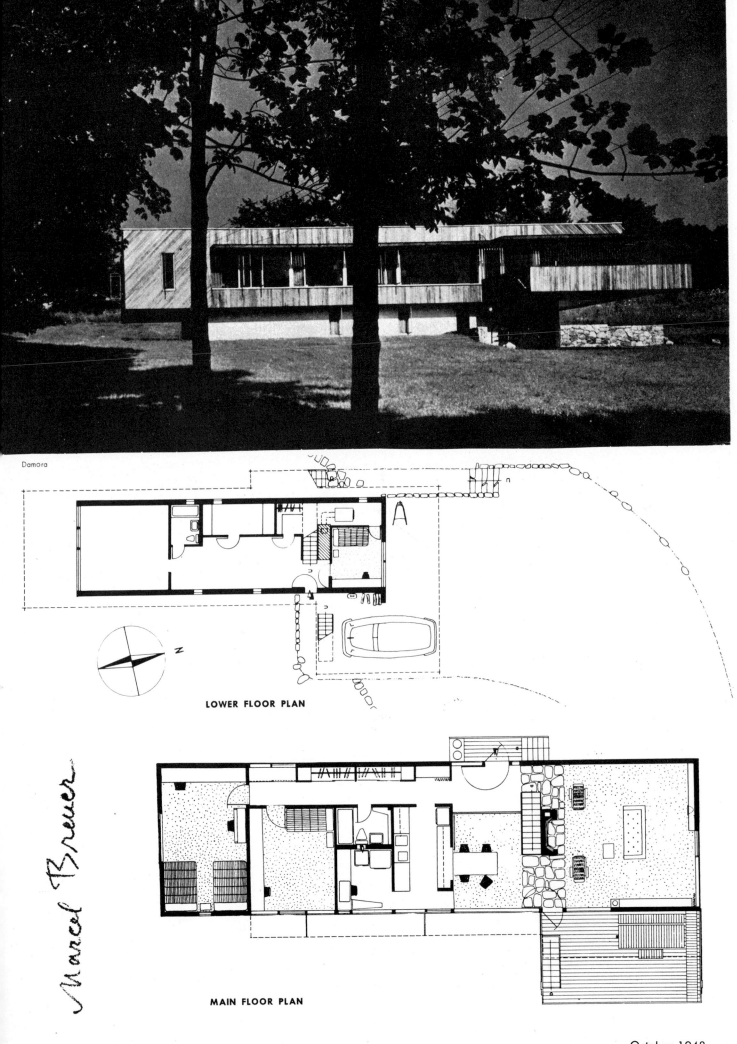

Damora

LOWER FLOOR PLAN

Marcel Breuer

MAIN FLOOR PLAN

MARCEL BREUER BUILDS FOR HIMSELF

For his own home Breuer has done a house which undoubtedly will find its way into future texts on architecture. Certainly there will be paragraphs pointing out to future students its sensuous qualities. For there is much in this house to warrant not only a lyrical note, but also to stand up under critical analysis. The sense of suspension which characterizes the design is readable in some degree in the photographs, is felt much more strongly by actual visitors. The suspension is a fact, not merely a feeling; the balcony porch is suspended on steel cables, as are also the sunshades. The stairs, too, actually hang from the hanging porch. Probably, nevertheless, the sense of suspension comes rather from the cantilever than from the actual suspension. The irresistible appeal of the cantilever is here developed to the ultimate degree. What Breuer has done, in effect, is to build a small basement story above ground, and then balance a full-size one-story house

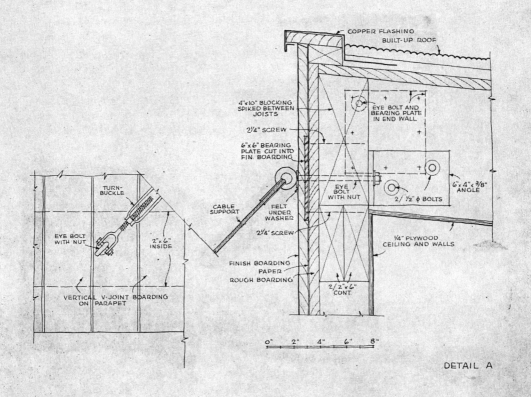

COPPER FLASHING
BUILT-UP ROOF

4"x10" BLOCKING
SPIKED BETWEEN
JOISTS

2¼" SCREW

6"x6" BEARING
PLATE CUT INTO
FIN. BOARDING

EYE BOLT AND
BEARING PLATE
IN END WALL

TURN-
BUCKLE

CABLE
SUPPORT

FELT
UNDER
WASHER

EYE BOLT
WITH NUT

6"x4"x3/8"
ANGLE

EYE BOLT
WITH NUT

2/ ½" Ø BOLTS

2"x6"
INSIDE

2¼" SCREW

¼" PLYWOOD
CEILING AND WALLS

FINISH BOARDING
PAPER
ROUGH BOARDING

VERTICAL V-JOINT BOARDING
ON PARAPET

2/ 2"x6"
CONT.

0"   2"   4"   6"   8"

DETAIL A

Construction is very similar to that of the so-called American frame house, but the frame was designed (with small dimensional lumber) to accommodate the long cantilevers — 10 ft. at either end. Floor members carry very little of the cantilevered load — the diagram on the front cover shows the floor joists running crosswise of the cantilever. Main load is carried by sheathing and weather boarding (though the latter is not considered as structural); both are used diagonally, the sheathing in one direc-

neatly atop it, cantilevered on all sides, with really long cantilevers at the ends. It looks as if the lower floor had been planned for its relatively small space needs, and the main floor planned separately for its needs, then the two combined. And that is exactly what happened.

The true story of this house, however, lies in the simple engineering logic with which its esthetic qualities were achieved. It was not done with any damn-the-expense design, but rather with what Breuer characterizes as "traditional frame construction adapted to achieve very large cantilevers without heavy framing members, or steel or concrete." Any Connecticut carpenter could understand, and approve, the almost primitive use of ordinary boards and rough lumber. And

Marcel Breuer

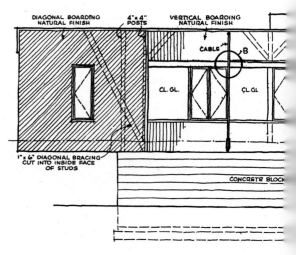

DIAGONAL BOARDING
NATURAL FINISH

4"x4"
POSTS

VERTICAL BOARDING
NATURAL FINISH

CABLE

B

CL. GL.

CL. GL.

1"x6" DIAGONAL BRACING
CUT INTO INSIDE FACE
OF STUDS

CONCRETE BLOCK

FRONT ELEVATION (EAST)

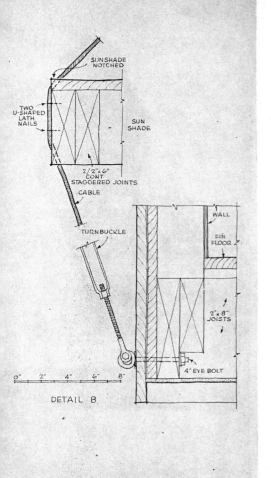

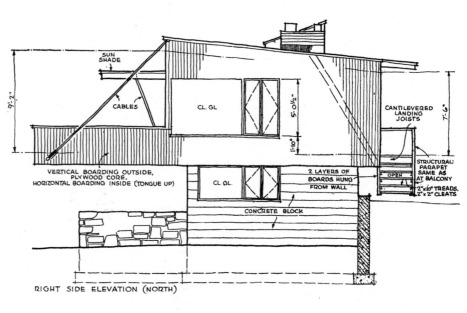

DETAIL B

SUNSHADE NOTCHED

TWO U-SHAPED LATH NAILS

SUN SHADE

2/2"x 6" CONT STAGGERED JOINTS

CABLE

TURNBUCKLE

WALL

FIN FLOOR

2"x 8" JOISTS

4" EYE BOLT

0" 2" 4" 6" 8"

SUN SHADE

CABLES

CL. GL

VERTICAL BOARDING OUTSIDE, PLYWOOD CORE, HORIZONTAL BOARDING INSIDE (TONGUE UP)

CL. GL.

2 LAYERS OF BOARDS HUNG FROM WALL

CONCRETE BLOCK

CANTILEVERED LANDING JOISTS

STRUCTURAL PARAPET SAME AS AT BALCONY

OPEN

2"x10" TREADS, 2" x 2" CLEATS

9'-2"

5'-0½"

1'-10"

7'-6"

RIGHT SIDE ELEVATION (NORTH)

tion, the outer boards in the other. The walls become in effect full-height trusses. Let-in bracing provides additional strength. Double 2 by 6's, in the position of the upper plate, carry the tension across the top of the house, and balance the pull from either end section. Four-by-four posts, in addition to normal studs, carry the extra weight. The porch is suspended (see details) by steel cables, using a type of hardware and turnbuckles used for the rigging of boats; they came from a Provincetown

hardware store and cost $22.00 all together. The end elevation shows how the weight is transmitted to the frame, the ordinary boarding again taking its share of the tension. Also there is some true cantilevering in the extension of the joists from house to porch. And the porch parapets enter into it too, being considered as structural plate trusses. The exterior stair is suspended from the floor of the porch, with a miniature concrete block to act as a stabilizer. Sunshades too are supported by tension cables

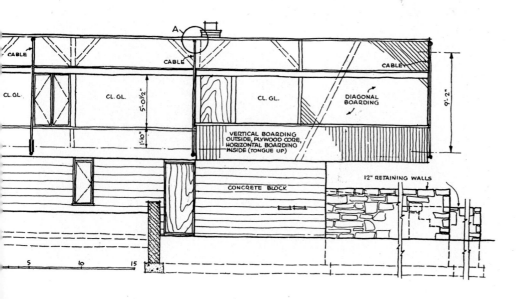

CABLE

CL. GL.

CABLE

CL. GL.

CL. GL.

CABLE

DIAGONAL BOARDING

VERTICAL BOARDING OUTSIDE, PLYWOOD CORE, HORIZONTAL BOARDING INSIDE (TONGUE UP)

CONCRETE BLOCK

12" RETAINING WALLS

5'-0½"

1'-10"

9'-2"

5   10   15

Marcel Breuer

any parsimonious Yankee could appreciate this particular victory over inflation in building costs.

Far from being an expensive house, it is surprisingly economical. Careful cost checks show a cube cost of just 75 cents, a total cost of $17,300. The total is less than half what most visiting architects have been guessing when they first register its expanse.

In the interior a similar approach to design has used essentially simple materials and ideas with equally good effect. The interior finish is painted plywood throughout, except the ceiling of the living-dining entrance space, which is cypress boarding, and the larger bedroom, which is natural gum plywood. Floor surfaces are Haitian mattings, bluestone and black asphalt tile.

Painting is white throughout, combined with natural wood surfaces, with certain walls in quite definite colors. The north wall of the living room is a strong cobalt blue, the low screen wall between dining room and entrance is the same color on both sides, so is one wall of the larger bedroom, with the adjacent walls one white and one a dark, neutral brown, the fourth a medium gray.

The house is planned for active living, including considerable entertaining, without servants. Visitors help in the kitchen. Connection from kitchen to other rooms is without doors, sliding cupboard doors connect dining table to kitchen. And from the centrally placed kitchen everything in the house and outdoors can be supervised — children, deliveries, also guests.

Marcel Breuer

The bedrooms are used also in the daytime as living rooms. The large bedroom has a piano, a large counter-desk for drawing, painting, correspondence, etc. The smaller bedroom too has room for a similar counter, also for comfortable seats.

The lower portion houses all auxiliary functions — heating, storage, second bathroom, workshop combined with guest room, playroom, and another bedroom for a five-year-old son, close to playroom, workshop and outdoors. And the lower level is a dirt and noise trap, appreciated alike by parents and children.

STUDIO-HOME OF THE

DEL MAR, CALIFORNIA

John Lloyd Wright, Architect

Handley Photos by Schneider

Merging into its luxuriant four-acre site so well that it seems to be a part of the landscape, this studio home of John Lloyd Wright and his author-wife, Frances Wright, successfully separates working and living areas though keeping them within the main body of the house. Mr. and Mrs. Wright like to work together, so the drafting room is located on a mezzanine opening via a screen mural to the writing area below. An upper-level entrance is provided for the architectural office to keep business activities "out of the house."

Of wood frame and reinforced concrete construction, the house has exterior walls of handmade adobe burned brick (orange terra-cotta) from a nearby canyon. White stucco is "woven through" the exterior creosoted wood; the shingles of the pitched roof are redwood.

October 1948

JOHN LLOYD WRIGHTS

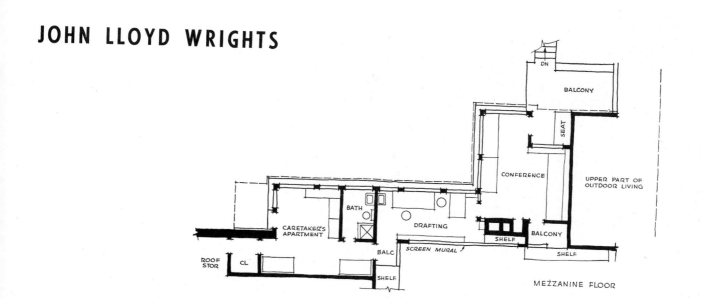

MEZZANINE FLOOR

Across-page: top, patio from kitchen snack bar; center, the forecourt;
bottom, patio from swimming pool. Although the house is essentially
single-level, a mezzanine provides office and drafting room space for
Mr. Wright and a fully-equipped caretaker's apartment (see plan above)

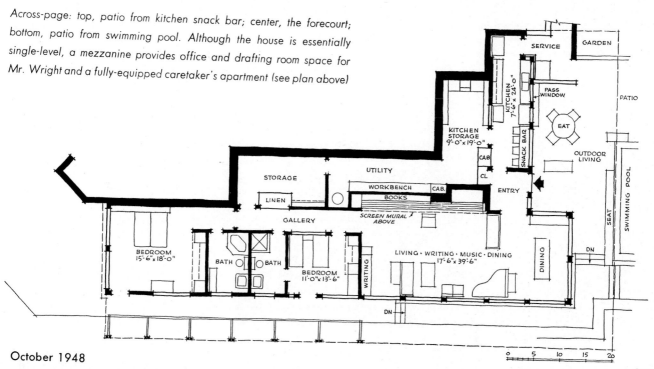

October 1948

Left: living room and dining area; windows overlook swimming pool. All interior woodwork is stained with pastel water colors, with ceilings in sunset coral tints. Floors are red quarry tile in living areas, gray ceramic tile in bedrooms

Right: entrance door is enriched with eucalyptus acorns from premises

Left: the mural screens shielding the mezzanine were painted by Mr. Wright in Tokyo in 1916, represent his conception of Toyland. A strip of paneled translucent glass provides special lighting over book shelves and fireplace. Mrs. Wright's writing corner in left background

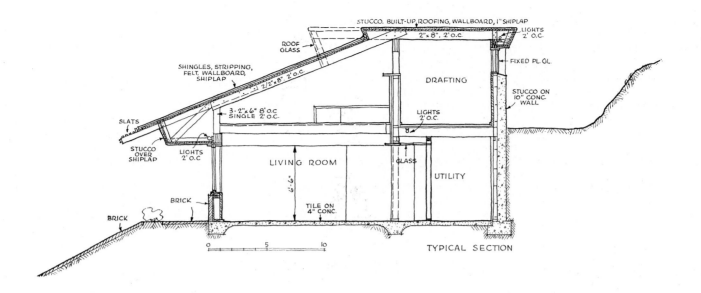

STUCCO, BUILT-UP ROOFING, WALLBOARD, I" SHIPLAP

2" x 8", 2' o.c.

LIGHTS 2' o.c.

ROOF GLASS

SHINGLES, STRIPPING, FELT, WALLBOARD, SHIPLAP

2 1/2" x 8" 2' o.c.

FIXED PL. GL.

DRAFTING

STUCCO ON 10" CONC. WALL

SLATS

3-2"x 6" 8' o.c. SINGLE 2' o.c.

STUCCO OVER SHIPLAP

LIGHTS 2' o.c.

LIGHTS 2' o.c.

LIVING ROOM

GLASS

UTILITY

9'-6"

BRICK

BRICK

TILE ON 4" CONC.

0   5   10

TYPICAL SECTION

The house occupies a flat area bulldozed through the side of the cliff and rests on a re-inforced concrete mat. All windows are stationary plate glass with ventilating panels in the wall below. Left: kitchen walls are pale yellow tile, ceiling is dusty blue, floor pale gray ceramic tile

Handley Photos by Schneider

Right: the drafting room terrace

Fred Gund Photos

DESIGNED ON THE MODULAR PRINCIPLE

Walter T. and Robert W. Vahlberg, Architects

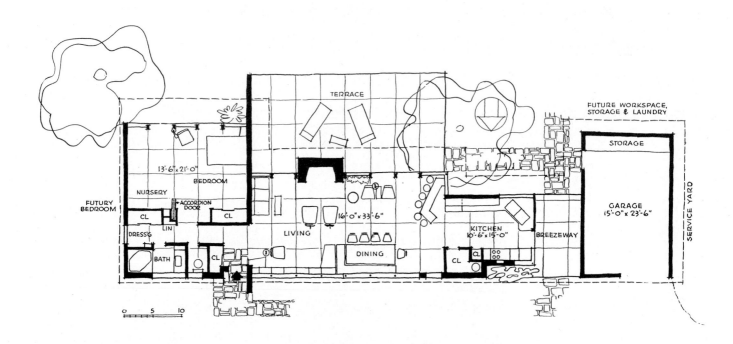

Shown above, the south wall is planned on a 4-ft. module; the north wall is 10-in. cavity brick. Roof is framed with built-up wood trusses, the finish ceiling being applied directly to them

September 1948

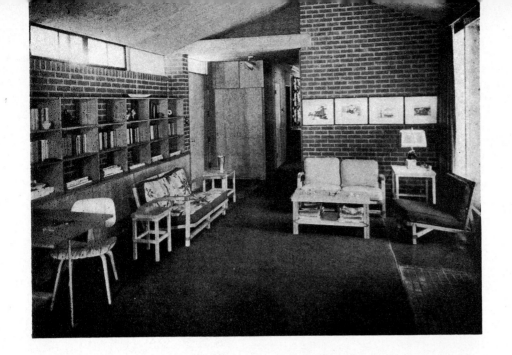

Left: the living room, looking past main entry to bedroom hall, beyond which future bedroom space may be added, see plan

Residence of Mr. and

Mrs. H. Barney Crawford,

Oklahoma City, Okla.

Right: with the exception of the chimney, sliding sash occupies all of the south wall of the living room. Ceilings over the living area are striated plywood; elsewhere smooth plywood. Interior wall surfaces are plywood and common brick

Left: breakfast bar is practically outdoors when sash is moved aside. Well-ventilated kitchen has divided door at end opening on breezeway. Floors are waxed red concrete

Roger Sturtevant Photos

A SMALL HOUSE OF IMPRESSIVE STATURE

House for Dr. and Mrs. Alex J. Ker,

Marin County,

California

CONTEMPORARY design in California seems bent on confounding critics who use such terms as "nude," "ascetic," or "dull." For this house, which won first award in a recent competition by *House and Garden*, is ample demonstration that modern can be as imaginative, as impressionistic, as anybody could wish. It makes full use of extended structural members, contrasting forms and materials, and long, strong lines to create dramatic interest. And, incidentally, the several accessory spaces implicit in such planning add important utility to the small country house, and greatly enhance its stature.

Fred Langhorst, Architect

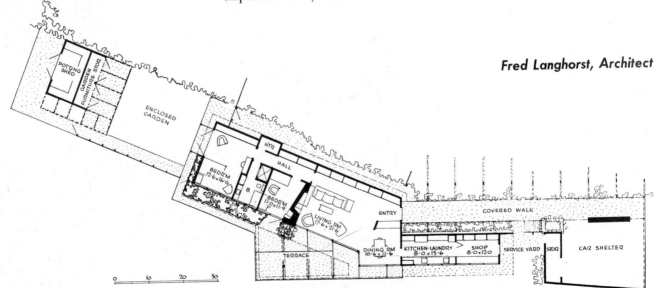

All rooms have been related to a southerly exposure, which fortunately coincides with the view from this hillside site. The rooms have all been related also to appropriate corresponding outdoor living areas, an outdoor living area in these views, in other photographs an enclosed garden, a service yard, a covered entry

While the site comprised several acres, the topography was rugged. An extensive grading operation created a long level area of varying width, running east and west. The house is set close to the hill to leave maximum free area to the south

The house is closely tied to the hillside, structurally as well as visually. This placing provides the maximum level area at the other side, south, for enjoyment of sunshine and view. Roof members of the car shelter extend to piers on hillside

View of dining room as seen from living room. Note living room light shelf over doorway. Walls redwood, ceilings gypsum board

The architect explains that, since this house was definitely designed for adults, he waived one of his basic rules — that a living room should not be a passage. Except for the high windows the room is closed to the crowding hillside, but expansively open to the valley view. A light shelf on two walls provides indirect general lighting. Stone hobs in the fireplace are "andiron eliminators" and serve as an informal place for sitting close to the fire. Heating is by gas-fired, forced warm air furnace

Roger Sturtevant Photos

Morley Baer Photo

HOUSE FOR INFORMAL LIVING, Carmel, California

George H. Woolsey, Designer

Stolte, Inc., Contractors

THE problem presented was to provide on the small irregular lot a maximum of space for informal living, both indoors and out. A maximum of privacy was desired on the exposed lot, which dictated a fence to enclose an outdoor living terrace and the service yard. Indoor and outdoor living areas are merged by sliding glass panels. The kitchen readily serves either indoor or outdoor dining preparations, though the barbecue is the center of interest for outdoor meals. Both the service entrance and the entrance to the living area are provided through the carport and service yard. A convenient lavatory is tucked away next to the kitchen. The house is heated by an electric radiant system consisting of two zone-circuits of half-inch steel cable laid in concrete and connected to thermostatically controlled low voltage transformers. The finished floor is ceramic tile.

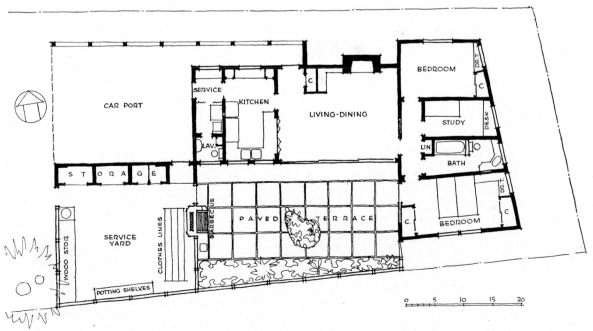

The fireplace merely provides supplementary heat since the embedded electric radiant cables produce a floor temperature of 70° to 74°, supplying between 35 and 50 Btu. per square foot with a power consumption of 10 to 15 watts

Above, an abundant supply of towels is always available on the simple but ingenious wall rack in the bathroom. Below, the kitchen is well-lighted day or night and is provided with adequate cabinets. Louvered shutters close the pass cabinet from kitchen to dining room

HOUSE FOR MR. AND MRS. LYLE B. CLOTHIER,

Tucson, Arizona

Arthur T. Brown, Architect

Western Ways Photos

Privacy on the street front is achieved by high windows with louvrex obscure glass. The shingled housing for the heater, next to the front door, forms a pleasant contrasting note in the long brick facade. Logical variations in ceiling heights add attractiveness to both interior and exterior

WHILE this house for Mr. and Mrs. Clothier and their 18-year-old son faces south on a busy street, it commands an expansive view of the Catalina Mountains to the north. It therefore appears to be a "solar" house in reverse, with maximum glass area on the north to take advantage of the view, and high windows on the south for privacy. The house is planned so that the doorbell can be answered from the kitchen and service porch without disturbing the living and dining area. High bookshelves form a screen between the entrance passage and the living room to insure privacy and still preserve a sense of openness. The living room never becomes a corridor for other rooms. The service space has been arranged for convenient servantless living and the "service porch," as part of the kitchen, provides a pleasant uncramped area for laundry and sewing activities.

While not large, the house seems unusually spacious because of the openness of the living and dining area with the high ceiling, and because porches to the north and east provide for convenient shaded outdoor living. Heating and cooling are provided from a central location adjoining the door

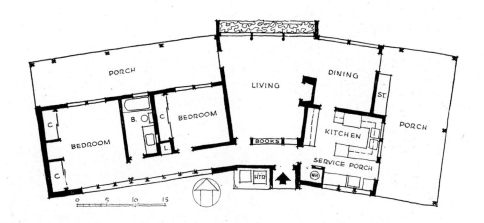

The gracious living room spreads its splayed walls to embrace the view of the Catalinas. The exposed ceiling beams also direct one toward the view. Pictures are unnecessary when one whole wall of the room becomes an ever-changing vista. The dining area is open to the living room, except for the fireplace

Western Ways Photos

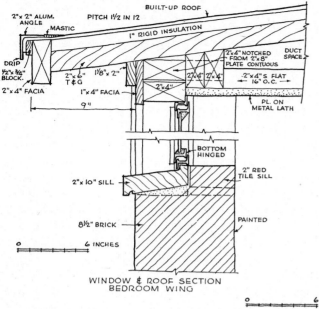

BUILT-UP ROOF

PITCH 1½ IN 12

2"x 2" ALUM. ANGLE

MASTIC

1" RIGID INSULATION

DRIP

½"x ¾" BLOCK.

2"x 4" FACIA

2"x 6" T & G

1⅛"x 2"

1"x 4" FACIA

2"x 4"

2"x 4" NOTCHED FROM 2"x 8" PLATE CONTUOUS

2"x 4" 2"x 4"

2"x 4" S FLAT 16" O.C.

DUCT SPACE

PL. ON METAL LATH

9"

BOTTOM HINGED

2"x 10" SILL

2" RED TILE SILL

8½" BRICK

PAINTED

0   6 INCHES

WINDOW & ROOF SECTION BEDROOM WING

Details of the window and roof construction of the bedroom wing show the use of frame members as jambs, heads and facias, and the reduction of the number of pieces to a minimum consistent with good construction and design. Metal windows in some climates can be installed as simply and directly as here shown

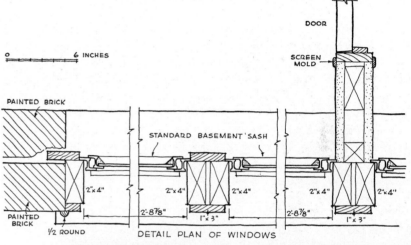

0   6 INCHES

DOOR

SCREEN MOLD

PAINTED BRICK

STANDARD BASEMENT SASH

PAINTED BRICK

½ ROUND

2"x 4"

2"x 4"   2"x 4"

2'-8⅞"

1"x 3"

2"x 4"   2"x 4"

2'-8⅞"

1"x 3"

DETAIL PLAN OF WINDOWS

Cabinets between the kitchen proper and the laundry-sewing area, called service porch on the plan, open from both sides. Duct work for heating and cooling is visible only in the kitchen above the convenient cabinets

FIRST FLOOR

STORAGE

UTILITY 8'-0" x 31'-0" KITCHEN

SCR'NED PORCH

GARAGE
20'-0" x 26'-6"

CL

2 CL

UP

LIVING-DINING
16'-0" x 22'-6"

PORCH

LAV.

ENTRY

WALK

PORCH

RECREATION
12'-6" x 16'-0"

SCR'NED PORCH

0 5 10 20

SECOND FLOOR

CL CL

BEDROOM
11'-6" x 16'-0"

DN

CL

LIN

BATH

BEDROOM
16'-0" x 21'-0"

SCREENED PORCH

CL

CL

CL

BEDROOM
11'-6" x 14'-6"

BATH

CL

CL

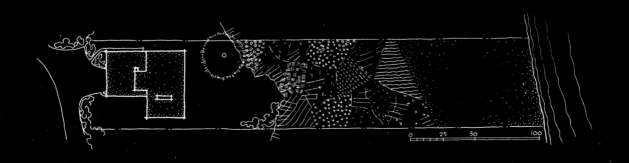

0 25 50 100

BROAD IN VISION THOUGH NARROW IN LAND

George Fred Keck, William Keck, Architects

Hedrich-Blessing Photos

THIS attractive, livable house in Illinois is shown by night and by day, as it appears from the edge of the terrace overlooking Lake Michigan. All major rooms open to the east for the lake view and breezes. Although the house cannot be classified as "small," the basic ideas developed in its design — the simple, open plan; good circulation; multiple use of space, the integration of radiant panel heat, solar heat, and roof overhang — these and many other details are all adaptable to the small house as well as the large. George Keck has done this in his smaller houses as well as in designs he has drawn for a manufacturer of prefabricated houses. Thus the architect becomes the innovator, and his client the sponsor, of new concepts of modern living which, if they could reach the small-house field to any impressive degree, would enormously benefit the average citizen.

Above: this view of the recreation room shows high windows to the south in the masonry end wall, and to the west in the wall toward the entrance drive. There is foam-glass insulation between the inner and outer stone surfaces, rock wool in wooden walls and roof. Below, a sturdy china and glass cabinet screens the dining space from the stair hall. Note the convenient pass-cabinet between dining room and kitchen with doors which close flush

Above: the living room fireplace occupies one-half the width of the chimney, the other half backing the fireplace in the recreation room beyond. All interior walls and ceilings are of varnished exterior cypress; a radiant panel heating system is used throughout

Hedrich-Blessing Photos

Right: the handsomely appointed kitchen has the service entrance, utility room and door to the garage at the farther end, in this photograph; entrance to living-dining room is at left of camera. A distinctive feature of this house is that all windows are double-glazed fixed sash, with transoms and louvred openings provided for ventilation. On the blustery shores of Lake Michigan, this is doubtless a practical and effective solution, but in more protected locations it is debatable whether such a system would completely replace operating sash in the affections of the public

These two views of the children's rooms which occupy the center section of the upper floor show how the rooms may be divided by the folding partition or opened up as a play area. The built-in wardrobes and chests encourage youthful orderliness. The intelligent and considerate planning of children's rooms is one of the notable developments of contemporary residential architecture

Right: the master bedroom, like the other bedrooms, opens on the screened porch which runs the length of the house. The highly organized storage space, seen here and elsewhere in the house, is built in and eliminates the need for much of the usual profusion of protruding and dust collecting furniture

Paul Davidson Photos

INGENUITY PROVIDES SPACIOUSNESS

House for Mr. and Mrs. Albert Tarter; Los Angeles, Calif.

Gregory Ain, Joseph Johnson & Alfred Day, Architects

B^Y means of a number of ingenious devices, the designers of this small house have succeeded in providing the spacious feeling, as well as the actual facilities, of a much larger place in the limited floor area of 908 sq. ft. Most important, as contributing to this happy feat, are two rigid, sliding wall panels which allow a very flexible use of the available space, and the preservation of an almost uninterrupted ceiling over more than half the rooms, which gives them a feeling of size considerably beyond their actual dimensions. The entrance side of the house is seen above; the opposite side below. Exterior walls are redwood shiplap siding; roof is white-surfaced, built-up composition; interior floors are asphalt tile. The plans and interior photographs are shown on the following two pages.

Above: the living room as it appears from the study, with the sliding panel drawn back against the wall of the entrance hall. All interior walls are Douglas fir plywood. Note storage cabinets at left of chimney. In addition to other devices previously mentioned, the large windows also help materially to increase the apparent size

Above: the broom-coat closet is held to a 6-ft. 8-in. height so that the living room, entry and kitchen appear as one space, a feeling which is further heightened by the large opening between living room and kitchen. Below, left: the rigid plywood panel, which runs on floor sheaves, here closes off one end of the living room; at right, the same wall opened up reveals the study as part of living room

Left: the dining table fills the openi[ng]
between living room and kitchen, is a p[art]
of both, yet wastes little floor area wh[en]
idle. In the floor plan, note the oth[er]
sliding panel, between bedrooms, whi[ch]
makes a child's play space when ope[n;]
also the divided bathroom, with laund[ry]

Paul Davidson Photos

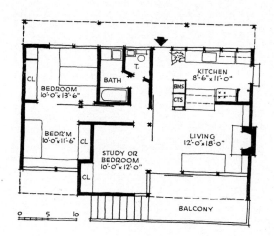

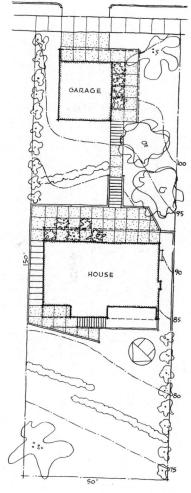

The garage, a corner of which is shown at
left, is near the street and at a considerably higher level than the house. It is
reached by means of a flight of steps

AN ARCHITECT'S HOUSE

HUGH STUBBINS, JR., ARCHITECT

Entrance side. Left to right: kitchen, social rooms, clerestory light over bathrooms, children's wing (toward rear); passage, garage

IN MASSACHUSETTS

ARCHITECTURAL
RECORD

SCHOOLS   MARCH 1948

Ezra Stoller Photos

THE way this house serves plain, hearty American family life, without reaching for tricks and effects, is, we believe, the important contribution in its very straightforward and brilliantly sensible scheme.

The house conspicuously avoids a certain kind of contemporary design ostentation, a kind that manifests itself not in colonnades, urns, or broken pediments, but in elaborate "zoning" separations, broken masses, fancy materials, and tricky detailing.

The surroundings were mostly found not made; like the pioneer cabin the house is a ship-shape dwelling set in a "clearing." Here young Hughdie, aged eight, can have the American boy's traditional privilege of growing up among trees, rocks, slopes, fields. For an architect's family of five, this had to be done economically and simply.

Though the first impact is of a charming family setting and not a diagram, the plan (overleaf) shows a quite consummate "zonal" arrangement, all within a simple rectangle of a house, set among natural terraces. At the center, like a control room, is the parents' bedroom. The left, or social, wing is based perhaps less on the four-square living-dining room than on the family kitchen, convenient alike to interior and exterior living. The right wing gives the children their own four-square living and play area, isolated from adults. Underneath, again separately accessible, is the father's architectural office. (The superhighway from which the trees shield the house gets him in twenty minutes to his other work at Harvard in the Graduate School of Design.)

Using plain materials, straightforward construction, uncomplicated plans, the architect built his house in 1946-7 at $8.50 a square foot, and financed it all through conventional lending agencies.

South view, on "solar" side, shows how ground drops to permit lower-floor office of cement block protected by cantilevering

Covered walk from garage to house (view at right) visually intersects the rectangular house. Vista ends in Mrs. Stubbins' garden, which in turn invades the house (see color illustration on our cover). Stone fence and retaining walls (of clean-cleaving local fieldstone) tie house to ground, afford four living terraces

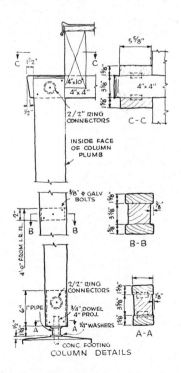

COLUMN DETAILS

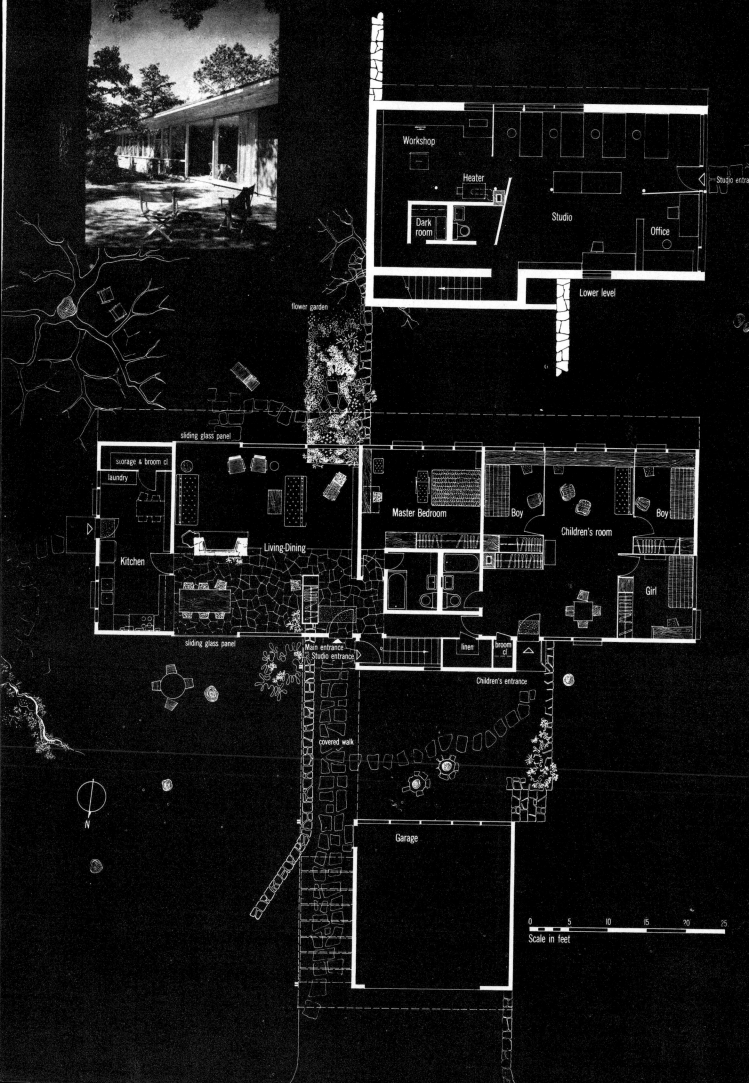

Workshop

Heater

Dark room

Studio

Office

Studio entrance

Lower level

flower garden

sliding glass panel

storage & broom cl

laundry

Kitchen

Living-Dining

Master Bedroom

Boy

Children's room

Boy

Girl

sliding glass panel

Main entrance
Studio entrance

linen

broom cl

Children's entrance

covered walk

N

Garage

Scale in feet

0   5   10   15   20   25

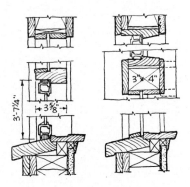

Living room view at right lets us see Mr. and Mrs. Stubbins and daughter Patricia before the ample fieldstone fireplace. The large sliding glass door, or panel, which opens the large square room to the out-of-doors, has its square frame painted Chinese red, which stands out strongly against the light gray vertical beveled pine boards, the varnished soffit, the white facia and trim. (Detail at bottom of page.) The fishnet curtain (March 1948 cover) is supplemented when desired by heavier drapes. Other openings are fixed glass or steel projected sash. Details shown are typical; the architect believes that mastery is shown in reduction, not multiplication, of details

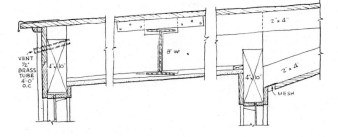

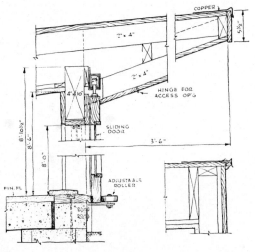

Above, detail of sliding glass panel (reduplicated on opposite side of room). Garden (left) carries into room (see March 1948 cover)

March 1948

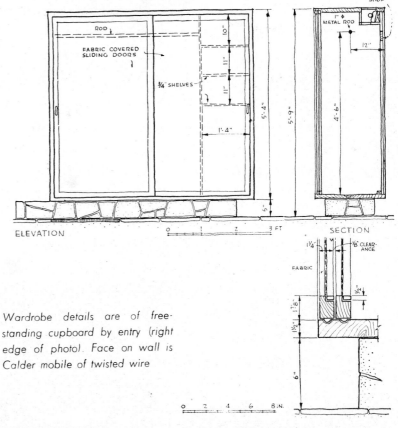

ROD

FABRIC COVERED
SLIDING DOORS

¾" SHELVES

10"

11"

11"

1'-4"

5'-4"

5'-9"

5"

HOOK
STRIP

1" Ø
METAL ROD

12"

4'-6"

ELEVATION

0   1   2   3 FT

SECTION

1¼"   ⅛" CLEAR-
ANCE

FABRIC

1½"

1½"   ⅞"

6"

0   2   4   6   8 IN.

Wardrobe details are of free-
standing cupboard by entry (right
edge of photo). Face on wall is
Calder mobile of twisted wire

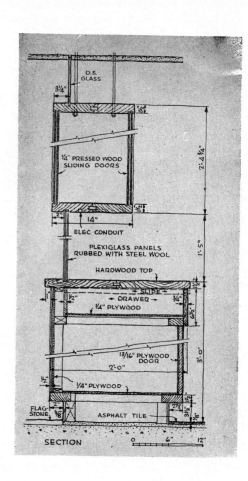

Pass-through cabinet creates division between kitchen and dining room, which is separated in turn from living area by fireplace wall, from entry by coat closet. Glass and china cabinet, suspended from ceiling, has pressed-wood sliding doors opening both ways. Pass-through panels are Plexiglas rubbed with steel wool; counter is teakwood, which also serves as bread board and cutting surface. Marble counter, to right of electric range, is heat-resistant, serves as pastry board. Dining room floor is gray slate rubbed with hot wax. Large square sliding glass panel, opening dining room to terrace, balances similar panel in the living room, as seen on previous page

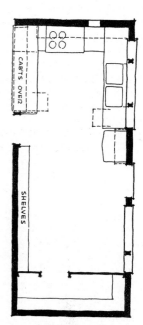

Lower half of kitchen is laundry and storage cabinet

Children's recreation room, right. Partition walls of vertical sugar pine were installed after floors and ceiling had been finished, so as to permit easy rearrangement whenever family requirements may change. Furniture, such as chair in foreground, was designed by the architect for domestic use

Master bedroom has built-in closets of detail similar to coat closet (page 341) with fluorescent lighting to illuminate both closet and room in general. Furniture, below, combines make-up table, desk, radio (mirror above produces illusion of through passage)

Clerestory light over bathrooms (bottom of page) is brought down close over roof, but has caused no leaks as yet through snow accumulation

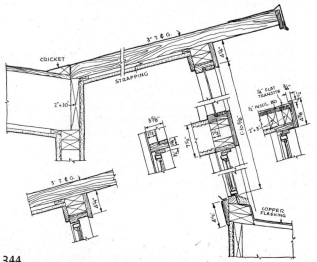

THE BOW FRONT FACES THE BLUE PACIFIC

House for Capt. and Mrs. W. S. Chitarin, Carmel, California

Albert Henry Hill, designer

Eckbo, Royston and Williams, Landscape Architects

AN EMERGING aspect of the small home, which may have increasing significance for architects, is indicated in the frequency with which clients who have built a small house for temporary occupancy — pending construction of a larger place — have found the compact and convenient dimensions of the smaller, "servantless" house unexpectedly workable and pleasant. The house shown on these three pages was originally planned for use by an invalid — which accounts for certain design features — and subsequently as a guest house, but is now proving a satisfactory home pending completion of plans for a larger house adjoining. The glazed bow front provides a pleasant protected gallery-deck behind the open flower-fronted porch, and the broad roof overhang shields both.

The Chitarin's living room features an experimental fireplace of peculiar design. "In such a small living area it was dangerous to bring the fireplace into the room. Against this was the fact that the minute it was on or set into the wall, it lost its intimacy, (and destroyed the exterior wall surface)." A curved screen of firebrick acts as a heat reflector at the rear, with the chimney flue on a thick slab supported by metal rods. A cone added inside the chimney throat keeps the smoke going in the right direction

Above: view into the kitchenette from the living room. Below: plot plan shows relation of house to stable, car port and future house. Prevailing wind is westerly and brisk

Roger Sturtevant Photos

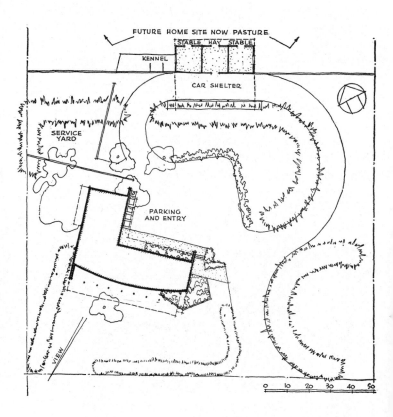

FUTURE HOME SITE NOW PASTURE

STABLE HAY STABLE

KENNEL

CAR SHELTER

SERVICE YARD

PARKING AND ENTRY

VIEW

0   10   20   30   40   50

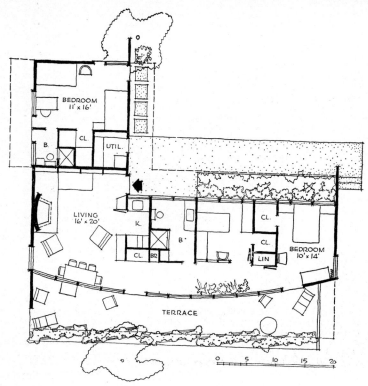

BEDROOM
11' x 16'

B.

CL.

UTIL.

LIVING
16' x 20'

K.

CL.

BR

CL.

B.

CL.

LIN

BEDROOM
10' x 14'

TERRACE

0   5   10   15   20

Above, left: the long level slab at the entrance was originally designed to facilitate use by an invalid in a wheelchair, which also accounts for level floors, wide doors, and the wide gallery connecting living room with bedrooms. The separate bedroom was intended for a nurse but is adaptable for guest use. Below: stable, car shelter and, further down the hill, the house

Roger Sturtevant Photos

Ritchie Lowry House,

Burlingame, Calif.

SPACIOUS PRIVACY ON A SMALL LOT

Expert disposition and interrelation of elements achieve qualities here of mountain remoteness amid suburban surroundings, and of almost manorial spread within dimensions strictly appropriate to the needs and means of a young couple. Northern placement of the house protects out-of-door spaces from witness and weather, prevailing from this direction. The pitch of roof and wide overhang give shade to the terrace side in suitable season, and during the cold months admit maximum sun to the living room. Detachment of garage, with interconnecting arbor, contributes to the general effect of seclusion and expanse.

Stone and Stecatti Photos

Left: roof is tar and gravel laid on 1-in. sheathing; screened vent to insulation space (discernible along edge of carrying beam) is matched by similar provision at rear of house. Below: glass-roofed arbor shields traffic from garage to house without precluding sun. Garden and landscaping designed by Douglas Bayliss

Francis Ellsworth Lloyd, Architect

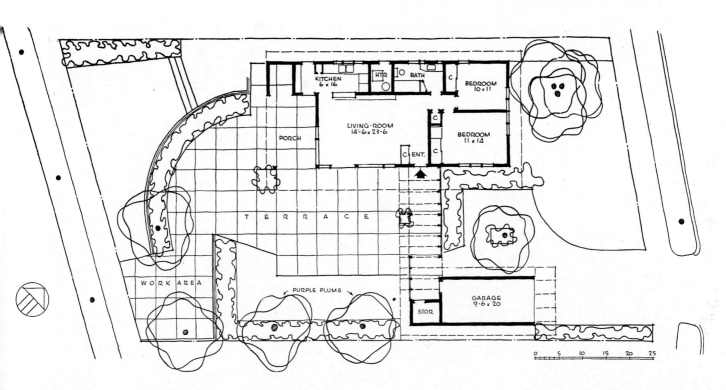

Right: kitchen placement (see plan) provides equal ease in service to living room and garden. Center: inside finishes are plaster board and combed plywood; exterior walls are rough board and batten

Stone and Steccati Photos

June 1948

The concrete terrace extending along the living-dining area commands a fine view of desert and mountains. The end of the terrace, west of the dining room, is planned to be roofed and screened. Below, the overhang of the roof shields the glass from the hot summer sun, permits it to penetrate in winter

Richard A. Morse and

William Y. Peters

Architects

Above: Maynard L. Parker Photo. Below: Ivan Burkhart Photo

ARCHITECTS' VERSION OF A G.I. HOME

Residence of Mr. and Mrs. William B. Schimmel

Tucson, Arizona

THE owner of this house, an artist, is a veteran of World War II; his home was built under government regulations in effect in 1946 and finished at the end of that year. Present sleeping accommodations — the most that could be provided under law — are somewhat inadequate for a family of two adults and two teen-age children, and another bedroom and bath, for later addition, were therefore provided in the original scheme, as indicated on the plan at right. Despite this temporary deficiency, it seems probable that when this house is brought to the attention of the general public a considerable number of ex-G.I.'s who have bought homes since the end of the war will have occasion to make rueful comparison between this house and what was sold to them. Whitewashed local common brick, exposed on the inside, is the principal structural material. The forced warm-air heating system is integrally combined with an evaporative cooler for summer use.

A new bedroom wing will extend out from blank wall at left in this photograph; entrance to house from carport, at extreme right, is through the walled service yard. Roof is built-up composition over 4-in. mineral wool insulation

Maynard L. Parker Photos

Floors throughout are colored cement on concrete slab. Except in kitchen and bath, ceilings are V-jointed pine boards, oiled and waxed. Walls are painted

Maynard L. Parker Photo

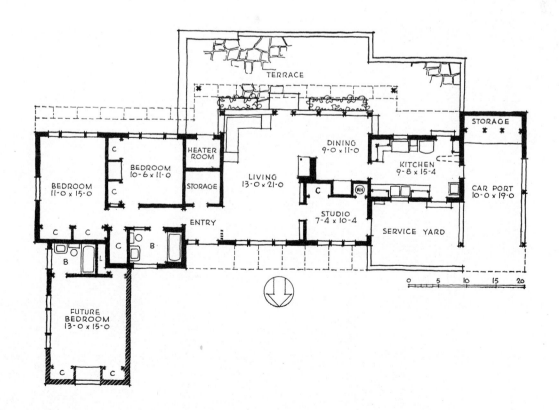

TERRACE

STORAGE

HEATER
ROOM

DINING
9-0 x 11-0

KITCHEN
9-8 x 15-4

BEDROOM
10-6 x 11-0

STORAGE

LIVING
13-0 x 21-0

CAR PORT
10-0 x 19-0

BEDROOM
11-0 x 15-0

STUDIO
7-4 x 10-4

SERVICE YARD

ENTRY

B

C

B

B

L

0   5   10   15   20

FUTURE
BEDROOM
13-0 x 15-0

TIME-SAVER STANDARDS

FOR HOME BUILDING

THE HOUSEHOLD LAUNDRY

Planning Considerations

Larch C. Renshaw, A.I.A.

There is every indication that the postwar house will be planned and equipped both to add to the joy of living and to eliminate most of the drudgery. Mechanical and electrical servants will perform the household tasks. The task of providing fresh clean linens, personal and household, will be made lighter and more efficient through the well-equipped home laundry planned on the production - line principle. Therefore these Time-Saver Standards which show a number of plans to meet various requirements and conditions, whether the home laundry is to be a separate room or to be combined with the kitchen, utility room or with other facilities.

LOCATION OF THE LAUNDRY

The best location is naturally convenient to other work centers, such as the kitchen, and to the drying yard, so that there will be a minimum of carrying necessary. A light, sunny, airy location can make laundering a pleasure. The day when the laundry tubs were relegated to an obscure corner of the basement has long since passed. Working in a damp, dark basement is both inefficient and depressing.

Laundering may be done in a room designed especially for this one purpose or in a combination room, sharing space with the kitchen, a recreation room, or a bathroom. Or it may be in conjunction with a canning, deep-freezing, or storage area, or with a sewing room, or with the heating and hot water services. In some southern states, installations may be in the garage or other buildings adjacent to the home.

ADVANTAGES OF A HOME LAUNDRY

Some of the advantages of a well-designed laundry in the home are:

1. Home-laundry processes prolong the life of linens and clothing, make for less frequent replacements and mending.
2. Investment in better quality linens and clothes is warranted, for they will receive the more gentle personal care of the owner.
3. Saving in cost or cash outlay which would normally go to a commercial laundry for its service.
4. Since some laundering must always be done at home, particularly if there are small children, the home laundry lightens the task of laundering fine linens, children's things, wash dresses, etc.

5. Clothes, linens, etc. cannot get mixed, lost or stolen, as they remain on the premises.
6. Clothes can be dried naturally by sun and outside air.
7. Laundry dates are determined by the housewife, not by the management of an outside agency.
8. Time saving: Important articles will be "out of use" for a shorter time, as washing can be done as often as desired. There are no delays or long waits for laundry to be returned.
9. Provision of an efficient home laundry adds to the resale value of the house, prevents obsolescence.

These advantages must be weighed against the advantages of a commercial laundry. Some of the advantages of a commercial laundry may be listed as:

1. Small charges for service can be met each week, whereas initial investment in a home laundry may seem to be prohibitive.
2. Area required by a home laundry can be eliminated or utilized for other purposes if budget is limited.
3. Commercial laundries do careful work and offer wide range of services — charging accordingly. They provide special skills and equipment not available in the home for certain classes of work, such as collars, shirts, etc.
4. It is sanitary and hygienic.
5. Special "quick service" is possible during normal times.

PLANNING FOR EFFICIENCY

The sequence of laundering operations determine the planning of space and facilities and the placing of equipment. Convenience, time-and-step saving are easily achieved by placing the elements in their natural order of use, viz: (1) Clothes chute (with or without bins or hampers); (2) Sorting table or counter; (3) Washing machine; (4) Laundry trays; (5) Dryer; (6) Ironer or mangle; (7) Ironing board; (8) Rack, "horse" or table for finished laundry. In addition, storage closet or cabinets will be necessary for soaps, powders, bluing, bleaches, starch, basket, clothespins, iron, etc. A hot plate is usually needed for starch preparation.

The facilities and equipment to be provided are therefore:

1. **Storage closet.** With space for soaps, sewing kit, spoons, sieves, bleaches, baskets, bluing, stain removers, starch, clothespins, etc. It may be a built-in unit or a special

free-standing cabinet.

2. **Clothes chute.** Should have its opening near a sorting table or counter so that clothes will not have to be handled more than necessary. It may be made of metal, metal-lined wood, wood, glass or a number of the composition materials. The chute should be vertical as curved sections are likely to cause clothes to clog the chute. The only possible curved section may be at the bottom of the chute as shown on the diagrams.

3. **Sorting table.** Should be either on casters or be a counter with bins below. There should be a hot plate on the counter for boiling clothes and starch making. If the sorting unit is of the cabinet type, it may be similar to the type of cabinet used in kitchens—with ventilated front for air circulation.

4. **Laundry tray or trays.** Or sink and tray. Should be near the washing machine and be equipped with mixing faucets. One tray should be at least 10 in. deep. The usual tray unit is about 24 in. long and 22 in. from front to back.

5. **Washing Machine.** Capable of washing and damp drying. Should be near the dryer or service door so that wet clothes may be carried a minimum distance, and may be dried either indoors or out. Postwar machines will come in many styles and types. However, to date, there is no indication that they will increase in overall dimensions. It would, however, be well for the architect to ascertain, as far as possible, the type of unit to be installed.

6. **Drying.** May be done by an electric or gas dryer, or clothes may be hung outdoors. It may also be well to include an adjustable rack hung from the ceiling for occasional indoor drying. Several manufacturers are planning a postwar radiant-heat electrical drying unit of a "tumbler" design. This type of dryer will fluff clothes and leave them soft. At least one manufacturer will combine complete drying with the washing machine equipment.

7. **Mangle or ironer.** Will require considerable space, as a work table is formed by sides which fold down when not in use. It is easily moved and may, therefore, be rolled out from the wall location when in use, if so desired.

8. **Ironing board.** Hand finishing will require provision for ironing board which can be folded into wall.

Kitchen-Laundry Plans

Scale ¼" = 1'0"

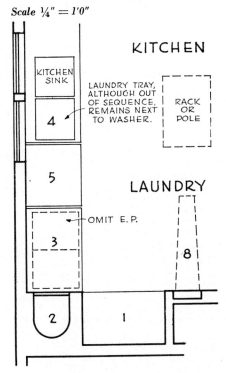

KITCHEN

KITCHEN
SINK

4

LAUNDRY TRAY,
ALTHOUGH OUT
OF SEQUENCE,
REMAINS NEXT
TO WASHER.

RACK
OR
POLE

5

LAUNDRY

3

OMIT E.P.

8

2

1

A. AT ONE CORNER OF KITCHEN
MINIMUM

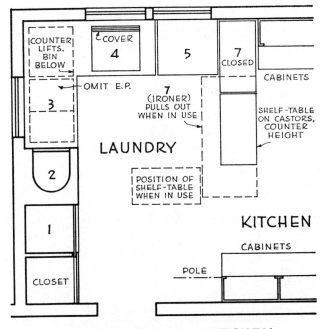

COUNTER
LIFTS.
BIN
BELOW

COVER
4

5

7
CLOSED

CABINETS

OMIT E.P.

3

7
(IRONER)
PULLS OUT
WHEN IN USE

SHELF-TABLE
ON CASTORS,
COUNTER
HEIGHT

LAUNDRY

2

POSITION OF
SHELF-TABLE
WHEN IN USE

1

KITCHEN

CABINETS

POLE

CLOSET

B. AT ONE END OF KITCHEN
COMPLETE EXCEPT FOR DRYER. NEEDS NO
ELECTRIC PLATE BECAUSE KITCHEN IS NEAR.
ADEQUATE OR MEDIUM

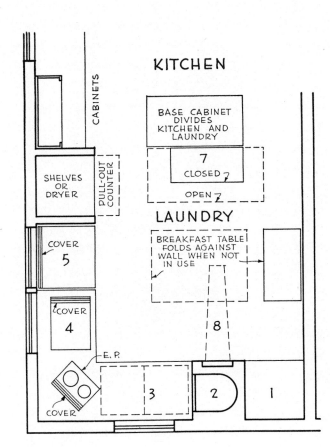

CABINETS

KITCHEN

BASE CABINET
DIVIDES
KITCHEN AND
LAUNDRY

7
CLOSED

OPEN

SHELVES
OR
DRYER

PULL-OUT COUNTER

LAUNDRY

BREAKFAST TABLE
FOLDS AGAINST
WALL WHEN NOT
IN USE

COVER
5

COVER
4

8

E.P.

3

2

1

COVER

KEY

1. STORAGE CLOSET
2. CLOTHES CHUTE (VENTILATED)
3. SORTING SHELF EQUIPPED WITH ELECTRIC
   PLATE; VENTILATED BINS BELOW.
4. LAUNDRY TRAY WITH MIXING FAUCET
   AND COVER
5. WASHING MACHINE
6. DRYER (SHOULD BE VENTILATED)
7. IRONER
8. ELECTRIC IRON AND IRONING BOARD

NOTES

INDICATIONS ON PLANS PROVIDE
FOR THE USUAL FLOOR SPACE
REQUIREMENTS. EACH PIECE FITS
INTO A SEQUENCE WHICH WILL MOST
NEARLY ACCOMPLISH A "PRODUCTION
LINE" EFFICIENCY IN HOME LAUNDRY WORK.

E.P. = ELECTRIC PLATE.

CHUTE EMPTIES ONTO SORTING SHELF
OR INTO A BASE CABINET ADJACENT
TO A BIN BELOW THE SHELF

◄ C. AT ONE END OF KITCHEN
IMPROVED VARIATION

THE HOUSEHOLD LAUNDRY

A Kitchen-Laundry Plan

Larch C. Renshaw, A.I.A.

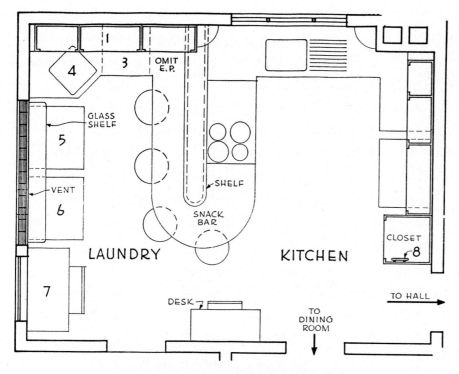

KEY

1. STORAGE CLOSET
2. CLOTHES CHUTE
3. SORTING SHELF
4. LAUNDRY TRAY
5. WASHING MACHINE
6. DRYER
7. IRONER
8. IRONING BOARD

D. COMPLETE KITCHEN AND LAUNDRY LAYOUT

By courtesy of Edison General Electric Appliance Company, Inc. of Chicago, Ill.

Separate Laundry Rooms

Scale ¼" = 1'0"

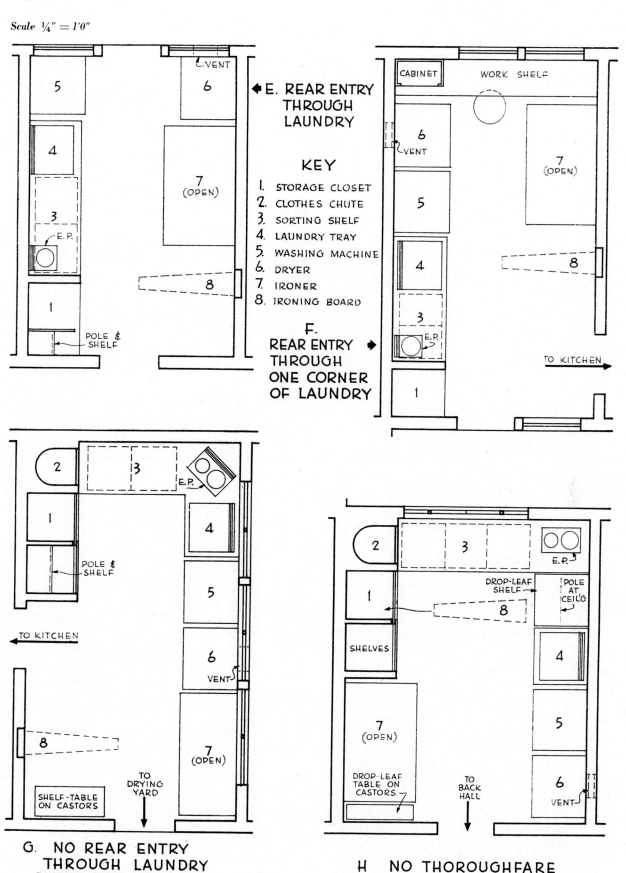

E. REAR ENTRY THROUGH LAUNDRY

KEY

1. STORAGE CLOSET
2. CLOTHES CHUTE
3. SORTING SHELF
4. LAUNDRY TRAY
5. WASHING MACHINE
6. DRYER
7. IRONER
8. IRONING BOARD

F. REAR ENTRY THROUGH ONE CORNER OF LAUNDRY

CABINET WORK SHELF

VENT

7 (OPEN)

8

TO KITCHEN

POLE & SHELF

TO KITCHEN

SHELF-TABLE ON CASTORS

TO DRYING YARD

G. NO REAR ENTRY THROUGH LAUNDRY
BETTER PRODUCTION LINE

DROP-LEAF SHELF

POLE AT CEIL'G

SHELVES

DROP-LEAF TABLE ON CASTORS

TO BACK HALL

H NO THOROUGHFARE
COMPLETE PRODUCTION LINE

THE HOUSEHOLD LAUNDRY

Multi-Use Laundry Rooms

Scale ¼″ = 1′0″

Larch C. Renshaw, A.I.A.

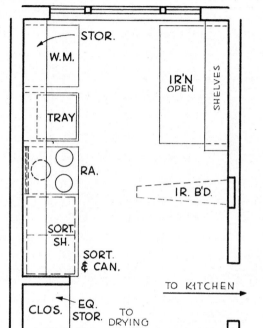

I. MINIMUM
NO FREEZER, NO DRYER, NO CHUTE

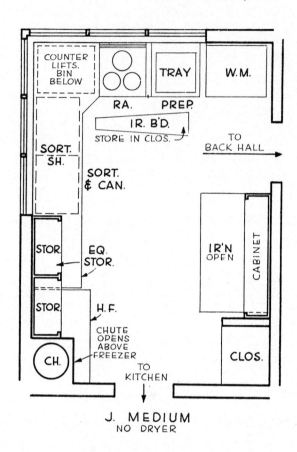

J. MEDIUM
NO DRYER

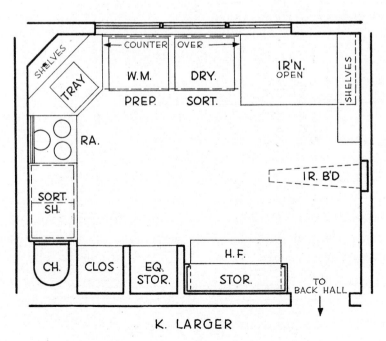

K. LARGER

KEY FOR LAUNDRY

CLOS.	STORAGE CLOSET
CH.	CLOTHES CHUTE
SORT. SH.	SORTING SHELF
TRAY	LAUNDRY TRAY
W. M.	WASHING MACHINE
DRY.	DRYER
IR'N	IRONER
IR. B'D	IRONING BOARD

KEY FOR CANNING - FREEZING

EQ. STOR.	CANNING EQUIPMENT STORAGE
SORT.	SORTING
PREP.	PREPARATION
RA.	RANGE (WITH COVER)
CAN.	CANNING & PACKAGING
H. F.	HOME FREEZER
STOR.	STORAGE FOR CANNED FOOD

LAUNDRY - CANNING - FREEZING

Scale ¼″ = 1′0″

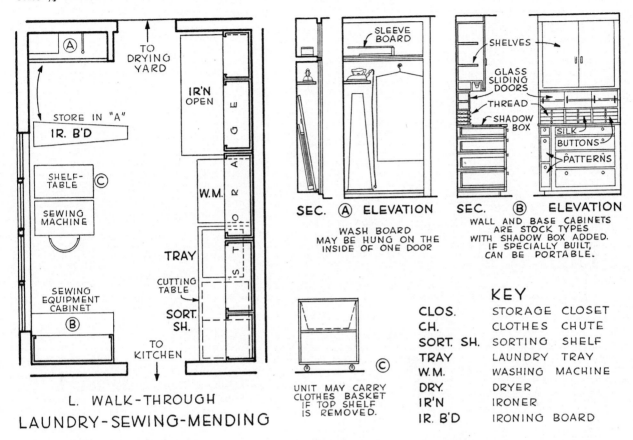

SEC. Ⓐ ELEVATION
WASH BOARD
MAY BE HUNG ON THE
INSIDE OF ONE DOOR

SEC. Ⓑ ELEVATION
WALL AND BASE CABINETS
ARE STOCK TYPES
WITH SHADOW BOX ADDED.
IF SPECIALLY BUILT,
CAN BE PORTABLE.

UNIT MAY CARRY
CLOTHES BASKET
IF TOP SHELF
IS REMOVED.

L. WALK-THROUGH
LAUNDRY-SEWING-MENDING

KEY

CLOS.	STORAGE CLOSET
CH.	CLOTHES CHUTE
SORT. SH.	SORTING SHELF
TRAY	LAUNDRY TRAY
W.M.	WASHING MACHINE
DRY.	DRYER
IR'N	IRONER
IR. B'D	IRONING BOARD

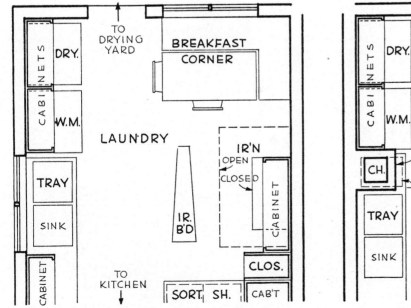

M. AT ONE END OF KITCHEN
LAUNDRY-BREAKFAST CORNER

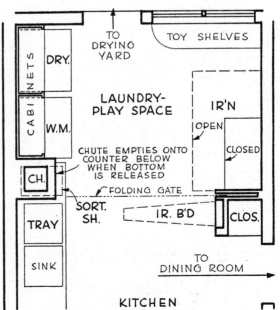

N. ALTERNATIVE USE
LAUNDRY-PLAY SPACE

HOUSEHOLD CLOSETS, PART I

Basic Elements — SHELVES   **Research by Larch Renshaw**

PURPOSE

The standards given on these four pages show the usual elements or fixtures that are assembled to produce an efficient storage space or closet. The choice and arrangement of the fixtures depend on the amount and nature of the materials to be stored. Data relating to elements of closet fixtures or equipment are thus made available for easy reference and for grouping to fit any particular purpose.

The standard elements are, 1. Shelves, 2. Poles, 3. Drawers, 4. Hooks, and 5. Special Fixtures. Practically any object can be stored efficiently by one or other of these means. For convenience and quick reference one page has been devoted to each of the standard elements, and the variations in sizes and types have been indicated by key numbers.

GENERAL CONSIDERATIONS

"A place for everything and everything in its place" is the slogan for closet designers as well as housewives. Modern closets should be planned for the storage of the particular clothing or objects of the individual or the group using the

space for storage. An accurate list of the objects to be stored is necessary for the scientific allotment and arrangement of space and facilities. A "margin of safety" of some 25 per cent increased capacity should be allowed for the usual accumulation of additional

belongings. It is better to have too much space than not enough. Much can be stored in little space if sufficient thought is given to the arrangement of the space and the equipment. Too many closets have unused and unusable space, due to poor planning.

TYPES OF CLOSETS

Closets may be classified according to purpose, place or user, or all three. The various types of closets and their particular arrangements will be considered in subsequent Time-Saver Standards. Most types are, however, equipped with the major elements here shown.

Modern closets by the efficient arrangement of space and fixtures accomodate much more clothing and material than the inconvenient, dark, space-wasting closets of a few decades ago. The modern closet thus often replaces pieces of furniture and provides a greater amount of free, uncluttered space in the room.

DOORS

Doors should open the full width of the closet wherever possible, two doors for a five foot closet. This eliminates dark, inaccessible,

USEFUL SHELF SIZES

S-1, S-2 8", S-3 10", S-4 12", S-5 16", S-6 18", L-VARIABLE 24"

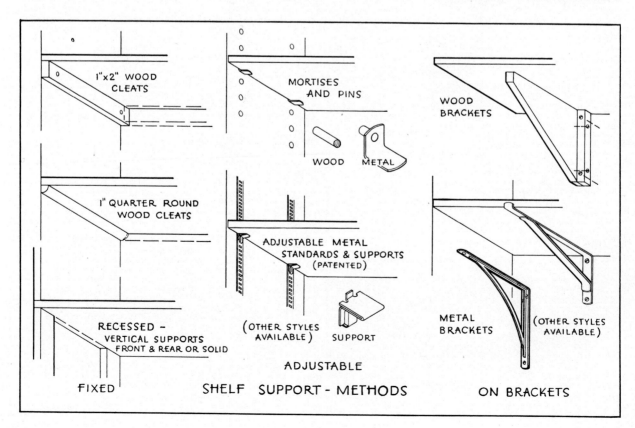

I"x2" WOOD CLEATS

I" QUARTER ROUND WOOD CLEATS

RECESSED - VERTICAL SUPPORTS FRONT & REAR OR SOLID

FIXED

MORTISES AND PINS

WOOD   METAL

ADJUSTABLE METAL STANDARDS & SUPPORTS (PATENTED)

(OTHER STYLES AVAILABLE)   SUPPORT

ADJUSTABLE

WOOD BRACKETS

METAL BRACKETS   (OTHER STYLES AVAILABLE)

ON BRACKETS

SHELF SUPPORT - METHODS

hard-to-clean corners. By the use of sliding doors the entire interior of the closet is exposed to view and every inch of space is immediately accessible. Such doors do not block traffic, bark shins or provide excuse for black eyes.

Sliding doors do not permit the use of special door fixtures such as tie racks, shoe racks or bags, hat hangers, mirror and the like, which are handy and easily reached when attached to a hinged closet-door.

SIZES

For general closets, bedroom or dressing-room closets, 2 ft.-0 in. is standard depth (2 ft.-6 in. if a hook-strip is to be used). This permits clothing to be on hangers on poles, with sufficient clearance. Clothes closet width, parallel to the doors, should be from 3 to 6 ft. per person depending on amounts of clothing and whether drawers or trays are to be provided in the closet or wardrobe for such items as have in the past been kept in bureaus

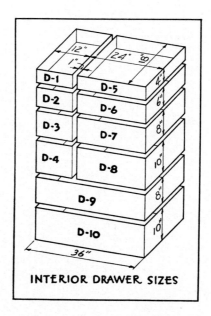

INTERIOR DRAWER SIZES

or other pieces of furniture.

Additional usable storage space is gained by limiting the height of

the closet proper to easy reaching height (7 ft. max.) and placing cupboards above for seasonal storage, things that are "put away" for the summer or winter.

LIGHTING AND VENTILATION

Lighting is now considered essential and standard in the modern closet unless room lights are so located as to fully illuminate all portions of the closet. A single tubular or bulb light placed just above the door at the front of the closet, with a diffusing reflector is usually sufficient. Automatic door switches are convenient.

Ventilation has rarely been considered necessary in closets as clothing is usually dry, clean and aired before being placed in the closet. Where such is not the case, ventilation can be supplied by louvres in the lower part of the door and a duct from the closet ceiling, or a grill from the upper part of the closet.

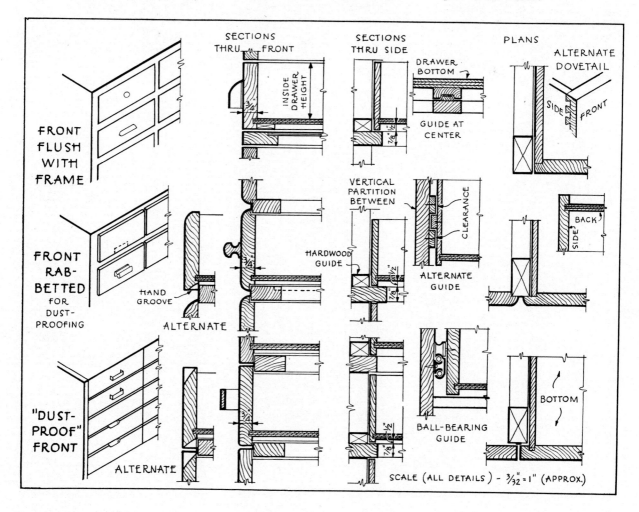

HOUSEHOLD CLOSETS, PART I

Basic Elements — POLES AND HANGERS   **Research by Larch Renshaw**

SHELVES

Shelves are simple and inexpensive to install, require a minimum of effort to use and are adaptable to the storage of many types of things, especially those of odd or bulky shape, folded articles, and of course books, magazines, etc. However, being open, they are most exposed to dust. Also small objects become hidden behind one another if the shelves are deep. A 12 in. shelf is usually adequate for most things. Things of known larger dimensions or greater depth should have their special places; linens, for instance, are frequently folded for an 18 or 24 in. shelf.

POLES

Hanging pole length can be estimated roughly at 3 in. per hanger for men's suits, 2 in. per hanger for women's. Height of pole above floor 5 ft. 6 in. average, but should be adjusted to the individual. Clearance between pole and shelf above, 3 in. Hardwood poles 1 in. in diameter should have intermediate supports if over 4 ft. in

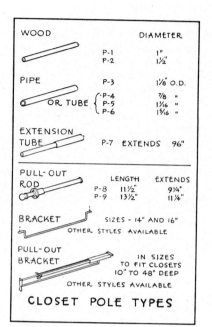

CLOSET POLE TYPES		
WOOD		DIAMETER
	P-1	1"
	P-2	1½"
PIPE	P-3	1⅛" O.D.
OR TUBE	P-4	⅞ "
	P-5	1¹⁄₁₆ "
	P-6	1⁵⁄₁₆ "
EXTENSION TUBE	P-7	EXTENDS 96"
PULL-OUT ROD	LENGTH	EXTENDS
	P-8 11½"	9¼"
	P-9 13½"	11¼"
BRACKET	SIZES – 14" AND 16" OTHER STYLES AVAILABLE	
PULL-OUT BRACKET	IN SIZES TO FIT CLOSETS 10" TO 48" DEEP OTHER STYLES AVAILABLE	

length. Consult manufacturers for special-purpose hanging rods, extension poles, brackets, etc.

DRAWERS

Drawers are growing in popularity in closet design because they accomodate numerous and sundry articles with a minimum of space and a maximum of convenience. They provide practically dust-free storage and present a neat appearance even when carelessly used. Drawers of different widths and depths make possible classified "filing" of different items, a great saving in time and an incentive to orderliness. A cabinet made up of a battery of standard drawers, selected for the storage of the known possessions of the user can easily be made from a comprehensive list, with allowance made for the accumulation of additional items.

Drawer construction is cabinet work requiring both skillful craftsmanship and the best materials. They must operate freely under all seasonal and climatic conditions to avoid lost tempers as well as inaccessible articles.

Various standard manufactured units shown, Knape & Vogt Manufacturing Co.

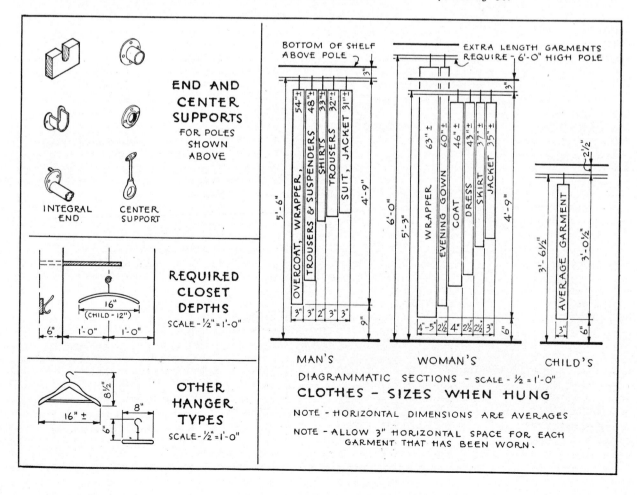

END AND CENTER SUPPORTS FOR POLES SHOWN ABOVE

INTEGRAL END

CENTER SUPPORT

REQUIRED CLOSET DEPTHS
SCALE – ½" = 1'-0"

OTHER HANGER TYPES
SCALE – ½" = 1'-0"

MAN'S   WOMAN'S   CHILD'S

DIAGRAMMATIC SECTIONS – SCALE – ½" = 1'-0"

CLOTHES – SIZES WHEN HUNG

NOTE – HORIZONTAL DIMENSIONS ARE AVERAGES

NOTE – ALLOW 3" HORIZONTAL SPACE FOR EACH GARMENT THAT HAS BEEN WORN.

Basic Elements — HOOKS, RACKS, ETC.

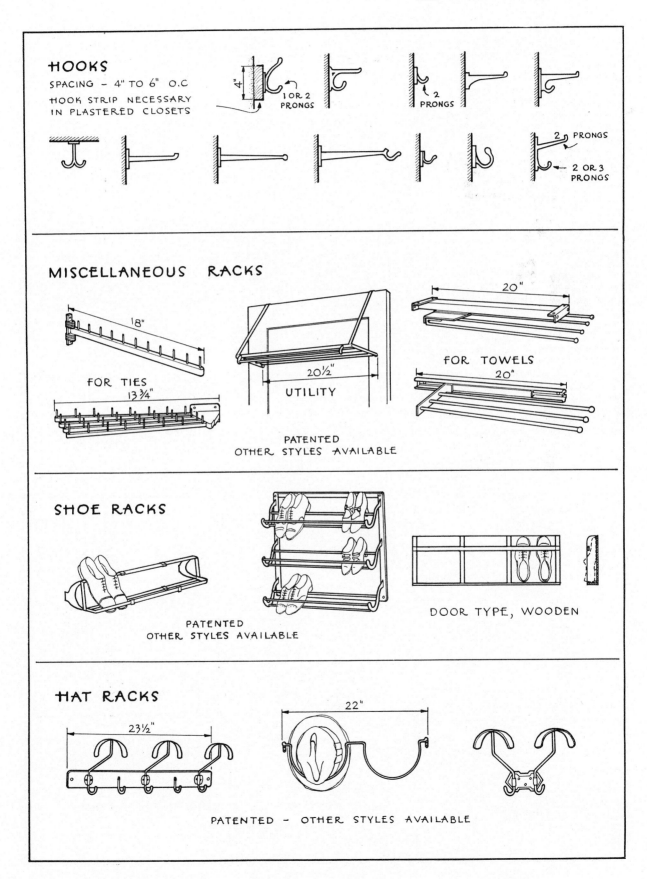

HOOKS
SPACING – 4" TO 6" O.C
HOOK STRIP NECESSARY
IN PLASTERED CLOSETS

4"

1 OR 2 PRONGS

2 PRONGS

2 PRONGS

2 OR 3 PRONGS

MISCELLANEOUS RACKS

18"

FOR TIES
13 3/4"

20 1/2"

UTILITY

PATENTED
OTHER STYLES AVAILABLE

20"

FOR TOWELS
20"

SHOE RACKS

PATENTED
OTHER STYLES AVAILABLE

DOOR TYPE, WOODEN

HAT RACKS

23 1/2"

22"

PATENTED – OTHER STYLES AVAILABLE

HOUSEHOLD CLOSETS, PART II

Assemblies of Basic Units　　　　**Research by Larch Renshaw, A.I.A.**

These schematic diagrams of closets are a continuation of the Time-Saver Standards Part I, which were published in the November, 1943 issue. Part I covered basic elements of household closets (such as shelves, poles, drawers, and accessories) which can be assembled to serve various storage needs. Part II shows possible and useful standards for assemblies of the basic units as suggestions for architects and designers planning closets for the personal use of a man, a woman, and a child. Dimensions are approximate and will differ with the structural details.

CRITERIA

Good closet design requires planning, arrangement and fixtures contributing to:

A. Convenience
1. Ease of access
2. Maximum visibility
3. Orderliness
4. Maximum availability or reachability
5. Maximum of used space

B. Preservation
1. Of pressed condition
2. Of freshness (ventilation)
3. From moths
4. From dust
5. From pilfering

These are not all simultaneously obtainable and some are mutually exclusive, for instance, eliminating doors gives maximum availability, but minimum security from dust, moths, and pilfering; or maximum reachability would involve unused space at top and bottom of closet.

DOORS AND PLANS

The obvious, and in most cases most efficient and economical, doors are the usual flush single and double swinging doors. They are omitted from the chart at right which shows alternate closet closing schemes. Hooks, racks, and accessories on swinging doors increase efficiency, using space in the closet otherwise unoccupied.

The alternate closet closing methods may involve more complicated or more expensive construction, though they may obviate the objection that swinging doors form an obstruction in the room.

Banks of wardrobe type closets with sliding or rolling doors are becoming more and more popular. Fitted with drawers or trays, they take the place of bureaus, chests, and chiffoniers and make for more spacious uncluttered rooms.

Doors which expose the full width of the closet are preferable for both visibility and reachability. "Walk in" or "walk through" closets naturally use more area than others with no "circulation." In some cases, however, a single door to a large "walk in" closet may be justified by the need for maximum wall space for furniture.

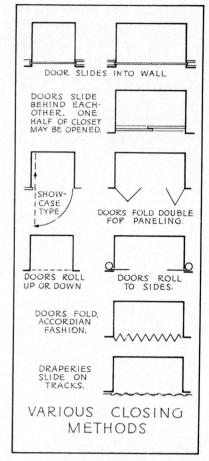

VARIOUS CLOSING METHODS

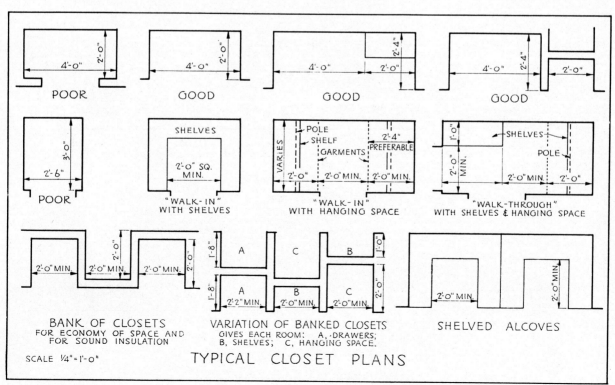

TYPICAL CLOSET PLANS

Bedroom Closets for Men

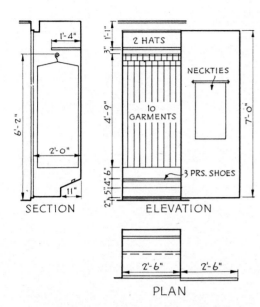

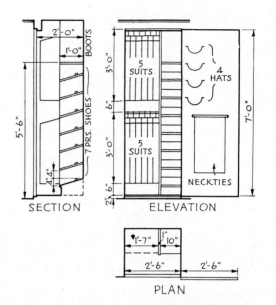

A minimum size closet of a usual type. Shoes can be stored on the raised shelf-rack and three additional pair on the floor in front of the rack. Door could be arranged for hats as shown below, leaving shelf for other storage.

Minimal closet arranged to make shoes more visible and reachable. There is space for hats without crushing or for night clothes hooks if hats are normally stored in a hall closet. Neckties might be in two tiers.

SCALE OF ALL DIAGRAMS ON THIS PAGE ¼" = 1'-0"

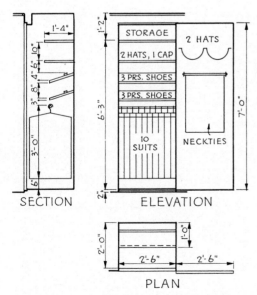

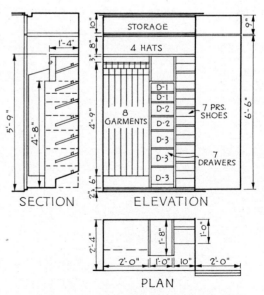

An alternate to the scheme above giving maximum view of shoes and an additional shelf. Trousers would have to be folded over the crossbar of the suit hanger rather than being hung separately from the pole with trouser-hangers.

A four-foot closet with seven drawers for shirts, socks, underwear, etc., and a vertical tier of shoe racks (as above). Night clothes and bathrobe hooks are best on the right hand door, necktie racks flat against the left hand door.

HOUSEHOLD CLOSETS, PART II

Bedroom Closets for Men (continued)

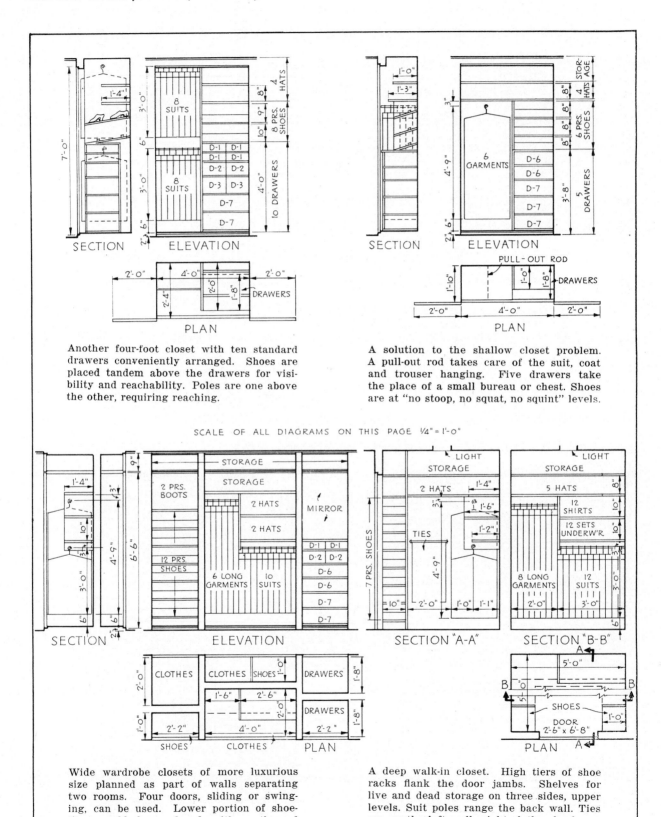

SCALE OF ALL DIAGRAMS ON THIS PAGE 1/4" = 1'-0"

Another four-foot closet with ten standard drawers conveniently arranged. Shoes are placed tandem above the drawers for visibility and reachability. Poles are one above the other, requiring reaching.

A solution to the shallow closet problem. A pull-out rod takes care of the suit, coat and trouser hanging. Five drawers take the place of a small bureau or chest. Shoes are at "no stoop, no squat, no squint" levels.

Wide wardrobe closets of more luxurious size planned as part of walls separating two rooms. Four doors, sliding or swinging, can be used. Lower portion of shoe-tiers could be replaced with mothproof "dead-storage" drawers.

A deep walk-in closet. High tiers of shoe racks flank the door jambs. Shelves for live and dead storage on three sides, upper levels. Suit poles range the back wall. Ties are on the left wall, night clothes hooks on right wall.

Bedroom Closets for Women

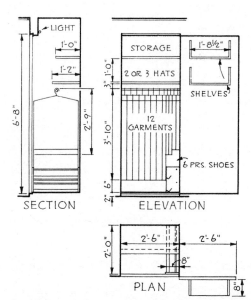

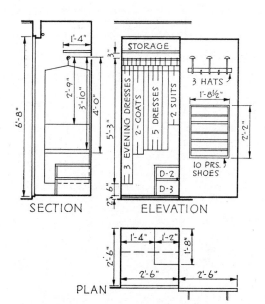

A small closet with shoe racks at the side under short hanging garments. Additional shoe pockets might be placed on the door under the hanging shelves. These handy shelves fold into the space in front of the hat and storage shelves.

An alternate minimum closet arrangment with a high pole for long dresses. Two drawers below the shorter hanging garments. Depth of closet permits a door type shoe rack and a hat rack. Wide hats can go on upper shelf.

SCALE OF ALL DIAGRAMS ON THIS PAGE ¼" = 1'-0"

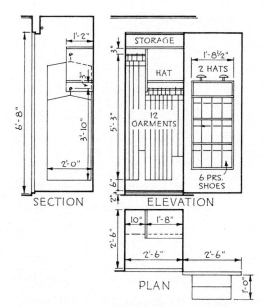

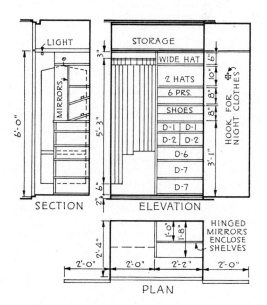

Alternate to closet above. It provides a high pole for hanging evening dresses and a lower pole for other dresses and suits. A large hat shelf is provided above the low pole as well as a hat rack and shoe pockets on the door.

A four-foot closet combining hanging and shelf space with drawers for stockings, underthings, and what-not. Shoes are easily seen and chosen from the almost eye-level cleat rack above the drawers. Hat storage on the shelves.

HOUSEHOLD CLOSETS, PART II

Bedroom Closets for Women (continued)

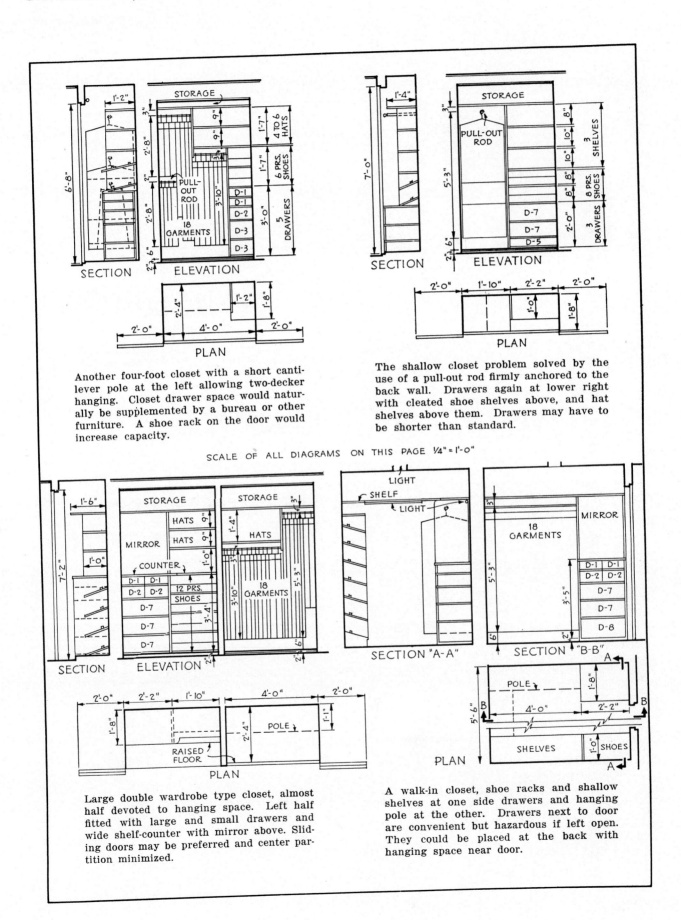

SCALE OF ALL DIAGRAMS ON THIS PAGE ¼" = 1'-0"

Another four-foot closet with a short canti-lever pole at the left allowing two-decker hanging. Closet drawer space would naturally be supplemented by a bureau or other furniture. A shoe rack on the door would increase capacity.

The shallow closet problem solved by the use of a pull-out rod firmly anchored to the back wall. Drawers again at lower right with cleated shoe shelves above, and hat shelves above them. Drawers may have to be shorter than standard.

Large double wardrobe type closet, almost half devoted to hanging space. Left half fitted with large and small drawers and wide shelf-counter with mirror above. Sliding doors may be preferred and center partition minimized.

A walk-in closet, shoe racks and shallow shelves at one side drawers and hanging pole at the other. Drawers next to door are convenient but hazardous if left open. They could be placed at the back with hanging space near door.

Bedroom Closets for Children

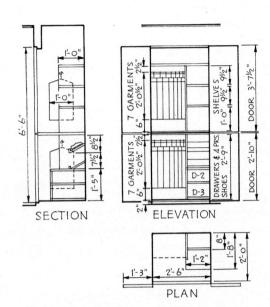

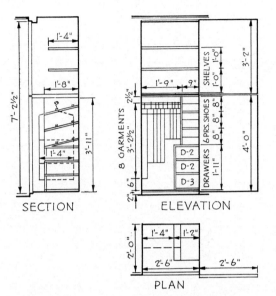

SCALE OF ALL DIAGRAMS ON THIS PAGE ¼" = 1'-0"

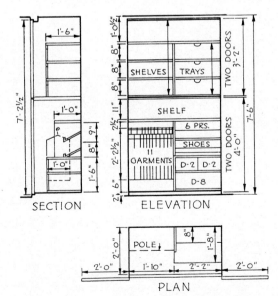

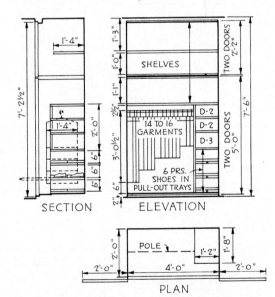

Closet for infants up to about 5 years old. Low hanging pole shelves and drawers permit habits of care and orderliness to be developed at an early age. Upper part would be used by adults. Note two sets of doors.

Small closet designed for a child of from 6 to 10 years. Pole at higher but easily reached level. Drawers and shoe racks at convenient heights. Ample shelf room provided above for the storage of possessions.

Alternate, and larger, closet for an infant up to 5 years of age. Trays or drawers for folded garments at an upper level for adult use. Hanging space, drawers and shelf available to child using the lower doors.

Closet for youngster up to 10 years old, providing greater length of hanging pole and different shoe arrangement, trays instead of cleat racks. A large shelf for hats, toys, or "collections" available to child.

HOUSEHOLD CLOSETS, PART III

Hall Closets   ***Research by Larch Renshaw, A.I.A.***

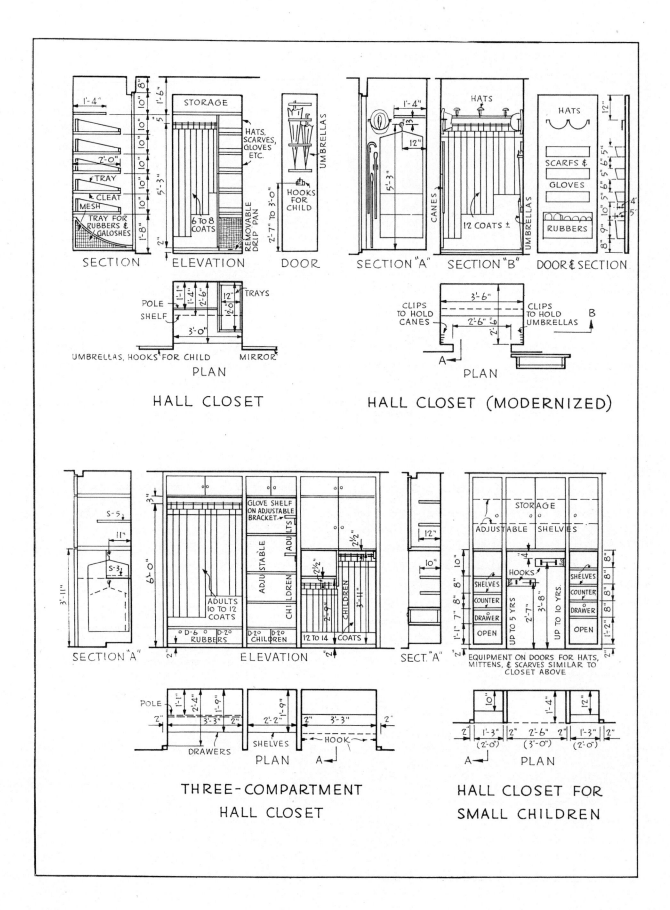

Hall Closets (continued)

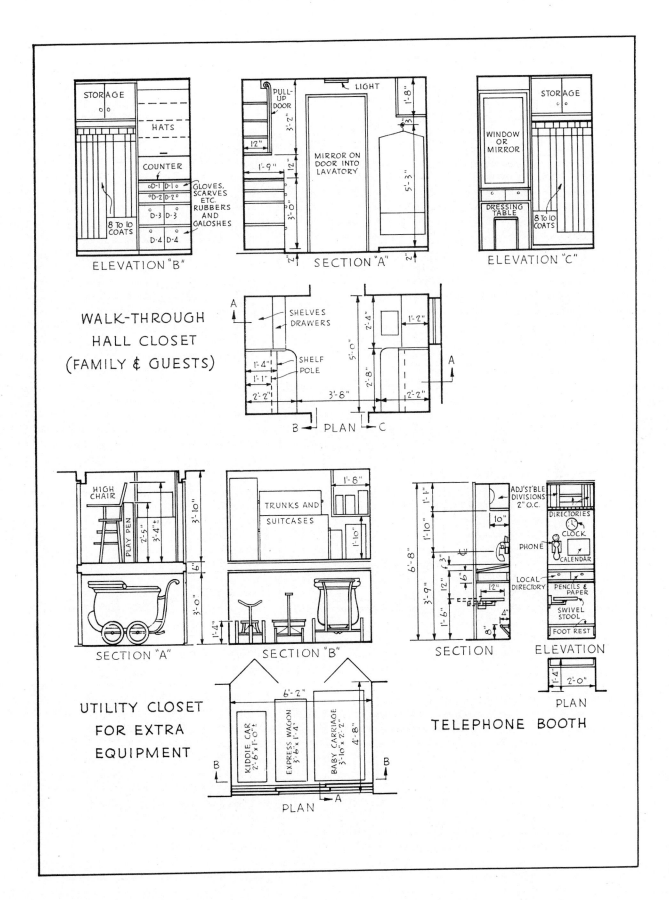

ELEVATION "B"

SECTION "A"

ELEVATION "C"

WALK-THROUGH HALL CLOSET (FAMILY & GUESTS)

PLAN

UTILITY CLOSET FOR EXTRA EQUIPMENT

SECTION "A"

SECTION "B"

PLAN

TELEPHONE BOOTH

SECTION

ELEVATION

PLAN

HOUSEHOLD CLOSETS, PART IV

Miscellaneous Closets ● *Research by Larch Renshaw, A.I.A.*

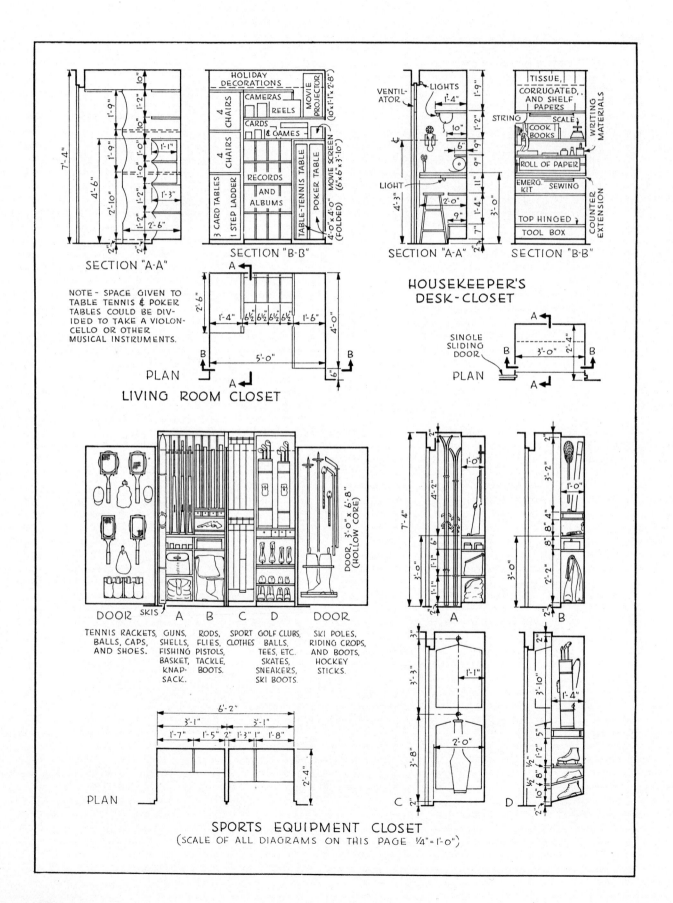

SECTION "A-A"

NOTE - SPACE GIVEN TO
TABLE TENNIS & POKER
TABLES COULD BE DIV-
IDED TO TAKE A VIOLON-
CELLO OR OTHER
MUSICAL INSTRUMENTS.

SECTION "B-B"

HOLIDAY DECORATIONS
CAMERAS
REELS
MOVIE PROJECTOR
CARDS & GAMES
4 CHAIRS
4 CHAIRS
3 CARD TABLES
1 STEP LADDER
RECORDS AND ALBUMS
TABLE-TENNIS TABLE
POKER TABLE
MOVIE SCREEN

PLAN
LIVING ROOM CLOSET

SECTION "A-A"

VENTILATOR
LIGHTS
LIGHT

SECTION "B-B"

TISSUE, CORRUGATED, AND SHELF PAPERS
STRING
SCALE
COOK BOOKS
WRITING MATERIALS
ROLL OF PAPER
EMERG. KIT
SEWING
COUNTER EXTENSION
TOP HINGED
TOOL BOX

HOUSEKEEPER'S DESK-CLOSET

SINGLE SLIDING DOOR

PLAN

DOOR   SKIS   A   B   C   D   DOOR

TENNIS RACKETS, BALLS, CAPS, AND SHOES.

GUNS, SHELLS, FISHING BASKET, KNAP-SACK.

RODS, FLIES, PISTOLS, TACKLE, BOOTS.

SPORT CLOTHES

GOLF CLUBS, BALLS, TEES, ETC. SKATES, SNEAKERS, SKI BOOTS.

SKI POLES, RIDING CROPS, AND BOOTS, HOCKEY STICKS.

DOOR, 3'-0" x 6'-8" (HOLLOW CORE)

A   B

C   D

PLAN

SPORTS EQUIPMENT CLOSET
(SCALE OF ALL DIAGRAMS ON THIS PAGE ¼"=1'-0")

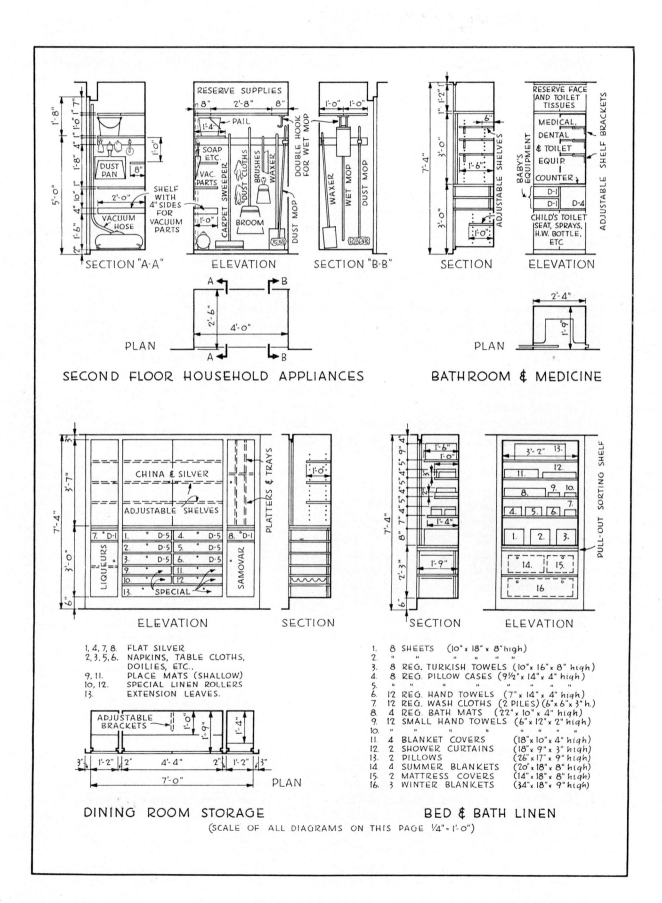

SECOND FLOOR HOUSEHOLD APPLIANCES

SECTION "A-A"   ELEVATION   SECTION "B-B"

PLAN

BATHROOM & MEDICINE

SECTION   ELEVATION

PLAN

DINING ROOM STORAGE

ELEVATION   SECTION   PLAN

1, 4, 7, 8. FLAT SILVER
2, 3, 5, 6. NAPKINS, TABLE CLOTHS, DOILIES, ETC.,
9, 11. PLACE MATS (SHALLOW)
10, 12. SPECIAL LINEN ROLLERS
13. EXTENSION LEAVES.

BED & BATH LINEN

SECTION   ELEVATION

1.   8 SHEETS   (10"x 18" x 8" high)
2.   "   "   "   "   "   "
3.   8 REG. TURKISH TOWELS (10"x 16"x 8" high)
4.   8 REG. PILLOW CASES (9½"x 14"x 4" high)
5.   "   "   "   "   "   "
6. 12 REG. HAND TOWELS (7"x 14"x 4" high)
7. 12 REG. WASH CLOTHS (2 PILES)(6"x 6"x 3" h.)
8.   4 REG. BATH MATS (22"x 10"x 4" high)
9. 12 SMALL HAND TOWELS (6"x 12"x 2" high)
10. "   "   "   "   "   "
11. 4 BLANKET COVERS   (18"x 10"x 4" high)
12. 2 SHOWER CURTAINS (18"x 9"x 3" high)
13. 2 PILLOWS   (26"x 17"x 9" high)
14. 4 SUMMER BLANKETS (20"x 18"x 8" high)
15. 2 MATTRESS COVERS (14"x 18"x 8" high)
16. 3 WINTER BLANKETS (34"x 18"x 9" high)

(SCALE OF ALL DIAGRAMS ON THIS PAGE ¼"=1'-0")

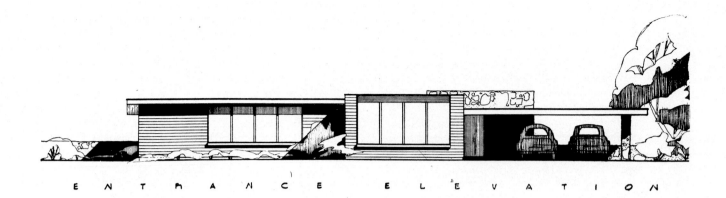

E N T R A N C E   E L E V A T I O N

WHERE THE WHOLE GARDEN MOVES INTO THE HOUSE

Fred Langhorst, Architect

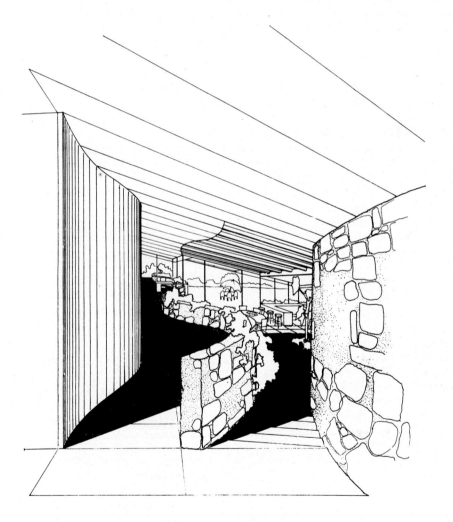

STARTING modestly with flower boxes in living rooms or entrance halls, the trend toward interior gardens has progressed, with planting strips creeping in through glass walls, until here we have the garden shaking off all inhibitions and dominating the whole house. In a warmer clime it would be the familiar patio, but here it is completely enclosed with skylight and glass doors. Thus it has a utility and an importance not accorded the patio; it becomes a central hall. All other rooms may merge with the garden room, or retire from it behind overhead rolling doors. The playfully curving wall accomplishes a change in level for the studio and two bedrooms, the upper hall becoming a terraced balcony overlooking the garden.

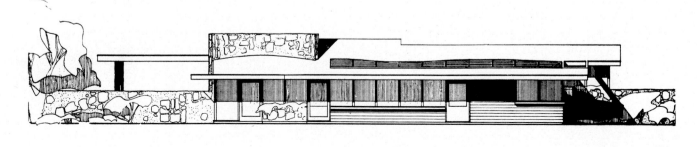

S O U T H   E L E V A T I O N

W E S T   E L E V A T I O N

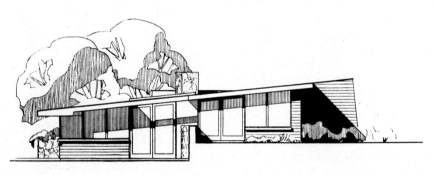

E A S T   E L E V A T I O N

This house, designed for Mr. and Mrs. Gerald Wright, Woodside, Cal., is planned so that it can be built in stages, the upper half of the plan representing a complete living unit while awaiting the complete realization of the larger concept. The house will be built on a concrete slab floor, with copper tubing panel heating coils in the slab. The larger windows will have fixed glass, with screened vents below and metal louvers above. Exterior walls will be 1 by 10 in. horizontal siding

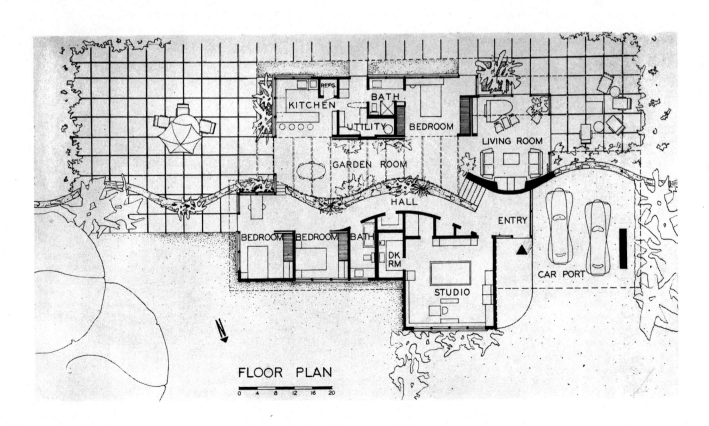

FLOOR PLAN

0   4   8   12   16   20

INDOOR-OUTDOOR PLANTING BEDS

By Henry B. Aul, Landscape Architect

For Construction Details see
TIME-SAVER STANDARDS
pp. 381 and 382

INDOOR planting beds have been enlivening more and more of the contemporary house plans. As one who has long plowed this particular furrow, I must begin by expressing hearty approval for the idea of bringing the garden inside. It is certainly a logical concomitant of bringing the view inside, of integrating indoor and outdoor living, of making the house a natural outgrowth of its site.

If, at the same time, some of the plans have a slightly experimental look, there is nothing to be deplored in that. The problems of indoor planting, both architectural and floricultural, are not so involved that the basic idea need suffer from improper handling.

Purposes of Planting

Indoor planting beds might be employed in a great many different varieties, for many different purposes. Flower beds that seem to extend from the outdoors right through a glass wall into the house establish a strong tie between the house and its site. Or, where windows are large and give an unobstructed view of the garden or landscape, the outdoor-indoor planting frames the view, or furnishes the foreground for it.

On the other hand, a window that overlooks a not too desirable view can be made a center of attraction not only with plantings about its base, but also with a tracery of vines across its face that will screen the less attractive scene outdoors.

Windows away from the garden side of the house, in the kitchen, bedrooms or hobby room, can be equipped to support plant growth, and thus introduce foliage and flowers in all parts of the house.

The entrance, regardless of its exposure, can be made a more cheerful spot to welcome guests.

Frequently it is possible to arrange indoor plantings which will form a partial screen or partition to separate one room from another.

Plants in the outdoor-indoor bed are staged where they are brought into unmistakable prominence. They are close at hand for the pleasure of the gardener and others and are convenient to work among. Since in most instances the planting is connected with large window areas, it is an assured way to have and enjoy plants in the house throughout the year.

Principles of Planting

To gain the closest tie between the outdoor and indoor plantings, it is best to have the plants arranged at approximately the same level throughout; and, if there is a curb or coping around the planting bed, have it contiguous. This means that the curb may be only a few inches above the floor and, depending on the distance of the terrace or porch below the floor level, will be six or more inches high around the outdoor planting.

In locations where, due to the exposure or the shelter of a porch roof or roof overhang, surface drainage is not a problem, it may be desirable to have the house floor and terrace floor at the same level, and the planting set into or raised above the floor level the same distance indoors and out.

Different growing conditions indoors and outdoors preclude the possibility

An indoor-outdoor, floor-level planting bed combined with a trellis for potted vines, to form a partition of plants between living and dining rooms. Flowers in pots can be enjoyed from either side, or from the terrace. Flowers may be changed with the seasons, or according to conditions of bloom. Upper sash provide ventilation. Roof overhang plus slat roller shades control sunlight around planting

Living porch planting bed in a corner sheltered from wind by glass screen. Soil bed might be heated by electric cable on a sub-soil thermostat. Plants may be grown directly in soil, or in pots on a layer of gravel

of using identical plant materials to gain exact continuity between the two areas. Besides, the seasonable change in weather in most parts of the country would upset such a planting plan, even if it were desirable. Considering the value of variety in most plantings and to most plantsmen, the idea is not practical.

Bench or table height plantings raised 24 to 30 inches above the floor can be continued from indoors out or vice-versa, just the same as floor level plantings. The bench-high planting has the advantage of bringing the plants up where they may be worked among conveniently and inspected and admired close at hand. The plant bench can be combined with a work bench in a hobby room or kitchen or between the indoor planting and a sheltered terrace work space that would please all gardeners.

Planning the Planting

It might seem that the easiest method to handle plants, both indoors and out, would be to set them directly in large pockets or beds of soil. It is possible to do this where the floor of the house is a concrete slab on the ground or close to the ground. But for the most satisfactory management of plants indoors, they should be grown and kept in pots. The pots are easily arranged or re-arranged in the planting bed according to their condition, size and appearance.

In pots, they can be shifted or turned to give them light on all sides, removed for treatment against disease or insect injury, for feeding and other handling. It is a method well worth considering for the terrace or other outdoor portions of the planting.

Indoors, the pots are placed on a one- to two-inch drainage base of fine washed gravel in the bottom of a lead, zinc or copper pan built to the shape of the planting bed. The metal pan forms an assured moisture barrier between the plants and the floor or walls.

An alternate plan is to fill the pan with peat moss or expanded mica in which to plunge and conceal the pots. This would be the method to follow when using potted plants outdoors. Of course, no metal pan is needed outdoors. For indoor beds, these pans should be from eight to ten inches deep and of a size that will permit removing them for cleaning once or twice a year.

Moisture Control

Except in unusually large installations, there seems to be little need to consider facilities for draining the pan-lined indoor planting bed. Where neces-

The entrance is a most logical place to gain the invitation of plants. Plants outdoors might be dwarf evergreens or ground covers. Plants indoors might be in a bed of soil, or might be in pots on shelves to screen hall

sary, a small sized pipe or copper tube can be led from the bottom of the pan to the basement drain, crawl space or through a weep hole in the outside wall.

Outdoor beds, filled with a 10- to 12-inch top layer of loam, humus and sand, are given a drainage base of coarse cinders or gravel with one or more lines of four-inch open joint land tile led off to a storm sewer or dry well. The surface of the bed is kept below the coping and adjacent windowsills, and is pitched away from windows and house wall at least one quarter inch to each running foot. Outdoor beds are surface mulched with peat moss or expanded mica to reduce mud splash on walls or windows, and to retain moisture in the soil around the plants.

Planting beds, set in flagstone, tile or other masonry floors, present little danger of moisture damage, and so may or need not be curbed, depending on the requirements of the design. On the other hand, plantings in proximity to wood framing, flooring and trim need to be separated from them by the metal pan liner and a curb of brick, stone, tile or slate, redwood, cypress or other moisture resistant wood. The curbing generally conceals the upper edge of the pan and the concrete base or framework of wood in which the pan is set. The top of the curb is a handy place to display small potted plants for special attention.

Windows connected with indoor-outdoor planting should, in most cases, be set in metal sash. They can be double glazed or single glazed with provision for winter storm sash. This will reduce perceptibly the amount of condensation and ice that forms during winter weather. Bottom sash should preferably be fixed with top louvers or movable sash to provide top ventilation not unlike that in a greenhouse. Movable sash

What better place for the cheer of flowers than right behind the kitchen sink? Pots are set on a gravel base in a metal pan, which is removable. Sash are fixed directly behind sink, with out-swinging casements at side

at the sides of the planting, and doors nearby, will aid general ventilation. Under certain conditions ceiling vents to exhaust fans are used.

Sun Control

Provision must be made to shade windows exposed to full or nearly full sunlight. The roof over a covered terrace or porch and the properly designed roof overhang or sun visor of the solar house furnish adequate shade. They also lessen the problem of splash and surface drainage around outdoor planting beds.

Louver-type insect screens, slat, roller shades, venetian blinds, slat and canvas awnings are other methods of shading the window. Most plantings do not crowd the window on the inside so closely that draw curtains cannot be

used. They are particularly attractive, not only for shade but to shut out the night and make a colorful background for the indoor planting at that time.

In some indoor plantings, not shade but the problem of sufficient light is uppermost. This is solved with flood or other types of incandescent lamps placed above the planting and turned on regularly when natural light is lacking.

Adequate heat is generally available from the regular house system. Water splashed over the gravel drainage material on which the pots are placed contributes humidity to counteract too much heat. Special plantings in sheltered porch or terrace floors can be kept going a good portion of the year with an electric heating cable such as is used to heat the soil in garden hot beds.

A bay window can easily be transformed into a small conservatory, with either soil-filled elevated beds or metal pans for pots. If door leads to terrace or garden, the indoor beds might be continued as raised beds outside. Out-swinging casements ventilate the bay, venetian blinds shade it, and full-length curtains can be pulled across the whole opening at night. Beds might be heated by an electric cable

INDOOR-OUTDOOR PLANTING BEDS, Construction Details

By Henry B. Aul, Landscape Architect

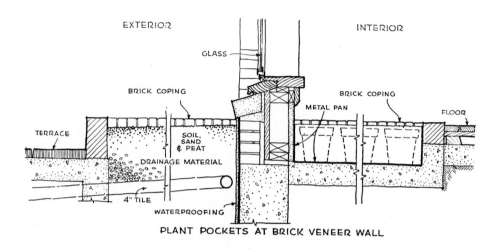

PLANT POCKETS AT BRICK VENEER WALL

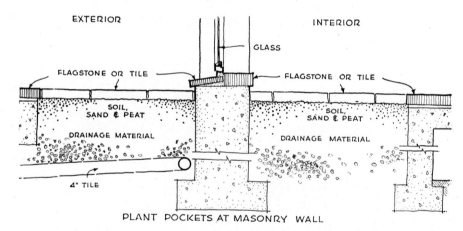

PLANT POCKETS AT MASONRY WALL

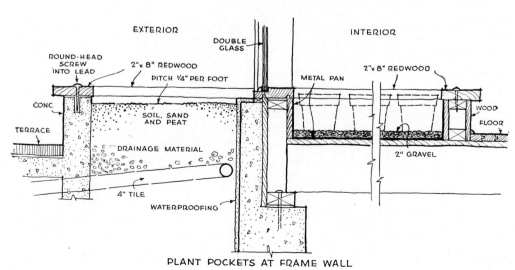

PLANT POCKETS AT FRAME WALL

INDOOR-OUTDOOR PLANTING BEDS, Construction Details

By Henry B. Aul, Landscape Architect

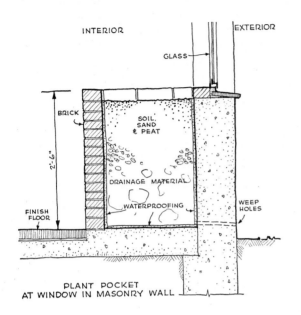

PLANT POCKET
AT WINDOW IN MASONRY WALL

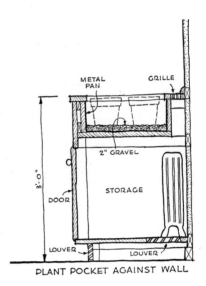

PLANT POCKET AGAINST WALL

For the client who takes his hobbies seriously, the potting bench outside may be combined with a bench-height plant display in a hobby room inside. Work bench outside is brick topped, and sheltered by roof overhang. Shelves above provide display space for plants and brighten up the prosaic potting bench. Top sash and end casement open to provide ventilation inside

INDOOR-OUTDOOR PLANTING BEDS Part 2

By Henry B. Aul, Landscape Architect

(For a selection of best indoor plants, see

TIME-SAVER STANDARDS, page 385)

THE MOST successful indoor window gardens present a reasonably attractive appearance not only during the months when the outdoor garden is dormant, but throughout the year. A glance up and down the column of the accompanying plant chart (pages 385 and 386) will show that foliage plants must be depended upon to form the foundation for this permanent planting. While this chart has room for only a fraction of the large number of plants available to the indoor gardener, it does include those that he is likely to grow with greatest success.

It will be noted that there are a limited number of plants attractive in both foliage and flower, and these should be given first consideration for the planting. There are also a few flowering plants that have a long season of bloom and should be teamed with the more permanent foliage plants. Seasonal flowering material including bulbs, azaleas and other plants received as gifts throughout the year can be depended upon to give the planting a colorful lift now and then.

Besides the evergreen foliage plants that have an upright, a spreading or round-shaped habit of growth and are suitable for a large part of the planting, there are excellent vines and trailers. Among these are the ivies, philodendrons, cissus and others that can be trained up the sides of the window or used to cover other supports connected with the planting bed. They are also used to face down the taller plants and to trail over curbs and the front edge of bench-high plant counters. In some arrangements they are displayed alone or in combination with foliage and flowering plants from hanging baskets.

Many of the foliage plants have unusually interesting and beautiful mottlings, stripes and other variegations in many different greens and other colors. The coleus, caladiums, bromeliads and begonias introduce reds, yellows, oranges, purples and other brilliant colors and color combinations to the foliage plant group.

Flowering maple, begonias in variety, bromeliads, the cacti and succulents,

impatiens, geraniums and African violets furnish a basis for flowers throughout the year. During the fall and winter they are reinforced with chrysanthemums, various annuals, lantana, and holiday gift plants. In the late winter and spring hardy bulbs and azaleas forced into bud, freezias, amaryllis and veltheimia in flower make this the brightest of all seasons in the indoor garden.

During the summer months when many of the plants, which have put on a long performance indoors, are resting and recuperating in the garden, the indoor planting is kept attractive with the most rugged of the foliage plants, the African violets, begonias and other standby flowering plants. They are augmented by the tuberous-rooted begonias, fuchsias, gloxinias, achimenes and fancy-leaved caladiums.

Frequently it is possible in connection with modern indoor-outdoor plantings to find a semi-shaded location outside the window where the summering indoor plants can be set in the ground and can continue to be a part of the window planting. Ferns, ivy and philodendron can be used indoors and out, begonias indoors and out, draceua and pandanus indoors and hosta outdoors to strengthen the continuity of the two plantings.

The tuberous-rooted and the fibrous-rooted begonias are excellent plants to create a tie between the indoor and outdoor plantings. Since growing conditions are so dissimilar between the two areas it is seldom desirable to duplicate the plantings on both sides of the window. It is enough that a number of the same

Indoor window garden filled with an assortment of flowering and foliage plants in pots. The planting has its greatest depths and height in the corner near the mirror. Indoor plants are thus effectively displayed, and the entire planting serve to frame the view of the outside garden

Monstera deliciosa, a foliage plant of unusual ornamental appearance; it has the odd common name of Swiss Cheese Plant

riety in foliage and plant forms prevents the transition from low to tall growing plants from becoming so even as to appear monotonous. Any arrangement that begins to resemble a dealer's counter where plants are displayed for sale should be suspect, for too much emphasis is being placed on individual plants. Group them without crowding to gain the true effect of a planting. If the planting can be arranged to form a partial partition between rooms, to fill a tall corner space or in other ways to serve some secondary purpose, it will prove effective. Flowering and colorful foliage plants are given a background of dark green foliage plants.

The first article in this series outlined various types of window plantings and

Cissus rhombifolia, ornamental foliage on a plant of trailing habit

plants, or plants of the same type, are used in both gardens. Many of the hardy, broad-leaved evergreen shrubs, such as the rhododendron, laurel, azaleas and andromeda are frequently used as background for the outdoor portion of the planting, while the various philodendrons, monstera, dieffenbachia, aglaonema and others fill the background with quite similar effect indoors.

Plants in the large window garden must be arranged to form a planting pleasing in appearance from inside the room, but at the same time they should frame, not block, the view into the garden. Tall-growers are placed toward the back and sides of the space, with the medium and low-growing specimens in the center and at the front edges. Va-

Hippeastrum or Amaryllis, a colorful winter and spring-blooming bulb

placed emphasis on the desirability of the metal or masonry-lined planting bed in which to arrange plants in pots on a two-inch drainage base of pebbles. Water, which is kept in the bottom of the pan and near the top surface of the layer of pebbles, supplies the humid atmosphere that is needed to grow plants successfully in modern heated rooms.

The pebbles present a clean, fresh surface on which to arrange plants in pots and simplify the task of watering. With this arrangement a normal room temperature can be maintained during the day, but it is desirable to have the night temperature drop ten to fifteen degrees.

Individual pot-grown specimens are easily turned for better display or to give them light on all sides. Plants that have passed their prime are removed and

replaced without trouble and, for variety, the entire planting may be rearranged at times. Plants suffering from diseases or insect attack can be removed for treatment.

Plants grown in a properly humidified atmosphere not only are less subject to insect attack than those in a hot, dry situation, but they are easier to water. They dry out less rapidly, thereby avoiding a drastic change from too wet to too dry. Nothing more elaborate than a medium sized watering pot with a long spout is required for watering the average collection of plants grown in pots. Exactly when to water is decided by each gardener as he learns to know his plants. Some gardeners go by appearance, others by weight or by the sound of the pot when rapped. Plants are given a good soaking only when they need it.

Gardens planted around modern windows benefit from the sun visor, roof overhang or other arrangements planned to keep the summer sun away from them. As indicated on the plant chart, plants have their individual preference as to the amount of light they like best, but even the ones that require the sun need some protection when it is the hottest. Slat roller shades, draw curtains and Venetian blinds are as welcome to the plants as to the plantsman, where there is no other provision for shading the window.

So long as gas is eliminated from the atmosphere plants do not require a large volume of fresh air. Window and door openings should be arranged in such a way that no strong drafts reach the window planting. However, when the weather is warm they can be given full exposure to the outdoors.

One of the Bromeliads, attractive in both foliage and inflorescence

INDOOR-OUTDOOR PLANTING BEDS: Part 2

By Henry B. Aul, Landscape Architect

PLANTS FOR INDOOR WINDOW GARDENS	Full Sunlight South Window	Some Sunlight East & West Windows	Full Light North Window	Flowering Plant	Foliage Plant	Vine or Trailer	Season of Top Attractiveness *	Rest Period Required	Rooting and/or Growing Period Required	Minimum Care Required	Tolerant of Gas	REMARKS
Abutilon hybridum Flowering Maple	X	X		X			Wntr					Pinch out tips of young shoots to keep bushy.
Achimenes grandiflora, etc.		X		X			Spr Sum	X	X			Gloxinia-like flowers.
Annuals—Alyssum, Nicotiana, Garden Balsam, Marigold, etc.	X			X			Wntr		X			Self-sown seedlings may be brought indoors in fall.
Aglaonema commutatum, Chinese Evergreen		X	X		X		All Year			X		Foliage plant of rugged constitution. Several species.
Azalea indicum, Kurume		X		X			Wntr Spr	X	X			Keep cool indoors. Plunge outdoors in summer.
Begonia scharffi, rex, semper florens, etc.		X	X	X	X		All Year					Flowering plants par excellent. Give full sun in winter.
Begonia tuber hybrida Tuberous Begonia		X	X				Sum	X	X			Spectacular summer bloomer. Store dry in winter.
Bromeliads—Billbergia, Cryptanthus, etc.	X	X	X	X	X		All Year	X		X	X	Ornamental flowers and foliage. Water sparingly.
Bulbs—Hardy forcing, Tulip, Daffodil, Hyacinth, Crocus, etc.	X			X			Wntr Spr	X	X			Unbeatable for cheerful flower color indoors.
Cacti and Succulents	X			X	X		All Year	X			X	Answer to hot, dry situation. Keep on dry side Nov., Dec.
Caladium bicolor Fancy-leaved Caladium		X			X		Sum	X	X			Colorful summer foliage plants. Dormant during winter.
Chrysanthemum hortorum Garden Chrysanthemum	X			X			Fall	X	X			Keep cool indoors.
Cissus rhombifolia, antartica, etc.		X			X	X	All Year			X		Deep colored vines. Withstand heat and dryness.
Coleus blumei Painted Nettle	X	X			X		All Year		X	X		Start new plants from cutting —each year
Dieffenbachia picta		X	X		X		All Year			X		Highly ornamental foliage plant.
Dracaena fragrans varieties Corn plant		X			X		All Year			X	X	Clean cut foliage plants.
Ferns-Boston, Holly, Birdsnest, Maidenhair		X	X		X		All Year					Keep moist at roots. Long favorite foliage plants.

* Wntr = Winter; Spr = Spring; Sum = Summer

INDOOR-OUTDOOR PLANTING BEDS: Part 2

By Henry B. Aul, Landscape Architect

PLANTS FOR INDOOR WINDOW GARDENS	Full Sunlight South Window	Some Sunlight East & West Windows	Full Light North Window	Flowering Plant	Foliage Plant	Vine or Trailer	Season of Top Attractiveness *	Rest Period Required	Rooting and/or Growing Period Required	Minimum Care Required	Tolerant of Gas	REMARKS
Ficus elastica, lyrata, pumila		X		X	X		All Year			X	X	Pumila is a climber. Lyrata is the fiddle-leaf fig.
Fressia species	X		X				Wntr Spr	X	X			Fragrant flowers.
Fuchsia speciosa		X	X				Sum	X	X.			Exotic summer bloomer. Rest on dry side in winter.
Hedera helix, species and var. English Ivy		X		X	X		All Year					Well known Evergreen Vine. Keep cool indoors.
Hippeastrum Amaryllis	X		X				Wntr Spr	X	X			Dramatically colorful.
Howea forsteriana Kentia Palm		X		X			All Year			X		Rugged constitution.
Impatiens sultani, holsti, etc.		X	X	X			All Year			X	X	Long season bloomers. Give sun in winter, part shade in summer.
Lantana camara	X		X				Wntr	X			X	Showy flowers. Start new plants from cuttings—annually.
Monstera deliciosa Swiss Cheese Plant		X		X			All Year			X		Unusual, indented leaves.
Pandanus veitchi Screw Pine		X		X			All Year			X	X	Graceful foliage plant.
Pelargonium hortorum Geranium	X		X				All Year		X			New plants started from cuttings.
Peperomia obtusifolia, sandersi, etc.		X	X				All Year					Keep cool. Tolerant of varied light conditions.
Philodendron cordatum Philodendron		X	X	X	X		All Year			X	X	Good color and constitution.
Phoenix roebelini	X		X				All Year					A graceful palm. Water sparingly.
Saintpaulia ionantha African Violet		X	X	X			All Year					Remarkable, small-flowering plant.
Schismatoglottis roebelini		X	X	X			All Year			X		Attractive exotic foliage. Keep moist.
Sinningia speciosa Gloxinia		X		X			Sum	X	X			Large colorful flowers. Store dry in winter.
Veltheimia vividifolia	X		X	X			Wntr	X				Good foliage and flower. Bulb—Keep dry in summer.

* Wntr = Winter; Spr = Spring; Sum = Summer

ROOF TRUSSES FOR SMALL HOUSES—for Dry Wall Construction

By Timber Engineering Company

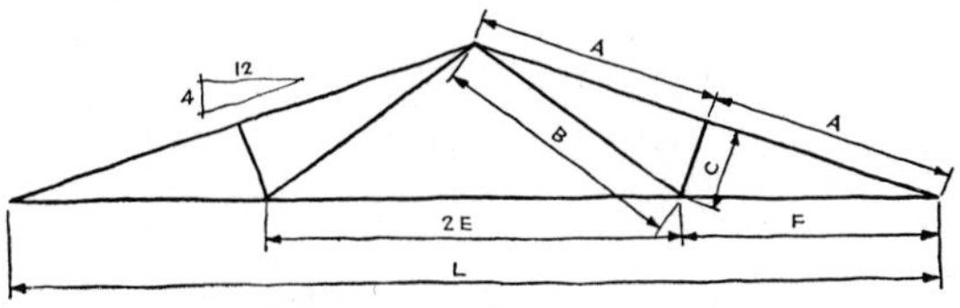

DIMENSIONS

SPAN LENGTH	A	B	C	E	F
20'	5'- 3¾"	5'- 6 11/16"	1'- 9 1/16"	4'- 5 3/16"	5'- 8 11/16"
22'	5'- 9 1/16"	6'- 1 5/16"	1'-11 3/16"	4'-10 11/16"	6'- 1 5/16"
24'	6'- 3 7/8"	6'- 8"	2'- 1 5/16"	5'- 4"	6'- 8"
26'	6'-10 3/16"	7'- 2 11/16"	2'- 3 3/8"	5'- 9 5/16"	7'- 2 11/16"
28'	7'- 4 9/16"	7'- 9 5/16"	2'- 5½"	6'- 2 11/16"	7'- 9 5/16"
30'	7'-10 7/8"	8'- 4"	2'- 7 5/8"	6'- 8"	8'- 4"
32'	8'- 5 3/16"	8'-10 11/16"	2'- 9¾"	7'- 1 5/16"	8'-10 11/16"

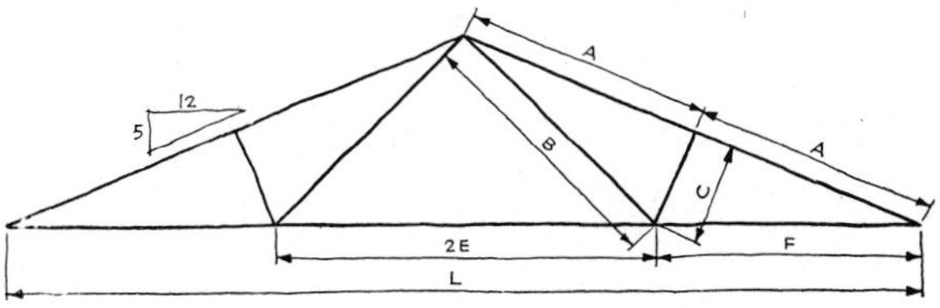

SPAN LENGTH	A	B	C	E	F
20'	5'-5"	5'-10 7/16"	2'- 3 1/16"	4'- 1 9/16"	5'-10 7/16"
22'	5'-11½"	6'- 5 7/16"	2'- 5 13/16"	4'- 6 9/16"	6'- 5 7/16"
24'	6'- 6"	7'- 0½"	2'- 8½"	4'-11½"	7'- 0½"
26'	7'- 0½"	7'- 7 9/16"	2'-11 3/16"	5'- 4 7/16"	7'- 7 9/16"
28'	7'- 7"	8'- 2 9/16"	3'- 1 15/16"	5'- 9 7/16"	8'- 2 9/16"
30'	8'- 1½"	8'- 9 5/8"	3'- 4 5/8"	6'- 2 3/8"	8'- 9 5/8"
32'	8'- 8"	9'- 4 11/16"	3'- 7 5/16"	6'- 7 5/16"	9'- 4 11/16"

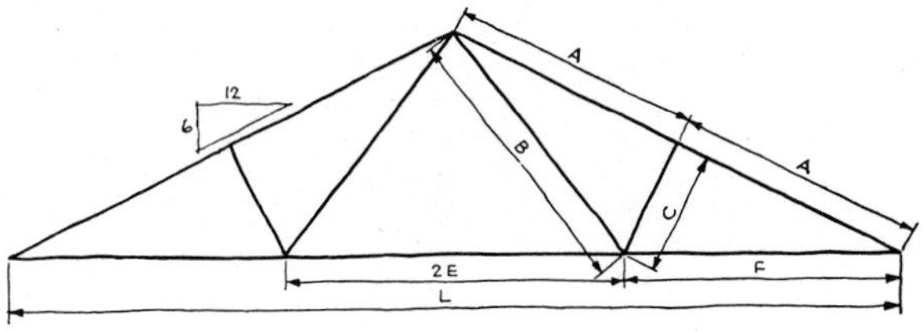

SPAN LENGTH	A	B	C	E	F
20'	5'- 7 1/16"	6'- 3"	2'- 9 9/10"	3'- 9"	6'- 3"
22'	6'- 1 13/16"	6'-10½"	3'- 0 7/8"	4'- 1½"	6'-10½"
24'	6'- 8½"	7'- 6"	3'- 4¼"	4'- 6"	7'- 6"
26'	7'- 3 3/16"	8'- 1½"	3'- 7 5/8"	4'-10½"	8'- 1½"
28'	7'- 9 15/16"	8'- 9"	3'-10 15/16"	5'- 3"	8'- 9"
30'	8'- 4 5/8"	9'- 4½"	4'- 2 5/16"	5'- 7½"	9'- 4½"
32'	8'-11 15/16"	10'-10"	4'- 5 11/16"	6'- 0"	10'- 0"

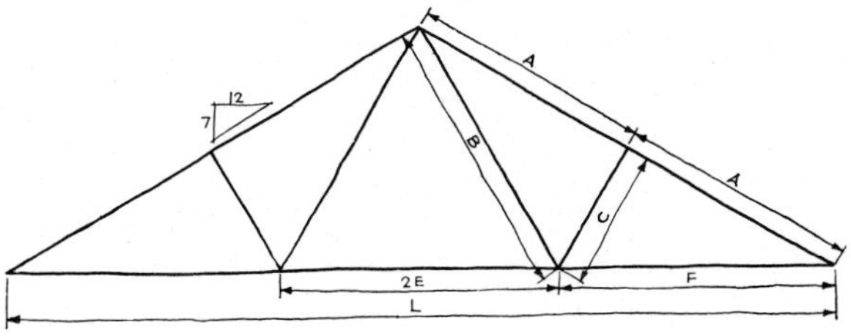

SPAN LENGTH	A	B	C	E	F
20'	5'- 9 7/16"	6'-8 7/16"	3'-4½"	3'- 3 9/16"	6'-8 7/16"
22'	6'- 4 7/16"	7'-4 7/16"	3'-8 9/16"	3'- 7 9/16"	7'-4 7/16"
24'	6'-11 3/8"	8'-0½"	4'-0 5/8"	3'-11½"	8'-0½"
26'	7'- 6 5/16"	8'-8 9/16"	4'-4 11/16"	4'- 3 7/16"	8'-8 9/16"
28'	8'- 1¼"	9'-4 9/16"	4'-8 ¾"	4'- 7 7/16"	9'-4 9/16"
30'	8'- 8 3/16"	10'-0 5/8"	5'-0 13/16"	4'-11 3/8"	10'-0 5/8"
32'	9'- 3 1/8"	10'-8 11/16"	5'-4 13/16"	5'- 3 5/16"	10'-8 11/16"

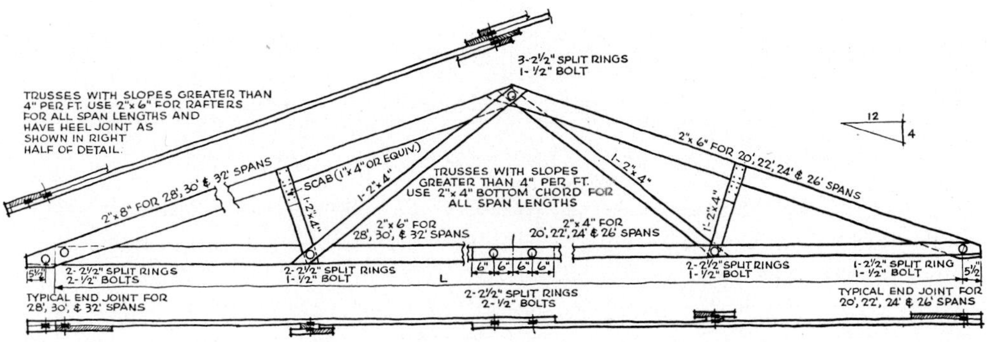

ROOF TRUSSES FOR SMALL HOUSES—for Plaster Finish

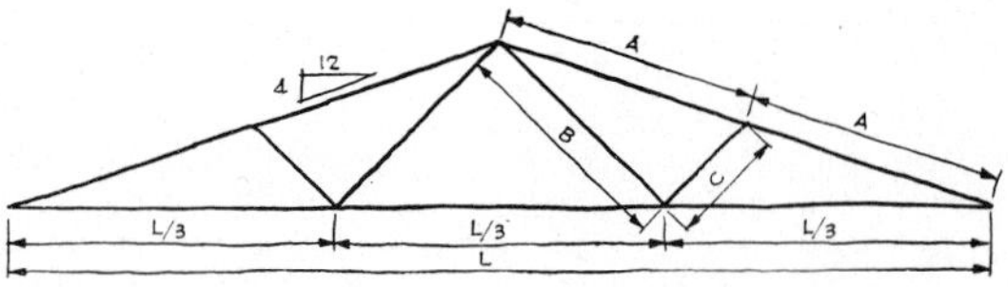
4
12
A
A
B
C
L/3
L/3
L/3
L

DIMENSIONS

SPAN LENGTH	A	B	C
20'	5'- 3 1/4"	4'-8 3/16"	2'-3 15/16"
22'	5'- 9 9/16"	5'-1 7/8"	2'-6 3/4"
24'	6'- 3 7/8"	5'-7 1/2"	2'-9 9/16"
26'	6'-10 3/16"	6'-1 3/16"	3'-0 7/16"
28'	7'- 4 9/16"	6'-6 13/16"	3'-3 1/4"
30'	7'-10 7/8"	7'-0 1/2"	3'-6 1/16"
32'	8'- 5 3/16"	7'-6 3/16"	3'-8 7/8"

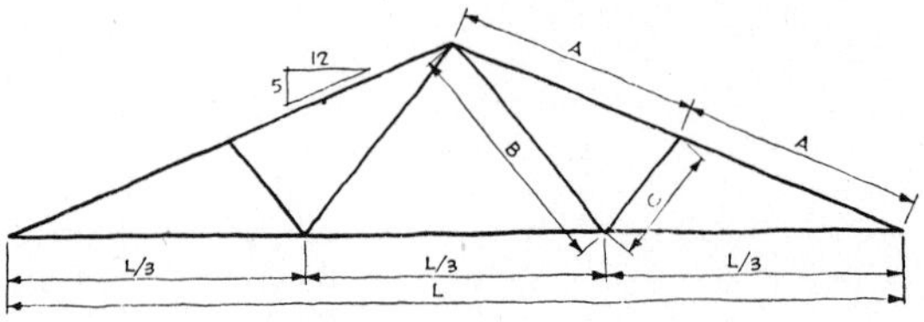
5
12
A
A
B
C
L/3
L/3
L/3
L

SPAN LENGTH	A	B	C
20'	5'- 5"	5'- 3 5/8"	2'- 7 5/8"
22'	5'-11 1/2"	5'-10 1/16"	2'-10 13/16"
24'	6'- 6"	6'- 4 7/16"	3'- 2"
26'	7'- 0 1/2"	6'-10 7/8"	3'- 5 1/4"
28'	7'- 7"	7'- 5 1/4"	3'- 8 7/16"
30'	8'- 1 1/2"	7'-11 11/16"	3'-11 5/8"
32'	8'- 8"	8'- 6 1/16"	4'- 2 13/16"

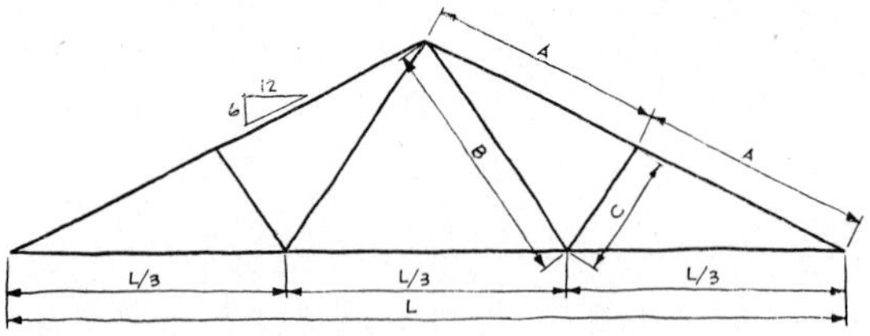
6
12
A
A
B
C
L/3
L/3
L/3
L

SPAN LENGTH	A	B	C
20'	5'- 7 1/16"	5'-11 11/16"	2'-11 5/8"
22'	6'- 1 13/16"	6'- 6 7/8"	3'- 3 1/4"
24'	6'- 8 1/2"	7'- 2 1/8"	3'- 6 7/8"
26'	7'- 3 3/16"	7'- 9 5/16"	3'-10 7/16"
28'	7'- 9 15/16"	8'- 4 9/16"	4'- 2 1/16"
30'	8'- 4 5/8"	8'-11 3/4"	4'- 5 11/16"
32'	8'-11 5/16"	9'- 6 15/16"	4'- 9 1/4"

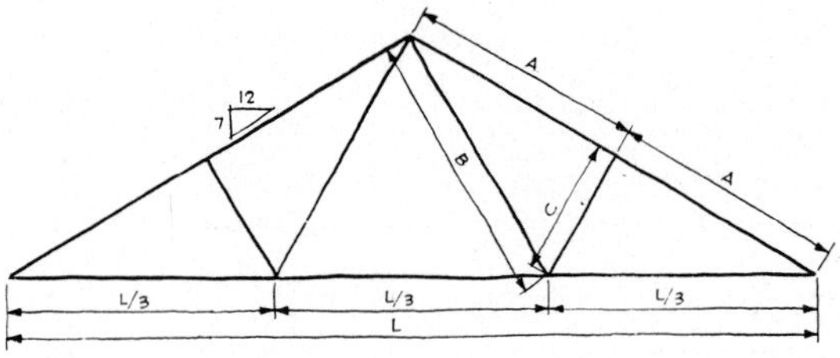
7
12
A
A
B
C
L/3
L/3
L/3
L

SPAN LENGTH	A	B	C
20'	5'- 9 7/16"	6'-8 3/16"	3'- 3 7/8"
22'	6'- 4 7/16"	7'-4 1/4"	3'- 7 15/16"
24'	6'-11 3/8"	8'-0 5/16"	3'-11 15/16"
26'	7'- 6 5/16"	8'-8 3/8"	4'- 4"
28'	8'- 1 1/4"	9'-4 7/16"	4'- 8"
30'	8'- 8 3/16"	10'-0 1/2"	5'- 0 1/16"
32'	9'- 3 1/8"	10'-8 9/16"	5'- 4 1/16"

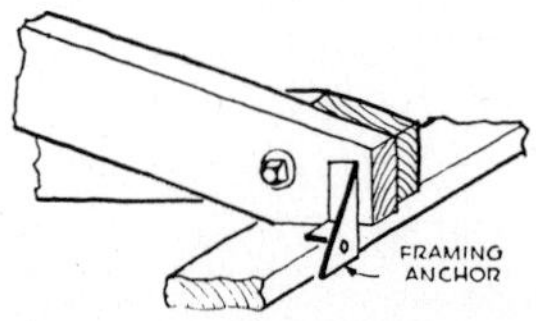
FRAMING ANCHOR

ANCHORAGE DETAIL

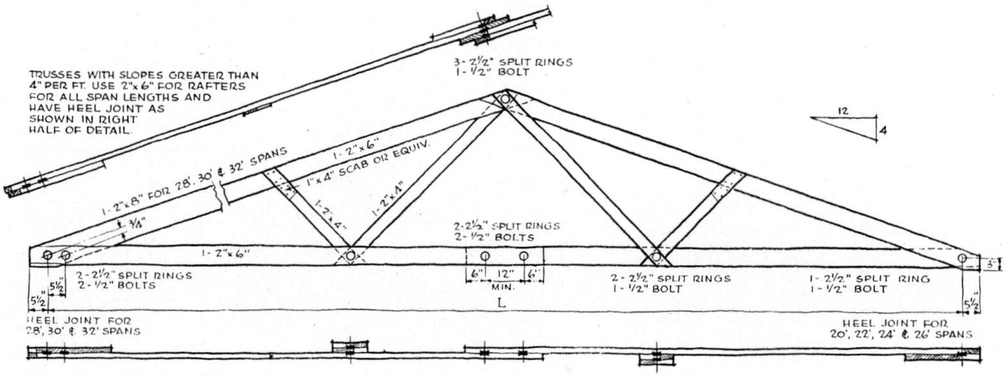
TRUSSES WITH SLOPES GREATER THAN 4" PER FT. USE 2"x6" FOR RAFTERS FOR ALL SPAN LENGTHS AND HAVE HEEL JOINT AS SHOWN IN RIGHT HALF OF DETAIL.
3-2½" SPLIT RINGS
1-½" BOLT
12
4
1-2"x6"
1"x4" SCAB OR EQUIV.
1-2"x8" FOR 28', 30' & 32' SPANS
2"x4"
2"x4"
3/4"
1-2"x6"
2-2½" SPLIT RINGS
2-½" BOLTS
2-2½" SPLIT RINGS
2-½" BOLTS
6" 12" 6"
MIN.
L
2-2½" SPLIT RINGS
1-½" BOLT
1-2½" SPLIT RING
1-½" BOLT
5½"
5½"
HEEL JOINT FOR 28', 30' & 32' SPANS
HEEL JOINT FOR 20', 22', 24' & 26' SPANS

Bolts used are ½ in. dia. machine bolts with 2 by 2 by ⅛ in. plate washers, 2⅛ in. dia. cast or malleable iron washers, or ordinary cut washers. Timber connectors shown are Split Rings and framing anchors as manufactured by the Timber Engineering Co., Washington, D. C.

This article is condensed from Aspects of Electrical Conduit Installations in Houses by Jefferson D. Brooks, Technical Bulletin No. 12, Jan. 1950, Housing and Home Finance Agency. Minimum requirements are given for safe installation of three commonly used types of steel conduits.

Types and Uses

1. *Rigid conduit* is an older, heavier type, softer than water pipe for easy bending, but sized for same tools. Internal diameter is a bit larger than nominal size. Galvanized or other rust-resistant finish is required if exposed to dampness. Enameled iron conduits may be used only indoors, with no severe corrosive influences. Materials especially suited to such conditions must be used; avoid dissimilar materials. Place conduit at least 18 in. under cinder fill subject to permanent moisture, or encase in 2 in. of non-cinder concrete. In wet locations, system must be water tight; leave at least ¼ in. air space between conduit or boxes and wall.

2. *Thin wall conduit* or *EMT* (electrical metallic tubing) is a lighter type, usually galvanized or similarly finished. It is used for exposed or concealed work where not subject to severe mechanical injury. Use is restricted in hazardous locations. Otherwise it is used as rigid conduit.

3. *Flexible conduit* is strong flexible tubing of spirally wound, interlocked steel strip, usually galvanized. Use in dry locations unless lead-covered or type RW (moisture resistant) wiring is employed. Do not use in hazardous locations. Conduits less than ½ in. size are used only for under-plaster extensions, fixtures, motor leads. Occasionally ⅜ in. size is permitted up to 48 in. (or longer) where larger size is not practicable.

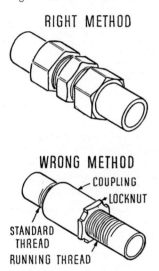

Fig. 1. Conduit connections

RIGHT METHOD

WRONG METHOD

COUPLING
LOCKNUT
STANDARD THREAD
RUNNING THREAD

Fittings

1. Running threads must not be used on rigid conduit for connections at couplings; unions must be used. Threads are finer than for standard pipe; threadless connectors are often used. The latter must be watertight if buried in masonry, concrete, fill, or used in wet places

2. Bushings must be used on ends of conduit unless box or fitting affords equal protection. A bushing may replace box where more than 4 conductors leave conduit at control apparatus, if wires are bunched, taped and painted; bushings must be of insulated type, except for lead-covered wires

3. All ends of conduit must be reamed to remove rough edges

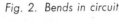

Fig. 2. Bends in circuit

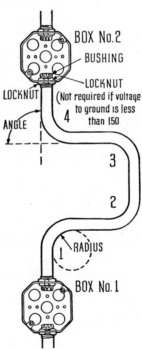

BOX No. 2
BUSHING
LOCKNUT (Not required if voltage to ground is less than 150
LOCKNUT
ANGLE
4
3
2
1 RADIUS
BOX No. 1

BEVEL WITH REAMER TO REMOVE ROUGH EDGE

Fig. 3. Reamed end of conduit

TABLE 1	Radius of bends in inches	
Conduit (trade size) (inches)	Ordinary conductors	Lead-covered conductors
½	3.7	6.2
¾	4.9	8.3
1	6.3	10.5
1¼	8.3	13.8
1½	9.6	16.1
2	12.4	20.6
2½	14.8	24.6
3	18.4	30.6
3½	21.3	35.5
4	24.1	40.2
4½	27.0	45.0
5	30.3	50.4
6	36.4	60.6

Bends must not injure conduit or effectively reduce internal diameter. Radius of the inner edge of any bend not made by manufacturer must not be less than shown in Table 1. Conduit between 2 outlets, fittings, or combination, must not have more than equivalent of 4 quarter bends (Fig. 2)

TABLE 2. Max Support Intervals For Conductors in Vertical Conduits

	Feet
No. 0 and smaller	100
No. 00 to No. 000	80
250 to 350 MCM	60
400 to 500 MCM	50
600 to 750 MCM	40
800 MCM and larger	35

Supports: conductors in vertical conduits must be supported by clamps, wedges or insulators at intervals not greater than shown in Table 2. All conduits must be securely fastened in place. Runs must be continuous from box to box with no splices

ELECTRICAL CONDUITS: 2—Installation and Selection

Miscellaneous Requirements

Wires must not be inserted in conduits until rough mechanical work on house is completed. Pull wires are inserted after making up conduit connections. Graphite, talc or approved compound are used as wire lubricant; cleaning agents must not be used.

Conductors of signal or radio systems must not occupy same conduit with those of light or power systems, except for elevators, sound recording and remote control. Conduits must not pass through dust or vapor removal ducts. Rigid conduit, or flexible conduit with lead covered conductors, may pass through air-conditioning ducts only where necessary, and must not obstruct fire dampers. Switch enclosures must not be used as junction boxes to make taps or feed through.

Secondary wiring to cold cathode lamps of 1000 volts or less may occupy same conduit as branch circuit conductors. Light and power circuits of 600 volts or less may occupy same conduit, whether a-c or d-c. Circuits over 600 volts must be separated from those under 600 volts. Prevent air circulation from warmer to colder areas through conduit.

Vertical conductors No. 1 or larger require the following gutter widths if deflected where they leave cabinet:

No. 1 . . . . 3 in.
No. 0 to 200 MCM . . . . 4 in.
250 to 900 MCM . . . . 6 in.

Where ungrounded conductors of No. 4 or larger are deflected more than 30 deg at ends of conduit run, an insulating bushing is required.

Conductors in Multiple

Where circuit capacity makes it impracticable to run all conductors in one conduit, additional conduits may be used if conductors in any one conduit are balanced in size and include one from each phase. Current in one direction must substantially equal current in opposite direction (fig. 4). With circuits supplying cold cathode tubes, x-ray apparatus, and underplaster extensions, currents are so small that a single conductor may be placed in a conduit without trouble from induction. Conductors in sizes No. 0 to 500 MCM

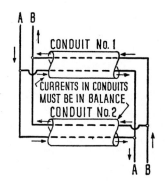

Fig. 4. Conductors in multiple

may be run in multiple if they are same length and have same area and type of insulation. Terminate both ends in manner to insure equal division of current. Except by special permission, not more than number of wires shown in Table 3 may be installed in multiple.

TABLE 3. Max No. of Wires To Be Installed in Multiple

No. of wires:	Size
3	No. 0
4	No. 00
5	No. 000 to 500 MCM

Wire Carrying Capacity

Standard tabulated carrying capacities of wires are based upon 3 or less wires in a conduit, and a surrounding temperature of not more than 86 F. Capacity must be reduced to 80 per cent of that listed for 4, 5 or 6 wires in a conduit; to 70 per cent for 7, 8 or 9 wires. A neutral conductor used with balanced circuits is not counted in applying percentages. If one of the system wires is missing

---

TABLE 4. Temp Reduction Factors (percentages)

Max Temp (°F)	Type of insulation			
	R, RW, RU, T, and TW	RH	V and AVB	AVA and AVL
104	82	88	90	94
113	71	82	85	90
122	58	75	80	87
131	41	67	74	83
140	. . . .	58	67	79
158	. . . .	35	52	71
167	. . . .	. . . .	43	66
176	. . . .	. . . .	30	61
194	. . . .	. . . .	. . . .	50

---

from circuit (as in a 3-wire circuit from a 4-wire system) the neutral conductor must be counted, for it carries the unbalanced current which would have been carried by the missing wire. All current-carrying capacity must be separately reduced for high surrounding temperatures by percentages given in Table 4. If room temp is within 18 deg of a maximum allowable temp, use insulation with next higher maximum.

Conduit Size Selection

Due to bunching effect of wires in conduit, all space inside conduit cannot be filled with wire (fig. 5). Percentages of allowable fill are calculated in sq in. of net cross-sectional area for standard size conduits, for various numbers of wires, in Table 5; Section A is for non-lead-covered wires, Section B is for lead-covered.

Where conduits cannot be replaced without damage to house, it is satisfactory to rewire conduits, for increased capacity, with more or larger wires which occupy more space than permitted for original installations. These increased values in sq in. are given in Table 5, Section C.

Cross-sectional areas of the various types of wires, in sq in., are given in Table 6. Values are added together for any combination of wires to be installed in a single conduit. This total permits ready selection of a conduit size, filled to a given percentage, from Table 5. Portion of conduit available for wires must be not less than shown for number and kinds of wires involved.

Where all wires are of one size, non-lead-covered, and for new installations, use Table 7 to select conduit size.

In general, one conduit must not contain more than 9 wires. Table 8 shows conduit capacity for a greater no. of wires, where specially permitted.

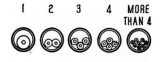

Fig. 5. Cross-sectional area of conduit which conductors may occupy

TABLE 5.—Net cross-sectional areas in square inches of conduit and tubing available for wires and cables for general use

Conduit (trade size) (in.)	Diameter (in.)	Area (sq. in.) (100 percent)	A. Conductors not lead-covered				B. Lead-covered conductors					C. Rewiring		
			1 conductor (53 percent)	2 conductor (31 percent)	3 conductors (43 percent)	Over 3 conductors (40 percent)	1 conductor (55 percent)	2 conductors (30 percent)	3 conductors (40 percent)	4 conductors (38 percent)	Over 4 conductors (35 percent)	1 conductor (60 percent)	2 conductors (40 percent)	Over 2 conductors (50 percent)
½.............	0.622	0.30	0.16	0.09	0.13	0.12	0.17	0.09	0.12	0.11	0.11	0.18	0.12	0.15
¾.............	.824	.53	.28	.16	.23	.21	.29	.16	.21	.20	.19	.32	.21	.27
1.............	1.049	.86	.46	.27	.37	.34	.47	.26	.34	.33	.30	.52	.34	.43
1¼............	1.380	1.50	.80	.47	.65	.60	.83	.45	.60	.57	.53	.90	.60	.75
1½............	1.610	2.04	1.08	.63	.88	.82	1.12	.61	.82	.78	.71	1.22	.82	1.02
2.............	2.067	3.36	1.78	1.04	1.44	1.34	1.85	1.01	1.34	1.28	1.18	2.02	1.34	1.68
2½............	2.469	4.79	2.54	1.48	2.06	1.92	2.63	1.44	1.92	1.82	1.68	2.87	1.92	2.39
3.............	3.068	7.38	3.91	2.29	3.17	2.95	4.06	2.21	2.95	2.80	2.58	4.43	2.95	3.69
3½............	3.548	9.90	5.25	3.07	4.26	3.96	5.44	2.97	3.96	3.76	3.47	5.94	3.96	4.95
4.............	4.026	12.72	6.74	3.94	5.47	5.09	6.99	3.82	5.09	4.83	4.45	7.63	5.09	6.36
4½............	4.506	15.95	8.45	4.94	6.86	6.38	8.77	4.78	6.38	6.06	5.57	9.57	6.38	7.97
5.............	5.047	20.00	10.60	6.20	8.60	8.00	11.00	6.00	8.00	7.60	7.00	12.00	8.00	10.00
6.............	6.065	28.89	15.31	8.96	12.42	11.56	15.89	8.67	11.56	10.98	10.11	17.33	11.55	14.44

TABLE 6.—Areas of conductors to be used in determining the number of wires of various sizes and combination that may be installed in a conduit

Wires—approximate area in sq in.

Wire size	RF–32;[1] R;[1] RH;[1] RW [1]	TF;[2] T;[2] TW;[2] RU [2]	Lead-covered RL and RHL—individual cables			AVA	AVB	AVL	Bare
			1 conductor	2 conductors	3 conductors				
18 ..	0.0167	0.0088	...	...	...	...	...	...	0.0013
16 ..	.0196	.0109	...	...	...	...	...	...	.0020
14 ..	.0327	.0135	0.062	0.115	0.273	0.047	0.033	0.080	.0032
12 ..	.0384	.0172	.066	.146	.301	.055	.040	.091	.0051
10 ..	.0460	.0224	.096	.180	.363	.064	.047	.102	.0081
8 ...	.0760	.0408	.132	.255	.528	.075	.057	.119	.0130
6 ...	.1238	.0819	.188	.369	.738	.122	.094	.145	.027
4 ...	.1605	.1087	.237	.457	.916	.155	.123	.181	.042
3 ...	.1817	.1263	...	...	...	...	...	...	.053
2 ...	.2067	.1473	.283	.578	1.146	.200	.166	.255	.067
1 ...	.2715	.2027	.352	.756	1.49	.268	.229	.300	.087
0 ...	.3107	.2367	.396	.859	1.70	.307	.264	.341	.109
00 ..	.3578	.2781	.454	.980	1.94	.353	.307	.390	.137
000 .	.4151	.3288	.515	1.123	2.24	.406	.358	.447	.173
0000	.4840	.3904	.593	1.302	2.68	.478	.425	.521	.219
250 .	.5917	.4877	.754	...	3.20	.616	.572	.715	.260
300 .	.6837	.5581	.850	...	3.62	.692	.649	.800	.312
350 .	.7620	.6291	.950	...	4.02	.778	.731	.885	.364
400 .	.8365	.6969	1.02	...	4.52	.850	.800	.960	.416
500 .	.9834	.8316	1.18	...	5.28	.995	.945	1.118	.520

[1] For general use.   [2] For rewiring existing conduits.

TABLE 7.—Number of conductors in conduit or tubing—for general use in new installations

Wire types RF–32, R, RH, RW, RU, TF, T, and TW

Wire size	Maximum number of wires in conduit or tube								
	1	2	3	4	5	6	7	8	9
18.............	½	½	½	½	½	½	½	¾	¾
16.............	½	½	½	½	½	½	¾	¾	¾
14.............	½	½	½	½	¾	¾	1	1	1
12.............	½	½	½	¾	¾	1	1	1	1¼
10.............	½	¾	¾	¾	1	1	1	1¼	1¼
8.............	½	¾	¾	1	1¼	1¼	1¼	1½	1½
6.............	½	1	1	1¼	1½	1½	2	2	2
4.............	½	1¼	1¼	1½	1½	2	2	2	2½
3.............	¾	1¼	1¼	1½	2	2	2	2½	2½
2.............	¾	1¼	1¼	2	2	2	2½	2½	2½
1.............	¾	1½	1½	2	2½	2½	2½	3	3
0.............	1	1½	2	2	2½	2½	3	3	3
00.............	1	2	2	2½	2½	3	3	3	3½
000.............	1	2	2	2½	3	3	3	3½	3½
0000.............	1¼	2	2½	3	3	3	3½	3½	4
250.............	1¼	2½	2½	3	3	3½	4	4	4½
300.............	1¼	2½	2½	3	3½	4	4	4½	4½
350.............	1¼	3	3	3½	3½	4	4½	4½	5
400.............	1½	3	3	3½	4	4	4½	5	5
500.............	1½	3	3	3½	4	4½	5	5	6

[1] 1 in. for services not over 50 ft long, with not more than 2 quarter bends, and using bare neutral.

TABLE 8—More than 9 conductors in conduit (between motor and controller, stage pockets, border circuits, sign flashers, and elevator control wires)

Wire types RF–32, R, RH, RW, RU, TF, T, and TW

Wire size	Maximum number of wires in conduit or tube						
	¾ in.	1 in.	1¼ in.	1½ in.	2 in.	2½ in.	3 in.
18.........	12	20	35	49	80	115	176
16.........	10	17	30	41	68	97	150
14.........	....	10	18	25	40	59	90
12.........	....	....	15	21	35	50	77
10.........	....	....	13	17	29	41	64
8.........	....	....	....	10	17	25	38
6.........	....	....	....	....	15	23

EXAMPLE—

Problem: what size conduit is required for 3 No. 14, 3 No. 10 and 2 No. 6 type RW wires for a new installation.

Solution: from Table 6 select:

$$\begin{aligned} \text{No. 14}&—0.0327 \times 3—0.0981 \\ \text{No. 10}&—\ \ .0460 \times 3—0.1380 \\ \text{No. 6}&—\ \ .1238 \times 2—0.2476 \\ \hline \text{Total}&\qquad\qquad\quad\ 0.4837 \text{ sq in.} \end{aligned}$$

From Table 5, for more than 3 conductors, 0.60 sq in. represents the smallest conduit, 1¼ in. size, which will receive the wires and be filled to not more than 40 per cent of its total cross-sectional area. However, a 1-in. conduit would receive the 6 smaller wires.

UNIFORM PLUMBING CODE FOR HOUSING

Sponsored by Housing and Home Finance Agency

CULMINATING 25 years of research and investigation the new *Uniform Plumbing Code for Housing* sponsored by the Housing and Home Finance Agency proposes a set of standards which if applied and adopted could result in these benefits:

1. Simplified, uniform installations.
2. Standard designs and fittings.
3. Economy in use of pipe.
4. Better sanitary safety.

Code Background

Efforts toward formulating a uniform plumbing code started when the Department of Commerce Building Code Committee issued *Recommended Minimum Requirements for Plumbing* (BH 13) in 1923.

A subcommittee of the Central Housing Committee prepared a plumbing manual in 1940 (*Building Materials and Structures Report BMS 66*) which served as a guide for agencies doing plumbing work or approving plumbing plans. (See ARCHITECTURAL RECORD. Nov. 1941.)

Added progress toward a uniform plumbing code came in 1941 when *Emergency Plumbing Standards* were developed by representatives of Master Plumbers and labor organizations together with representatives of federal agencies to conserve critical materials.

As the *Emergency Plumbing Standards* were mandatory during the war and were observed throughout the country, they proved to many municipalities not only that their own plumbing codes were either antiquated or extravagant, but also that a nationwide plumbing code is feasible and could result in better sanitation at lower cost. For these reasons the government's long-time efforts to launch a uniform plumbing code were encouraged.

National Housing Agency in 1946 sponsored a plumbing test project at the National Bureau of Standards and the formation of the Uniform Plumbing Code Committee which would: (1) engage in careful research into the nation's plumbing needs; (2) study and analyze existing practices and materials; and (3) on these findings make recommendations and draft a peacetime plumbing code suitable for nationwide adoption.

This committee, with Vincent T. Manas, chairman, is composed of members representing the Housing and Home Finance Agency, National Association of Master Plumbers, The United Association of Journeymen and Apprentices of the Plumbing and Pipe Fitting Industry of the United States and Canada (A.F.L.), National Bureau of Standards, and the United States Public Health Service.

National Bureau of Standards, directed by the Uniform Plumbing Code Committee, conducted an investigation of certain aspects of flow in housing drainage systems. One phase of this work was done using transparent piping so that the flow phenomena could be observed and photographed. Motion pictures were taken of pertinent phenomena so that the results could be more easily visualized and studied by the plumbing industry and officials or individuals connected with code formulation.

Tests and Results

The test setup at the National Bureau of Standards represented complete and accurate reproduction of some of the characteristic plumbing systems used in housing. It included complete systems ordinarily found in a small home with one bathroom, kitchen, and basement and in a two-story duplex house with bathrooms back to back on the first floor. This arrangement provided three systems for studying the major problems on which data were needed.

The first system provided the means for investigation of self-siphonage problems of plumbing fixture traps. The results of tests on this system gave information for the determination of the safe distance that a fixture could be extended without a vent.

The second system permitted the investigation of stack vented fixtures. This type of installation permits the grouping of the kitchen sink and bathroom lavatory, water closet, and bathtub or shower directly into the soil stack without individual back vents; it is the most economical for a one- or two-story residence.

The third system permitted the investigation of the merits of wet vented fixtures whereby one pipe

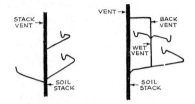

(See details on page 394)

serves the dual purpose of removing the waste water from a fixture and venting another fixture.

Some tests were performed not only with smooth, transparent pipe and fittings, but with standard materials because code requirements must be based on the use of standard pipe and fittings commonly used in a drainage system. On all tests 3-in. soil stacks were used.

The *Uniform Plumbing Code for Housing* (presented as Technical Paper No. 6 of the Technical Staff of Housing and Home Finance Agency, Leonard G. Haeger, director) includes the results of these tests as analyzed by the Uniform Plumbing code Committee. The requirements of the code are also based on the results of earlier research and on the practical experience of members of the Committee.

Principles provided for in the *Uniform Plumbing Code* will effect proportionate saving for either a small or large residence in design and installation. For instance, the roughing in for a complete bathroom may be enclosed in the space provided by a 2-by-4 if 3 in. copper tubing is used for the stack.

The use of house traps and fresh air has been definitely proven as not adding to sanitary safety. This in-

House traps not advisable

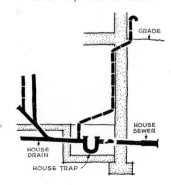

UNIFORM PLUMBING CODE FOR HOUSING

Sponsored by Housing and Home Finance Agency

FIXTURE WASTE LENGTH

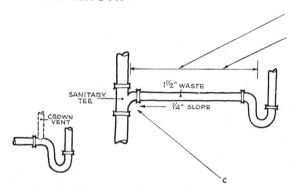

SANITARY TEE

1½" WASTE

¼" SLOPE

CROWN VENT

c

The distance from trap to vent of present codes in U. S. varies from 18 in. to as much as 12 ft.

Uniform Plumbing Code, based on tests at the National Bureau of Standards, has set this length under conditions shown at a maximum of 4 ft. 6 in. If ½ in. slope is provided for the waste the maximum distance is reduced to 3 ft. 0 in. (See table for other sizes)

Since the code requires 6 in. minimum from trap to vent, crown venting is not allowed

Where a long turn tee-Y is used instead of a sanitary tee, the maximum permissible distance for 1½ in. diameter waste at ¼ in. slope is 4 ft. 0 in. If the slope is increased to ½ in. per ft., the length of unvented waste is reduced to 2 ft. 0 in. (See table)

Full "S" traps are not permitted. Anti-siphon traps are not recognized as such

	DISTANCE OF TRAP FROM VENT			
	Permissible length, feet			
Size of Fixture Drain, inches	Sanitary Tee		Longturn TY or Combination Y and ⅛ Bend	
	¼" slope	½" slope	¼" slope	½" slope
1¼	4'-0"	2'-6"	1'-6"	1'-0"
1½	4'-6"	3'-0"	4'-0"	2'-0"
2	5'-0"	4'-6"	4'-6"	4'-6"
3	6'-0"	6'-0"	6'-0"	6'-0"
4	8'-0"	8'-0"	8'-0"	8'-0"

stallation creates greater resistance to flow and prevents the venting of the main sewer through the roof outlets of the building.

Further research and study remains to be done on loading of building drains, soil stacks and branches; loop and circuit venting; flow rate of plumbing fixtures; and ratification of present empirical values provided in most codes as they pertain to loading of the plumbing system.

Although the *Uniform Plumbing Code* applies to housing, many of the principles involved and many of the standards recommended are applicable to all classes of plumbing installations; they provide a foundation for investigation extended to all types of structures. The *Uniform Plumbing Code for Housing*, meanwhile, provides the basis for many communities to consider review of their present codes in an effort to encourage more and better housing at lower costs through (1) simplified, uniform installations with standard designs and fittings and through (2) reduction in the space needed to accommodate plumbing pipes and fixtures.

UNIFORM PLUMBING CODE FOR HOUSING

Sponsored by Housing and Home Finance Agency

STACK VENTING

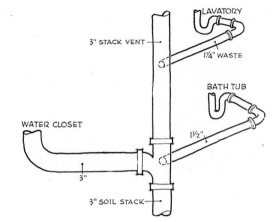

Maximum length of unvented lavatory waste: 4 ft. 0 in. at ¼ in. slope; 2 ft. 6 in. at ½ in. slope (See table page 153 for other sizes)

Maximum length of unvented water closet branch: 6 ft. 0 in. at either ¼ in. or ½ in. slope (See table)

Maximum length of unvented bathtub waste: 4 ft. 6 in. at ¼ in. slope; 3 ft. 0 in. at ½ in. slope (See table)

Fixtures are grouped around the stack with no individual vents needed

Materials allowed for drainage: **galvanized steel pipe, galvanized wrought iron pipe, cast iron soil pipe, copper tubing (type "M") and lead pipe.**

Stack venting is limited to one-story buildings or to the topmost branch interval of a building. Where the water closet and bathtub (or shower) wastes enter the stack at the same level, the system is adequately vented if the fixtures are installed within the limits of the table on page 393. No more than four fixtures can be stack vented above the stack vented water closet and bathtub (or shower)

WET VENTING

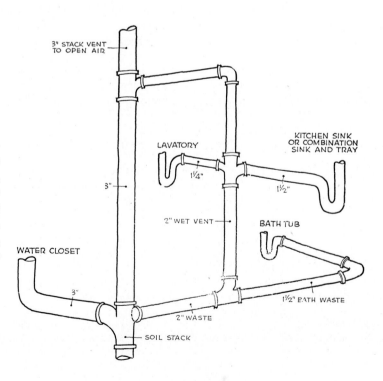

The waste pipe from lavatories, kitchen sinks or combination fixture may be used as a wet vent for bathtub or shower trap "provided that the wet vent connects with the waste in a vertical plane or not more than 6 in. therefrom;" and that not more than one fixture is drained into a 1½ in. wet vent or not more than four fixtures into a 2 in. wet vent. All fixtures must be installed within the limits of the table on page 393.

INSULATION OF CONCRETE FLOORS IN DWELLINGS

Suggestions Based on Research by Housing and Home Finance Agency *

THE extensive use in house construction of concrete slab floors, cast on the ground or over unheated crawl spaces, calls for special structural insulation to avoid cold floors. The most effective way is by insulating the concrete floor at its edge and insulating all crawl space walls.

Suggested insulation details grew out of a series of tests ** conducted by the National Bureau of Standards to determine the thermal characteristics of concrete floors. The findings again gave proof of the high conductivity of concrete floors which makes them feel colder to the touch than other floor materials at the same temperature.

The actual (surface) temperature of a concrete floor, however, can be just as satisfactory as other floors if resistance is placed in the paths of greatest heat flow.

The heat loss of slab floors laid on the ground is primarily through the edge. Heat loss through the center is relatively small due to the insulating value of the thick layer

of earth beneath it through which heat must flow to reach the outside air.

Over enclosed crawl spaces, heat loss also is principally through the edge, though the loss through the center is relatively higher than with floors laid on the ground.

For comfort, the floor temperature should not fall below 60° F. at approximately 1 ft. from the exterior wall when room temperature is maintained at 70° F. Farther from the wall, the floor will of course be warmer.

When properly insulated, a concrete floor presents a more uniform temperature over the entire surface than do most other floors. Cool air drops down along the inside of all exterior walls, cooling the floor at that point. Since concrete is a better conductor than most materials, heat is conducted more readily from the warmer central portion of the floor to the cooler edges.

In general, conditions of comfort can be obtained by:

1. Insulating the edges of the concrete slab laid on the ground and extending the insulation for a distance under its perimeter.

2. Insulating the slab edges of

concrete floors laid over crawl spaces and insulating the exposed wall of the crawl space.

These methods are generally more effective than insulation placed under the entire slab and are easier to install satisfactorily.

Insulating Materials: The selection of insulating materials depends upon several factors: durability; strength to withstand pressure of the earth and imposed loads; relative insulation value; and cost.

Insulating materials placed in or near the ground must resist moisture, mildew, termites, etc. Where a material depends upon a coating of asphalt or coal tar pitch for protection, it is necessary to select the coating carefully, bearing in mind that the solvents in pitch will affect asphalt. This is important where such coated materials are to be used in contact with roofing felt.

The accompanying table contains some information about several insulating materials which might be used; suggested details of construction will be found on the following Time-Saver pages.

---

* Abstracted from a report by Laurence Shuman, Mechanical Engineering Adviser, Housing and Home Finance Agency.
** Sponsored by Housing and Home Finance Agency; then National Housing Agency. Details are published in Report BMS-103, Government Printing Office, 10 cents.

INSULATING MATERIALS FOR CONCRETE FLOORS

Material:	Cellular Glass Enclosing Sealed-in Gas, such as *Foamglas*	Glass Fibers with Plastic Binder, such as *Fiberglas*, Coated or Uncoated
Thickness:	2, 3, 4, and 5 in.	¾, 1, 1½, and 2 in.
R (Resistance Value; per 1 in. thick)	1.82 to 2.22	3.33 to 3.85
Characteristics:	Crushing strength approximately 150 lb. per sq. in. Water absorption negligible. Easily cut, indented, etc. Will not adhere to masonry.	Supports about 12 lb. per sq. in. Water penetration into uncoated board is slow and disintegrates the binder; penetration into coated board is inconsequential unless exposed to constant head of water.
Suggestions:	Surface may gradually spall away if subjected to moisture and freezing. Dip in roofing pitch or asphalt for protection. Use tie wires for attaching to masonry.	Use coated board or apply coal tar pitch or asphalt. Where moisture is expected, coat all cut edges. Follow manufacturer's instructions for cutting.
Material:	Cane or Wood Fiber Boards, such as *Celotex*	Hard Cellular Rubber Enclosing Sealed-in Gas, such as *Hard Rubber Board or Rubatex*
Thickness:	½, 25/32, 1 in., etc.	½, ¾, 1, 1¼, 1½, and 2 in.
R (Resistance Value; per 1 in. thick)	2.50 to 2.86	4.00 to 5.00
Characteristics:	Crushing strength is adequate. Boards are subject to moisture penetration. Deteriorate under damp conditions.	Crushing strength is approximately 70 lb. per sq. in. Water absorption negligible. Easily cut, indented, etc. Does not adhere adequately to masonry.
Suggestions:	Coat boards and all cut edges heavily with coal tar pitch. Do not use in locations subject to considerable moisture.	Split board with leather splitting machine to reduce costs. Coat with asphalt or pitch, or use metal ties or cement keys where necessary to bond to masonry.

INSULATION OF CONCRETE FLOORS IN DWELLINGS

Suggestions Based on Research by Housing and Home Finance Agency

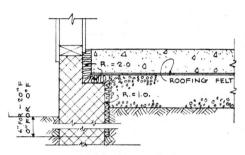

INSULATION AT INSIDE OF FOUNDATION WALL

Suggested Details show how heat loss through slab edges can be reduced satisfactorily by placing resistance in the paths of greatest heat flow. The drawings show some unconventional types of construction, the intention being to show insulating principles in graphic form while leaving the construction type to the choice of the designer.

The insulation shown is based on minimum desirable results for a heating design temperature of −20° F. Resistance values "R" are given rather than a specific thickness of insulation. (See Table of Materials on page 395 for resistance values of various materials.)

Variations in requirements for other design temperatures and for floor heating are given below.

Design Temperature	Relative Percentage for Values of R*	
	(No Floor Heating)	(Floor Heating)
−20° F.	100%	150%
0° F.	75%	113%
20° F.	50%	75%

For any homogeneous material, the resistance value (R) varies in proportion to the thickness of the material.

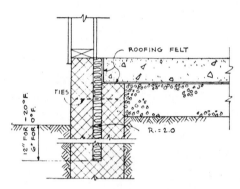
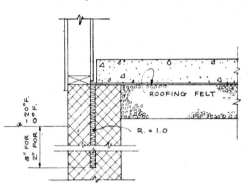

INSULATION AT CENTER OF FOUNDATION WALL

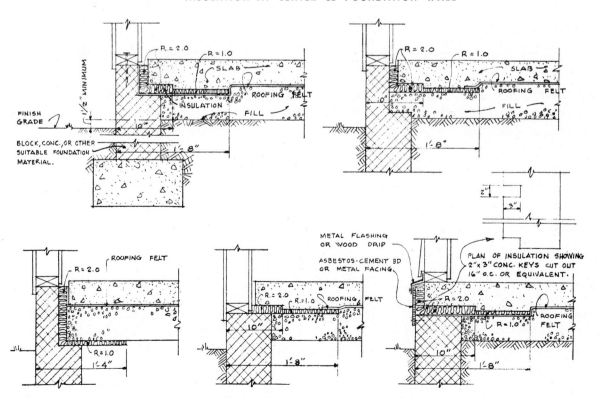

CONCRETE SLAB ON GROUND

INSULATION OF CONCRETE FLOORS IN DWELLINGS

Suggestions Based on Research by Housing and Home Finance Agency

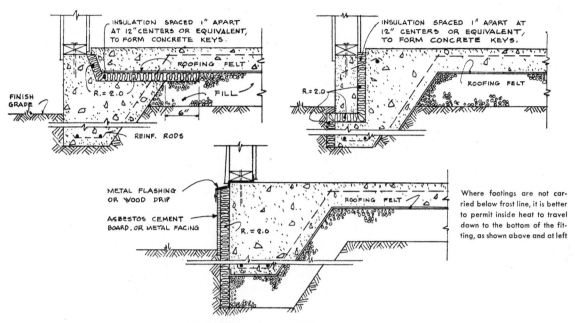

Where footings are not carried below frost line, it is better to permit inside heat to travel down to the bottom of the fitting, as shown above and at left

FLOATING SLAB FOUNDATIONS

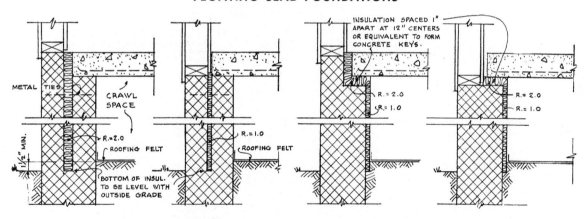

CONCRETE SLAB OVER CRAWL SPACE

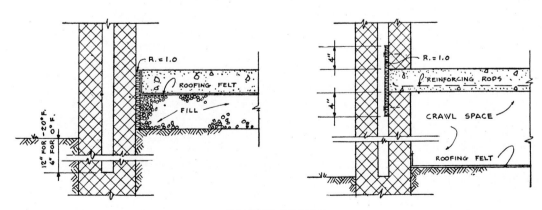

CAVITY WALLS

HEATING SYSTEMS FOR HOUSES

1 — One-Pipe Steam Systems: Design, Radiators

First of a series on heating systems for residences and other small buildings, covering steam, hot water, and radiant methods, prepared for ARCHITECTURAL RECORD by William J. McGuinness, Prof. of Mechanical and Structural Engineering, Pratt Institute.

Characteristics

While comparative installation costs vary periodically and according to geographic location, a one-pipe steam system is generally cheaper to install than a hot water system or a good forced-warm-air system. While its operating cost may be slightly higher than these systems, one-pipe steam is economical, rugged and easy to maintain. If well designed and maintained, and if boiler water is kept hot by an aquastat, it is prompt to respond to a call for heat. When rooms are at temperature or when outside temperature increases, it shuts off promptly and does not have any troublesome "carry-over" heating such as may occasionally be encountered in other systems.

Design

The first step in design of any heating system is determination of hourly heat losses in Btu from each room or space. Since each square foot of free-standing cast iron steam radiation emits 240 Btu per hour, it is necessary only to divide hourly heat loss by 240 to arrive at the amount of radiation needed. From the accompanying tables the designer may select a radiator of proper size to make up heat loss and to fit space available.

Pipe sizes are fixed by the amount of radiation served. They can be selected from the table given herein, keeping in mind that they fall into three categories: (1) mains; (2) runouts, risers and radiator connections; and (3) returns.

Not of least importance in general design is a space layout of the system to insure proper operation and architectural suitability. Good operation suggests adequate height from boiler to start of main, pitch of all pipes, proximity of radiator to riser, proper location of all air vents, space for servicing boiler, location of radiators below glass areas, and use of two or three radiators in large rooms. Space requirements include recessing of radiators if possible, maintenance of basement headroom and location of piping to permit finishing of basement rooms.

Maintenance

It is difficult and expensive to boil greasy water. New installations should have boiler and piping cleaned and blown out thoroughly after a short period of operation. Water should be drained and refilled, and the stack cleaned, yearly. Radiator control valves must be kept tight to prevent steam leakage into rooms. Air vents on radiators and mains must exhaust air quickly or heating will be slow and expense increased; this or the passing of steam may indicate need for their replacement. In the case of oil burners, efficiency tests are now quite standardized and easy to make. Taking stack temperature and analyzing flue gases will indicate whether combustion is complete and efficient. A slight adjustment in air intake, draftostat, etc., may result in great savings.

CAPACITIES OF PIPE IN SQ. FT. OF RADIATION

PIPE SIZE (inches)	STEAM MAIN** (Condensate and steam flowing in same direction)	RUNOUTS, RISERS, RADIATOR CONNECTIONS*	WET RETURN
1	—–	28	700
1¼	—–	62	1200
1½	—–	93	1900
2	386	169	4000

Courtesy Institute of Boiler and Radiator Manufacturers

* If runout to radiator exceeds 8 ft. in length increase pipe one size.
** Based on "Equivalent Length" of 200 ft. To determine equivalent length add to actual length (boiler to farthest radiator) 4.3 ft. for each elbow and 8 ft. for each tee.

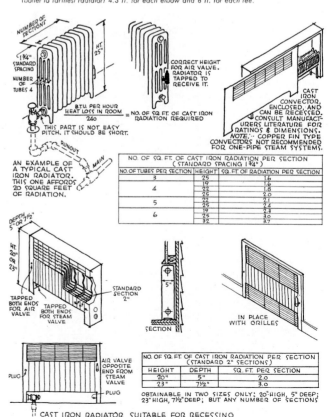

NO. OF SQ. FT. OF CAST IRON RADIATION PER SECTION (STANDARD SPACING 1¾")		
NO. OF TUBES PER SECTION	HEIGHT	SQ. FT. OF RADIATION PER SECTION
3	25	1.6
4	19	1.6
	22	1.8
	25	2.0
5	22	2.1
	25	2.4
6	19	2.3
	25	3.0
	32	3.7

NO. OF SQ. FT. OF CAST IRON RADIATION PER SECTION (STANDARD 2" SECTIONS)		
HEIGHT	DEPTH	SQ. FT. PER SECTION
20"	5"	2.0
23"	7½"	3.0

OBTAINABLE IN TWO SIZES ONLY: 20" HIGH, 5" DEEP; 23" HIGH, 7½" DEEP; BUT ANY NUMBER OF SECTIONS

CAST IRON RADIATOR SUITABLE FOR RECESSING

TYPES OF RADIATION

HEATING SYSTEMS FOR HOUSES

2 — One-Pipe Steam Systems: Boilers and Controls

By William J. McGuinness

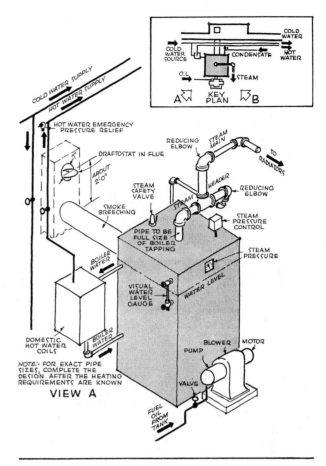

VIEW A

NOTE:- FOR EXACT PIPE SIZES, COMPLETE THE DESIGN AFTER THE HEATING REQUIREMENTS ARE KNOWN

Boiler and Piping

Selection of boiler depends on a number of things besides system capacity, including: whether the boiler is steel or cast iron; kind of fuel (oil, coal or gas); and whether or not generation of domestic hot water is included. Once these are decided, capacity should be calculated to include all radiation, allowance for domestic hot water, and allowances for pickup from a cold start and for loss in pipes. Manufacturers' recommendations should be consulted. Black iron pipe is most common and covering should be provided for mains, runouts and risers in exterior walls. Return lines are not usually covered. The boiler should be well insulated.

Domestic hot water can be produced by coils in a unit adjacent to the boiler as shown here, or by submerged coils within the boiler (both producing continuous flow of hot water); or smaller coils can be used to supply a storage tank for intermittent use. The former method is now the more popular.

Controls

In this system, **valves** at radiators must be fully open or fully shut. A small opening will cause hammering between steam and condensate. The **pressure control** shuts off the oil burner when steam pressure becomes excessive. High steam pressure will also operate the spring-loaded **safety valve** and afford a mechanical relief. The **aquastat** is adjustable to maintain boiler water at a temperature high enough to produce domestic hot water. It will turn the oil burner on and off to accomplish this. An additional advantage of this control is that when heat is called for the boiler water has a start and need not be heated up from a very low temperature. The **clock thermostat** turns the oil burner on and off to maintain an optimum temperature in the heated space. The clock attachment changes this temperature between day and night. The **low-water cutoff** will stop the fire if the boiler water level drops, saving the boiler from burning out. The **stack temperature control** will stop the oil pump and blower if the burner has failed to ignite within a time limit. The **oil burner switch** at the head of the basement stairs will cut off the system when a shut-down is desired.

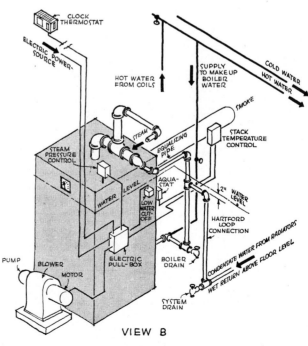

VIEW B

**TYPICAL OIL-FIRED BOILER
FOR A ONE-PIPE STEAM SYSTEM**

HEATING SYSTEMS FOR HOUSES

3 — One-Pipe Steam Systems: Mains and Returns

By William J. McGuinness

GENERAL NOTES

Pitch mains, returns, and radiator runouts ½″ in 10 ft. Main changes to return pipe size by a reducer, below boiler water level. Quick vent air valves must be at least 15″ away from the vertical drop at end of mains. To prevent boiler water backing into return, a Hartford loop connection should join the return with the equalizing pipe 2″ below boiler water level. Quick vent valves should be placed as high as possible by extending them above the main. It is preferable to connect the supply end of the main to a horizontal header instead of by a vertical pipe to the boiler. Basement radiators are possible only above boiler water level, if drained to a wet return.

SUGGESTED MAIN LAYOUTS

For small rectangular houses with center girder

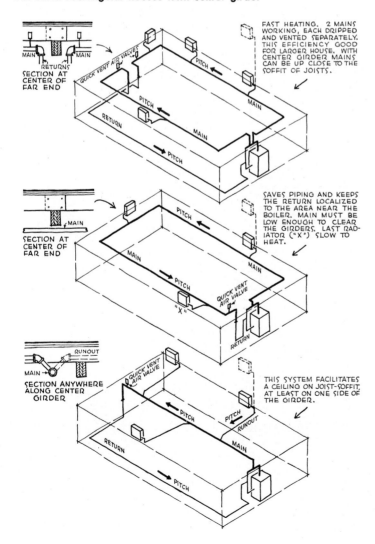

FAST HEATING. 2 MAINS WORKING, EACH DRIPPED AND VENTED SEPARATELY. THIS EFFICIENCY GOOD FOR LARGER HOUSE. WITH CENTER GIRDER MAINS CAN BE UP CLOSE TO THE SOFFIT OF JOISTS.

SAVES PIPING AND KEEPS THE RETURN LOCALIZED TO THE AREA NEAR THE BOILER. MAIN MUST BE LOW ENOUGH TO CLEAR THE GIRDERS. LAST RADIATOR ("X") SLOW TO HEAT.

THIS SYSTEM FACILITATES A CEILING ON JOIST-SOFFIT AT LEAST ON ONE SIDE OF THE GIRDER.

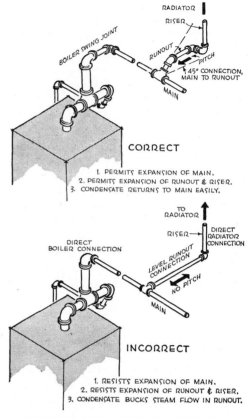

CORRECT

1. PERMITS EXPANSION OF MAIN.
2. PERMITS EXPANSION OF RUNOUT & RISER.
3. CONDENSATE RETURNS TO MAIN EASILY.

INCORRECT

1. RESISTS EXPANSION OF MAIN.
2. RESISTS EXPANSION OF RUNOUT & RISER.
3. CONDENSATE BUCKS STEAM FLOW IN RUNOUT.

CORRECT AND INCORRECT BOILER AND RADIATOR CONNECTIONS

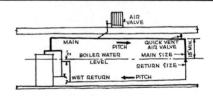

Usual type; can follow cellar wall near floor.

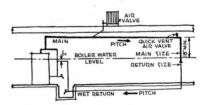

When return cannot be visible it may be buried in or below slab; coat outside of return with asphaltic paint; do not put return in water-bearing soil or cinders. Pit is required if system is to be drained.

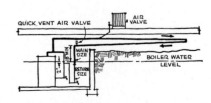

Space limitation may necessitate dry return; do not connect radiator runouts to it unless it is as high as main. Note position of quick-vent valve and minimum height of return above boiler water level.

REASONS FOR THREE KINDS OF RETURNS

HEATING SYSTEMS FOR HOUSES

Forced Hot Water Systems: 1—One-Pipe; Types, Equipment

Selection of a Type of System

Most residences can be served satisfactorily and most economically by a one-pipe forced circulation system with a single loop main. Larger residences call for the use of a multicircuit one-pipe system consisting of a main without any radiator branches supplying several branch mains each serving a section of the house and returning through a single return line and circulating pump to the boiler. The addition of extra flow control valves and pumps can easily turn this into a zoned system good enough for the largest house or for a small apartment building or similar structure. In very large installations or those calling for the greatest efficiency the two-pipe, reversed-return, forced-circulation system is certainly the most efficient, because the return water is handled very positively by a separate return main and is not able to cool the water flowing to other radiators in the circuit.

Characteristics of Hot Water Heating

Forced systems in which the boiler water is kept hot by water temperature controls are very fast in response to calls for heat. They are much faster than one-pipe steam systems. When the thermostat is satisfied, the circulating pump stops, but the heat emission of the radiators continues at a slowly diminishing rate which is much better than the speedy stopping of a steam system in which all the steam in a radiator has condensed and drawn air into the radiator. The possibility of circulating water at temperatures less than the actual design temperature makes hot water an ideal medium for moderate weather.*

Economy of Installation and Operation

The cost of a pump, flow control valves, special return fittings and

---

* A properly designed hot water system is quieter in operation than the best one-pipe steam system. It is free from the frequent complaint that one-pipe steam systems push into the room odor-laden air from the radiators whenever steam comes up.

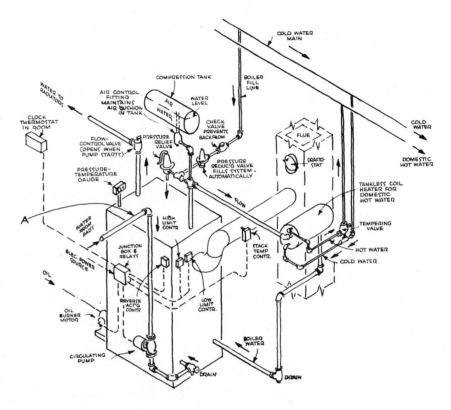

TYPICAL OIL-FIRED BOILER AND EQUIPMENT

For one- or two-pipe forced hot water systems

Note direct main connections (A, no swing joints); expansion not sufficient to cause trouble. Circulating pump is in return line, in either vertical or horizontal run according to pump requirements

Operation

1. When room thermostat calls for heat, oil burner and pump turn on simultaneously

2. If water drops below limiting temperature (160°), reverse-acting control turns off pump until oil burner has raised water temperature

3. Low-limit control turns on oil burner whenever water falls below 160°

4. High-limit control turns off oil burner when water temperature exceeds a high limit (often 200°), thus stabilizing water temperature during capacity operation

5. When room thermostat is satisfied, pump and oil burner turn off

6. Stack temperature control, an emergency control, shuts down burner if it does not ignite promptly

7. Pressure relief valve, an emergency control, opens to relieve any pressure in excess of a set value (often 30 lb. per sq. in.). This valve should be set above boiler, otherwise if it failed it would drain boiler, subjecting boiler to cracking

---

larger radiator often make the installation of a hot water system more costly than a steam one-pipe system. Because of the heat-retaining qualities of the circulated water it is usually cheaper to operate a hot water system than it is to operate a one-pipe steam system.

Fittings, Pipe and Covering

Copper tubing is very popular and adaptable to hot water systems and in a great many instances is replacing steel. In these cases bronze and copper solder fittings are often used. It is usual to cover all steel pipe for the conservation of the heat, but

TIME-SAVER STANDARDS

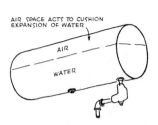

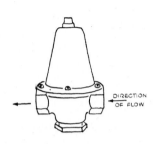

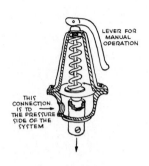

COMPRESSION TANK WITH AIR CONTROL FITTING
SELECT TANK SIZE TO FIT SYSTEM

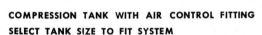

Capacity in sq. ft. of radiation	Tank capacity gallons	Tank dimensions
to 300 sq. ft.	15	12″ x 30″
300 to 500 sq. ft.	18	12″ x 36″
500 to 700 sq. ft.	20	12″ x 42″
700 to 1000 sq. ft.	24	12″ x 48″

PRESSURE REDUCING VALVE

Fill line to boiler; adds water when pressure drops below 12 lb. per sq. in.

Other side connected to city water pressure (40 to 50 lb. per sq. in.; too high for system) Full system is needed; it's easy to forget to add water to boiler. This valve adds it automatically

PRESSURE RELIEF VALVE

Spring-loaded diaphragm raises when system pressure exceeds 30 lb. per sq. in., permitting water flow through center tube

Drip. Valve seldom opens under proper operation, however, drip can empty into dry well or sink, *not* sewer

In systems where compression tank replaces high-gravity tank, pressure-relief valve is needed because system is otherwise closed. If air cushion in compression tank is too small (through improper operation), this valve operates to relieve system and prevent bursting of parts

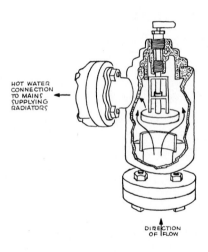

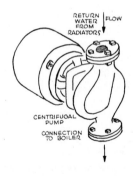

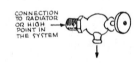

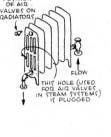

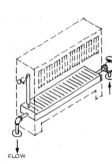

FLOW CONTROL VALVE

When circulating pump starts, water flow raises the valve seat. When the pump is not operating, it closes against circulation. This is important in summer when hot water must be retained in boiler (for domestic hot water) but must not flow through radiators

CIRCULATING PUMP

Electric motor turns on, forcing water through system, when heat is called for and if water is hot enough (160°). Select pump as directed in TSS page on "Design"

AIR VENT

When opened, pressure forces out air in the high place. When water starts to flow this valve must be closed. Automatic vents are available at slightly higher cost. Note (lower drawing): air vent must be extended high above cast iron or copper convectors to keep air out of the water passages

copper pipe is usually left exposed because it loses heat by radiation at a rate very much slower than steel.

Maintenance

The elimination of air is one of the most important things in the good operation of a hot water job. If the elimination is manually accomplished at the radiators it should be done several times during the heating season. The water level in the compression tank should be adjusted at the same time if this function is not automatic. It is important to provide proper lubrication for the pump. All equipment such as flow control valves, pressure relief valves etc. should be checked for proper adjustment.

The author and editors wish to acknowledge with thanks the assistance of several manufacturers of heating equipment, and of the Institute of Boiler and Radiator Manufacturers. For heating problems beyond the scope of these Time-Saver Standards, the reader is referred to the Institute of Boiler and Radiator Manufacturers, 60 E. 42 St., New York 17, N. Y.

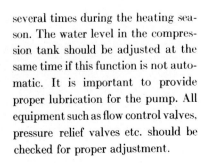

HEATING SYSTEMS FOR HOUSES

Forced Hot Water Systems: 2—Design of One-Pipe Systems

By William J. McGuinness

ONE-PIPE SYSTEMS

Radiators receive water from main and discharge back into same main

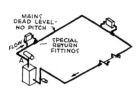

ONE-CIRCUIT ONE-PIPE SYSTEM

Approx. 7 radiators or 40000 Btu maximum

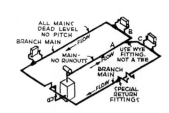

MULTI-CIRCUIT ONE-PIPE SYSTEM

Main A is sized to serve entire system; mains B and C are sized to serve respective circuits; same size held through to boiler. This system, with additional circuits, can serve the largest residence

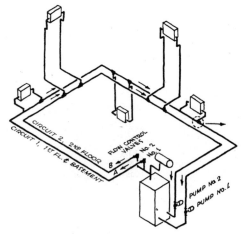

ZONED ONE-PIPE FORCED HOT WATER SYSTEM

Zoning

An advantage of forced-circulation hot water heating is adaptability to zoning. When Zone 1 calls for heat, pump No. 1 starts; flow control valve No. 1 opens, permitting flow in circuit 1. Flow control valve No. 2 remains shut preventing circulation in circuit 2. If instead, Zone 2 called for heat, pump and valve No. 2 would operate with flow in circuit 2 and not in circuit 1. Simultaneous action is possible. Separate thermostats operate pumps 1 & 2. Joint use is made of one boiler whose water is kept hot by water temperature controls

Basement and Second Floor Heating

Aside from zoning, sketch also illustrates several uses of special return tees

1. For 1st floor radiators, use of one special return fitting is common & riser size is found in Table 3, Section E. Two fittings are possible, in which case riser size is found in Table 3, Section A, and is smaller for same capacity

2. For 2nd & 3rd floor radiators, use of two special return fittings is common & riser is found in Table 3, Sections B & C. If one fitting is used, larger riser is chosen from Table 3, Sections F & G

3. For downfeed risers to basement, use of two special return fittings is necessary; size of riser is shown in Table 3, Section D

1. Average Water Temperature and Temperature Drop

In the following typical example, an average water temperature of 197 F will be assumed and the temperature drop in the system will be taken as 20 F. Water will leave the boiler at 207 F and return at 187 F.

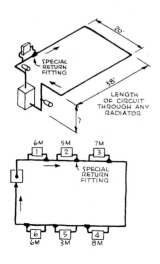

2. Water Flow Required to Make up Hourly Heat Loss in the System

The total heat loss is 35,000 Btu per hour. Dividing this by 9600 (see TSS on design of a two-pipe system) the answer is 3.63 gal. per minute.

3. Length and Equivalent Total Length of System

The length of the circuit through any radiator is:

Length	38
	38
Width	20
	20
Height	7
	7
Runouts (rad.)	8
	138 ft.

To arrive at the total equivalent length of system including the resistance of fittings, multiply by 1.5 (add 50 per cent). Total equivalent length is 207 ft.

HEATING SYSTEMS FOR HOUSES

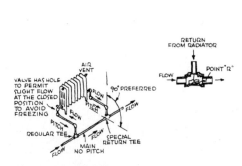

SPECIAL RETURN TEE

For one-pipe systems only; insert constricts flow, diverts some supply water into supply tee. Venturi action at R pulls water out of radiator. Note that colder water flows at bottom of main; hence radiator branches should be 90° to horizontal

Courtesy Bell & Gossett Co.

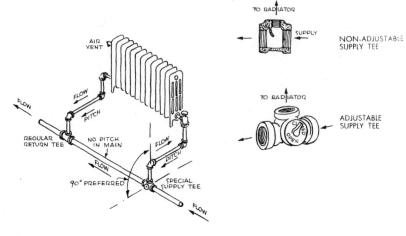

SPECIAL SUPPLY TEES can be used instead of special return tees

Courtesy H. A. Thrush & Co.

4. Select a Pump

Referring to Chart 1, it is found that the selection of a 1¼-in. pump will result in the need to maintain in the system frictional resistance the equivalent of 6.2 ft. of head.

5. Pressure Drop in the System

Section A of Table 1 indicates that for 6 ft. of head (the closest to our requirement) and a length of 200 ft. the friction loss will be 350 millinches per foot in the system.

6. Selecting Size of Main

In the 350-millinch column, Table 1, Section B, it will be found that a 1-in. main will carry 59,000 Btu per hour which is adequate. Our loss is 35,000 Btu. It is to be noted that 1 in. is a minimum for mains in one-pipe systems. In one-pipe systems the main size, selected on the basis of the total capacity, is carried at this size through the system and back to the boiler.

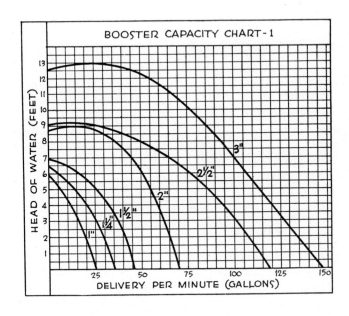

7. Sizing Runouts and Risers

Risers in one-pipe systems must be a little larger than for two-pipe systems. Table 2 lists the sizes needed for various capacities.

The largest radiator in the system carries 8000 Btu per hour and will

HEATING SYSTEMS FOR HOUSES

Forced Hot Water Systems: 4—One-Pipe Design Tables Continued   By William J. McGuinness

require ½-in. supply and return. Because this is a minimum it will be used for all the radiators. In larger systems there would be a noticeable difference between the risers in one- and two-pipe systems.

8. Selection of Radiators

An average temperature of 197 F will result in emission of 200 Btu per square foot of cast iron radiation or cast iron convectors. Dividing the hourly heat loss in each room by 200, the number of square feet of radiation can be determined. Radiator No. 1 will have to provide 30 sq. ft. In the entire system there will be 175 sq. ft.

9. Selection of Boiler

For 175 ft. of connected radiation it is possible to select a hot water boiler, specifying the type of firing. Allowances for pipe loss, pickup and normal domestic hot water requirements are usually included by the manufacturer in his ratings.

TABLE 1 — PIPE SIZING TABLE FOR MAINS
1 PIPE FORCED CIRCULATION HOT WATER SYSTEMS WITH SPECIAL RETURN FITTINGS

SECTION A

BOOSTER HEAD PRESSURES	TOTAL EQUIVALENT LENGTH OF PIPE IN FEET								
2'	40	48	60	68	80	96	120	160	240
2½'	50	60	75	86	100	120	150	200	300
3'	60	72	90	103	120	144	180	240	360
3½'	70	84	105	120	140	168	210	280	420
4'	80	96	120	137	160	192	240	320	480
4½'	90	108	135	154	180	216	270	360	540
5'	100	120	150	171	200	240	300	400	600
5½'	110	132	165	188	220	264	330	440	660
6'	120	144	180	206	240	288	360	480	720
6½'	130	156	195	223	260	312	390	520	780
7'	140	168	210	240	280	336	420	560	840
7½'	150	180	225	257	300	360	450	600	900
8'	160	192	240	274	320	384	480	640	960
8½'	170	204	255	291	340	408	510	680	1020
9'	180	216	270	308	360	432	540	710	1080
9½'	190	228	285	325	380	456	570	760	1140
10'	200	240	300	342	400	480	600	800	1200
10½'	210	252	315	360	420	504	630	840	1260
11'	220	264	330	377	440	528	660	880	1320
11½'	230	276	345	394	460	552	690	920	1380
12'	240	288	360	411	480	576	720	960	1440

SECTION B (Based on 20° Temperature Drop)

PIPE SIZE	MAIN CAPACITIES (In Thousands of BTU)								
					MILINCHES				
	600	500	400	350	300	250	200	150	100
1"	80	71	64	59	53	48	42	37	31
1¼"	170	160	140	130	118	102	90	78	63
1½"	260	240	210	185	175	156	140	121	94
2"	500	450	410	360	322	294	261	227	182
2½"	810	750	670	610	551	523	460	385	310
3"	1600	1400	1300	1150	1000	900	800	680	550
*3½"	2300	2100	1850	1650	1500	1350	1190	1020	825
*4"	3200	2900	2600	2300	2100	1950	1700	1350	1140

* Trunk main capacities only. Fittings are not made larger than 3".

NOTE — The figures shown in these tables apply to both steel pipe and Type L copper tubing, as capacity differences are not sufficient to cause design errors.

HEATING SYSTEMS FOR HOUSES

Forced Hot Water Systems: 3—One-Pipe Design Tables   By William J. McGuinness

TABLE 2 — PIPE SIZING TABLE FOR RISERS
1 PIPE FORCED CIRCULATION HOT WATER SYSTEMS WITH SPECIAL RETURN FITTINGS

(Based on 20° Temperature Drop)

CAPACITY OF RISERS WITH TWO FITTINGS (In Thousands of BTU)

	PIPE SIZE	600	500	400	350	300	250	200	150	100
						MILINCHES				
					Upfeed Risers—First Floor (See Note 1)					
A	½″	23	22	19	18	17	16	14	12	10
	¾″	43	41	37	33	30	28	26	22	20
	1″	80	73	64	60	55	50	45	39	32
	1¼″	180	140	120	110	100	93	80	74	62
					Upfeed Risers—Second Floor (See Note 2)					
B	½″	16	15	14	13	11	10	10	8	7
	¾″	31	28	25	24	22	21	18	15	13
	1″	58	52	45	43	37	33	32	28	25
	1¼″	122	108	92	90	79	72	68	59	50
					Upfeed Risers—Third Floor (See Note 2)					
C	½″	14	12	11	10	9	8	8	7	6
	¾″	26	24	23	21	19	18	16	14	12
	1″	47	43	38	36	34	31	29	28	25
	1¼″	99	91	81	77	70	66	59	56	46
					Downfeed Risers (See Note 3)					
D	½″	16	15	14	12	11	9	8		
	¾″	33	30	26	24	20	18	14		
	1″	58	52	43	41	34	29	25		
	1¼″	117	106	86	83	69	59	49		

FOR LESS THAN 200 MILINCH RESISTANCE. BASE CALCULATIONS ON PUMP WITH HIGHER HEAD PRESSURE.

NOTE — The figures shown in these tables apply to both steel pipe and Type L copper tubing, as capacity differences are not sufficient to cause design errors.

CAPACITY OF RISERS WITH ONE FITTING (In Thousands of BTU)

	PIPE SIZE	600	500	400	350	300	250	200	150	100
						MILINCHES				
					Upfeed Risers—First Floor					
E	½″	16.5	15	13	12	11	10.6	10	9.2	8
	¾″	29	27	25	24	21	19	18	17	15
	1″	50	48	44	41	37	35	33	31	28
	1¼″	95	88	78	76	69	62	55.6	48	40
					Upfeed Risers—Second Floor					
F	½″	11	10	9	8	7	7	6	6	4
	¾″	20	19	17	16	14	13	12	11	11
	1″	34	32	29	28	25	24	22	21	18
	1¼″	70	68	59	57	51	49	45	43	36
					Upfeed Risers—Third Floor					
G	½″	9	8	7	7	6	6	6	5	4
	¾″	18	16	14	14	12	12	11	10	9
	1″	31	29	28	27	24	22	21	20	18
	1¼″	63	60	56	52	48	45	43	41	36

READ THESE NOTES CAREFULLY BEFORE SIZING RISERS

NOTE 1. 1st FLOOR UPFEED RISERS—Capacities shown in the table are based upon horizontal branches not more than 3 feet long, with stubs 18″ long, or a total of 9 feet of pipe. 6 elbows, one valve and one union ell, and one C.I. radiator are added for the equivalent length.
For each additional 10 equivalent feet of pipe, move 2 milinch columns to the right.

NOTE 2. 2nd and 3rd FLOOR UPFEED RISERS—Capacities shown are based upon horizontal branches not more than 3 feet long, with risers 10 feet high and 20 feet high respectively. 8 elbows, one valve and one union ell, and C.I. radiator are added for the equivalent length.

For each additional 10 equivalent feet of pipe, move 2 milinch columns to the right.

NOTE 3. DOWNFEED RISERS—Capacities shown are based on a drop of seven feet to the *center of the radiator*, with not over 3 feet total in horizontal branches, 6 elbows, one valve and one union ell and one C.I. radiator.
For every additional 2 feet of vertical drop, move one column to the right in milinch table.
On downfeed jobs the main MUST be pitched up and a vent installed on end of main.

HEATING SYSTEMS FOR HOUSES

Forced Hot Water Systems: 5 — Two-Pipe Systems

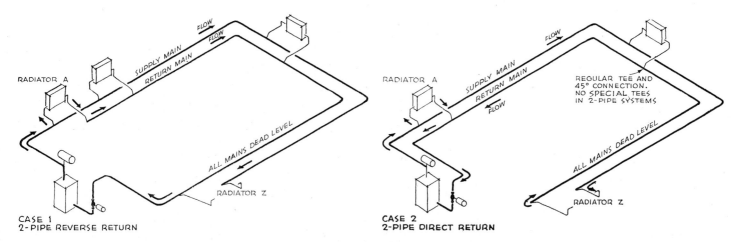

CASE 1
2-PIPE REVERSE RETURN

CASE 2
2-PIPE DIRECT RETURN

TYPES OF TWO-PIPE HOT WATER SYSTEMS

The 2-pipe direct return saves a little pipe but the reverse return is much preferable and usually chosen. Note (Case 1) that the length of circuit supply and return to "A" is identical with that to "Z" giving equal heating. In Case 2 note how much favored radiator "A" is by comparison with the long travel to and from "Z." On a straightway circuit the piping needed for Case 1 is even greater. It is chosen, however, for its equal length of run and return to every radiator

1. Average Water Temperature and Temperature Drop in the System

With closed systems under pressure it is possible to circulate water at or above the temperature of the boiling point of water if desired, without generating steam, because the boiling point of water increases with increasing pressure. A frequently used range of temperature and one that is used in this design is as follows: the average temperature of water in the system is 197 F. The drop in temperature between the boiler delivery and return water is 20 F. Thus the water will leave the boiler at about 207 F and return at about 187 F. This is in case we are running below the boiling point of water at atmospheric pressure.

2. Water Flow Required to Make Up Hourly Heat Loss

This house loses 118,000 Btu. per hour. The specific heat of water is one. This means it takes one Btu. to heat one pound of water one degree F.

In cooling, water will give off one Btu. for each pound losing one degree F. With a fixed heat loss and a fixed water temperature drop, the equation for quantity of water to be

circulated becomes — Gallons per minute x 8 pounds per gallon x 1 Btu. per pound x 20 degrees F equals Btu. per hour heat loss, or

GPM x 60 x 8 x 1 x 20 = Btu./Hr.

or $GPM = \dfrac{Btu/Hr.}{9600}$

which is a standard formula for these conditions. Substituting the actual value of 118,000 Btu. per hour heat loss we arrive at 12.2 gallons per minute to be circulated in order to make up the hourly heat loss.

3. Length and Equivalent Length of Circuit

In a two-pipe reverse return system the length of travel of water from the boiler through the supply main, through a radiator and through the balance of the return main is the same for any radiator. It should be computed accurately from the building layout. This installation has a length of travel of approximately 184 ft. as follows:

width	30 ft.
	30
length	50
	50
height	8
	8
runouts (1 rad.)	8
	184 feet

The "Equivalent Total Length" is a length of imaginary straight pipe equivalent to the run computed above plus an allowance for the resistance of fittings, boiler, valves, etc. On large jobs of unusual design it is customary to compute this accurately. For our purpose it is sufficient to add 50 per cent. The equivalent total length of this installation is thus 184 x 1.50 = 276 ft. This will be used in later calculations.

4. Select a Pump

Besides selecting a pump it is necessary to establish sizes for all pipes. One step depends on the other. The amount of water pumped through per minute must not vary. This is 12.2 gallons per minute. A powerful pump can circulate at this rate through very small pipes while a weak pump can deliver the same quantity per minute only through large pipes. If from Chart 1 (on p. 404) we select a 1½ in. pump we discover that it will pump our 12.2 gallons per minute against a "head" of 6.4 ft. Now it is necessary to select a piping system that offers resistance of the value of 6.4 ft. to assure flow of 12.2 gallons per minute.

HEATING SYSTEMS FOR HOUSES

Forced Hot Water Systems: 6—Design of Two-Pipe Systems   *By William J. McGuinness*

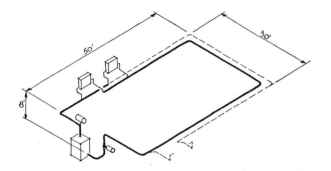

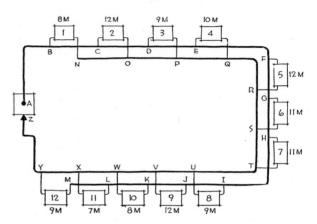

A TYPICAL DESIGN OF A 2-PIPE REVERSE RETURN FORCED CIRCULATION HOT WATER HEATING SYSTEM

Left: Sketch showing general dimensions of the system and the length of the circuit through one (any) radiator. Right: General plan layout identifying the mains, numbering each radiator and giving each room heat loss in thousands of Btu./hr. Example: 8M = 8000 Btu./hr.

5. Meaning of Pressure Drop in Millinches Per Foot

"Feet of head" means that the 1½ in. pump will deliver 12.2 gallons per minute if it is raising the water 6.4 ft. in height. Since the heating circuit is a closed one the water returns to the same level and the only resistance to pumping is a frictional one. The water must leave the pump at a pressure which would be caused by a 6.4 ft. height of water and at the end of the "equivalent length" the pressure will be zero. Thus the water loses 6.4 ft. of head in 276 ft. of pipe. A millinch is one one-thousandth of an inch. There are thus 12,000 millinches in one foot of height. Lost in the system will be 6.4 x 12,000 millinches or 76,800. The loss per foot will be $\frac{76,800}{276}$ or 270 millinches per foot. If this loss is maintained the circulation will be correct. It is possible to establish this millinch loss directly from Table 1 (ARCHITECTURAL RECORD, Sept. 1949, p. 405) which has the results of calculations such as we have completed above. In the left hand column of

Section A the closest head is 6½ ft. Go to the right until you reach the nearest total equivalent length. This is 260. Directly below in this column in the horizontal line labelled "Millinches" is the value 300 millinches per foot. This is close enough for our purpose to the accurately computed value of 270 arrived at previously. This table is used always instead of the calculation which was made to explain the process. We shall now use the "300 Millinch Column" in selecting all pipe sizes.

This is a good average pressure loss. High pressure drops result in speed and noise and low pressure drops result in slow speed and consequent slow response.

6. Selecting of Mains and Returns

Section B of Table 1 (ARCHITECTURAL RECORD, Sept. 1949, p. 405 and supplement herewith) gives the size of mains and returns at the left for any value of heat per hour to be delivered, the latter being read in the 300 millinch column. The supply mains are thus sized as follows:

Main	Capacity M Btu./Hr.	Size to be used
AB	118	1¼ in.
BC	110	1¼
CD	98	1¼
DE	89	1¼
EF	79	1¼
FG	67	1¼
GH	56	1¼
HI	45	1
IJ	36	1
JK	24	¾
KL	16	¾
LM	9	½

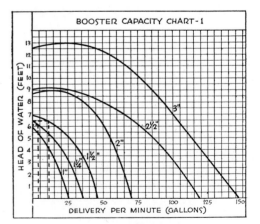

MAIN CAPACITIES (In Thousands of BTU.)									
(Supplement to Table 1, Section B, ARCHITECTURAL RECORD, Sept. 1949, p. 153)									
	MILLINCHES								
PIPE SIZE	600	500	400	350	300	250	200	150	100
½"	19:1	18.2	16.3	15.1	13	12.5	10.8	9.2	7
¾"	41	37.7	33	30.5	28	26.7	23.5	20	15

HEATING SYSTEMS FOR HOUSES

Forced Hot Water Systems: 7—Design of Two-Pipe Systems Continued

In reverse order the return mains would be sized in similar manner.

Return	Capacity M Btu./Hr.	Pipe Size to be used
NO	8	½ in.
OP	20	¾
PQ	29	1
QR	39	1
RS	51	1
ST	62	1¼
TU	73	1¼
UV	82	1¼
VW	94	1¼
WX	102	1¼
XY	109	1¼
YZ	118	1¼

7. Radiator Branch Size

The size of all radiator branches both supply and return will be ½ in. selected also from Section B of Table 1 on the same basis. There it is seen that a ½ in. pipe carries 13,000 Btu. per hour at this pressure drop which is more than that required by any radiator.

8. Selection of Radiators

The heat emission from one square foot of cast iron radiation depends upon the temperature of the steam or water inside and the temperature on the other, or room, side. The room side is 70 as in most systems, but instead of 212 F temperature as in steam systems the average temperature of the water is 197 F. So instead of 240 Btu. per sq. ft. per hour as in the case of steam radiation the hourly emission is somewhat less and can be found from standard tables. At 197 F this is found to be 200 Btu. per hour per sq. ft. of radiation by reference to Table 3. In each case then the hourly loss is divided by 200 to arrive at the sq. ft. of radiation required. Radiator No. 1 must have 40 sq. ft., No. 2 60 sq. ft. and so forth. The total radiation for the house is 590 sq. ft. The individual radiators may be selected from the standard sizes given in the table included in the section on one-pipe steam systems. (ARCHITECTURAL RECORD, Aug. 1949, p. 398). While copper convectors are quite popular, they have not been considered here because they involve

STRUCTURAL DETAILS

CASE 1

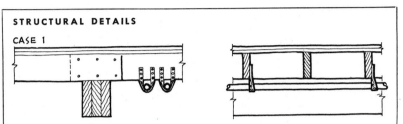

Mains not passing through girders can be supported dead level directly below joists but with slight clearance to prevent noise caused by expansion

CASE 2

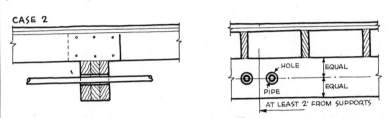

In average installations having mains of about 1″ diameter, holes slightly oversize for clearance will provide convenient passage for the pipes without weakening girder, if holes are kept at mid-height and away from supports

CASE 3

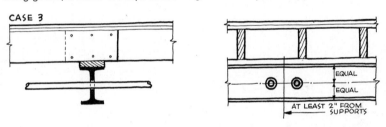

Similar arrangement with steel girder. In Cases 2 and 3 pipes should be supported on hangers, should not rest on bottom of girder-hole, which would result in noise during expansion. All mains and returns in forced systems can be level

TABLE 3

HEAT EMISSION—HOT WATER RADIATORS		
EMISSION PER SQ. FT.	AVERAGE RAD. TEMPERATURE	BOILER TEMPERATURE
240 BTU	215°	225°
225 BTU	210°	220°
200 BTU	197°	210°
180 BTU	190°	200°
160 BTU	175°	185°
150 BTU	170°	180°

slight variations from the standard procedure given here.

9. Selection of a Boiler

If this house has normal requirements for domestic hot water, the figure of 590 sq. ft. of radiation and the kind of firing, oil in this case, are the only items of information necessary to select a boiler to carry the load.

Most manufacturers rate their boilers at the connected load and make allowance for pipe heat loss and pick up from cold condition as well as an allowance for normal domestic hot water requirements. It is well to read the boiler ratings carefully in the manufacturer's catalogue.

HEATING SYSTEMS FOR HOUSES

Cast Iron Baseboard Heating Systems: 1

By William J. McGuinness
Professor of Architectural Engineering
Pratt Institute

Comparison With Other Systems

Baseboards distribute heat better than standing radiators and are less conspicuous. Properly installed, there is less wall streaking because of the top seal strip and non-concentrated convection currents. Lower parts of rooms are warmer, as shown in Charts A and B, making it most adaptable to basementless construction. Response to starting and shutting off is quicker with baseboards than with radiant heating.

Heating Medium

Hot water forced circulation is the most adaptable heat source for baseboards and can be used in any of the three circuits sketched. Operation is like any hot water system using conventional radiation and operation cost is about the same. If there is a minimum wall space for base, heat losses can be cut by further insulation, double glazing, etc.

Adaptability to Old Buildings

Baseboards can be used in conversion jobs where gravity hot water systems are in use. Two pipe steam systems in larger buildings can be used with baseboards, but in one-pipe systems, the long run of condensing radiation makes it almost impossible to get the condensate out the same end as the steam enters.

Steps in Design

1. Determine Heat Loss. The usual calculations for hourly heat loss in BTU should be completed and recorded for each room in the sketch.

2. Select Baseboards And/Or Radiators. The order of preference for baseboard location is a) under windows, b) on outside walls, c) on inside walls. As a trial length, outside walls are measured and recorded in each room. Heat loss of the room per ft of baseboard should be computed. The max required output (515 BTU per ft in the living room) sets the water

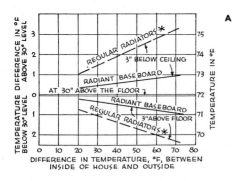

Chart A. *Room air temperature at various levels: at 70 deg inside to outside temp., a difference of 2 deg between floor and ceiling is shown for baseboards against almost 6 deg for radiators. *Small tube recessed radiators*

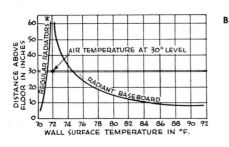

Chart B. *Radiant baseboard keeps lower walls warmer, overcomes cold floors. Overall mean radiant temp. is not higher with baseboards because radiators produce a hot ceiling. Studies made when temp. indoors at 30 in. level was 72 deg, outdoors 32 deg*

Circuits and Piping (Right)

I. Least expensive to install. Adequate heat but no individual control of units. If pipes drop to avoid doorways as at point A, drainage must be provided at point B.

II. Most popular for small and average size installations. Control of individual units by valves.

III. Best for large installations. Each base element controlled separately and receives water at max. temp. directly from supply main

Note: Charts A and B from University of Illinois Bulletin No. 358 — A Study of Radiant Baseboard Heating.

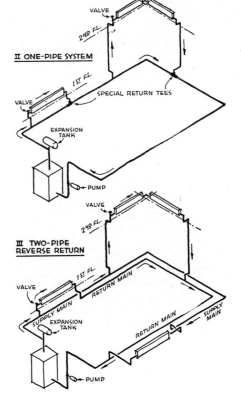

HEATING SYSTEMS FOR HOUSES

Cast Iron Baseboard Heating Systems: 2 — Types of Heaters

temperature which must be used throughout the system. In this case 200 F (the max recommended by some manufacturers) is chosen as the average water temperature and results in base lengths which fit the space. Base of the desired height and type may be selected from Tables 5–8 to make up heat losses. Cast iron radiators may be used with cast iron baseboards. Table 3 gives a heat emission of 210 BTU per hr for 1 sq ft of radiation at 200 F. Dividing the loss in the kitchen and bathroom by this rate (there is not room in these spaces for baseboard) we find that 26.7 and 10.9 sq ft respectively are needed. From Table 4 radiators may be selected to make up this footage. It is necessary in selecting baseboard lengths to leave space for expansion, piping and end cover boxes for valves.

3. *Select Boiler.* A boiler with a net rating of 45,000 BTU per hr will be adequate for this system. Boilers are made large enough to supply the pick up, pipe loss and domestic hot water needs, unless these are unusual.

4. *Select Air Cushion Tank.* To facilitate expansion in the system, allow 1 gal of tank volume for each 30 sq ft of radiation. Dividing 222.9 sq ft by 30, the min volume usable is 7.4 and the next larger stock size tank will be selected.

5. *Select Pump Size.* Tables used are based on a temperature drop in the system of 20 F. Since this is the drop we have chosen, use Table 9 to select a pump size. Since our heat loss is below 50,000 BTU per hr, a 1 in. standard pump is acceptable. The head developed by the pump in supplying water to make up the heat loss at the given temperature drop may be found from Table 10. For a 1 in. pump and nearly 50,000 BTU per hr, the head will be about 5.25 ft.

6. *Determine Main Size.* In determining the length of the system it is usual to allow 12 ft for each heating element in addition to the measured length of the main. The total of these

I-B-R means Institute of Boiler and Radiator Mfgrs. Col. 4 in table gives manufacturers' ratings.

MFR. TYPE & I-B-R RATING	DIMENSIONS	VIEWS FRONT BACK	SQ. FT./FT. RATING
AMERICAN RADIATOR R LOW 1.25			1.25
AMERICAN RADIATOR RC LOW 2.08			2.08
BURNHAM R LOW 1.25			1.25
BURNHAM RC LOW 2.08			2.08
CRANE R HIGH 1.77 LOW 1.25			HIGH 1.77 LOW 1.25
CRANE RC HIGH 2.92			2.92

Table I - BASEBOARD HEATER UNITS

HEATING SYSTEMS FOR HOUSES

Cast Iron Baseboard Heating Systems: 3 — Design   *By William J. McGuinness*

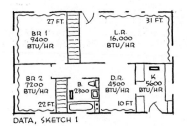

DATA, SKETCH 1

Heat loss and outside wall length

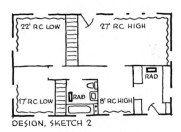

DESIGN, SKETCH 2

Length and type of baseboard

Temp. drop of water in system 20°
Length of System:

Measured length of main	130
Radiator allowance	
(6 heating elements x 12)	72
(Use 200' in Table 11)	202

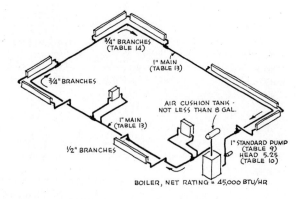

**DESIGN OF A RADIANT BASEBOARD HEATING
SYSTEM USING ONE-PIPE FORCED HOT WATER**

Table 2

	DATA, SKETCH 1			DESIGN, SKETCH 2		
1 SPACE	2 BTU/HR HEAT LOSS	3 LINEAR FT. OF EXTERIOR WALL AVAILABLE	4 BTU/LIN. FT. OF EXTERIOR WALL	5 TYPE AND HT. OF BASEB'D SELECTED	6 LENGTH OF BASE TO BE USED	7 SQ. FT. OF RADIATION
L.R.	16,000	31	515	RC HIGH	27'	78.8
D.R	4,500	10	450	RC HIGH	8'	23.3
K.	5,600	NONE, USE RADIATOR	—	RADIATOR	22"-4T-16SEC	28.8
BR 1	9,400	27	347	RC LOW	22'	45.8
BR 2	7,200	22	327	RC LOW	17'	35.4
BATH	2,300	NONE, USE RADIATOR	—	RADIATOR	22"-4T-6SEC	10.8
TOTALS	45,000					222.9

for the example given is 202 ft. Using this length and the head of 5.25 ft enter Table 11 and find that 1 in. is the right size for a main that will supply the BTU's required.

7. Determine Branch Sizes. Using the lengths of the baseboards in each room, it is found from Table 12 that branches are to be ½ and ¾ in. as recorded on the final piping diagram. Size of branches for small-tube cast iron radiation as used in the kitchen and bath is found from Table I, Sec-

tion B, ARCHITECTURAL RECORD, Nov. 1949, p. 408. Using the total heat loss of 45,000 BTU per hr and main size of 1 in., ½ in. branch size is satisfactory for each of the radiators.

References

For larger jobs, the reader is referred to: IBR Installation Guide No. 5, *Baseboard Heating Systems* of the Institute of Boiler and Radiator Mfgrs. (60 E. 42nd St., New York 17, N. Y.,

50 cents) through whose courtesy the tables have been partially reproduced here; *A Study of Radiant Baseboard Heating in the IBR Research Home* by Alonzo P. Kratz and Warren S. Harris, Engineering Experiment Station Bulletin Series No. 358, Univ. of Illinois, Urbana, Ill., 35 cents; *Heating a Basementless House With Radiant Baseboard* by R. H. Weigel and W. S. Harris, article in Heating Piping and Air Conditioning, Nov., 1948.

Table 3 — HEAT EMISSION RATES

AVERAGE RADIATOR TEMPERATURE	BTU/HR PER SQ FT
170	150
175	160
180	170
185	180
190	190
195	200
200	210
205	220
210	230
215	240

Table 4 — SMALL TUBE CAST IRON RADIATORS

NO. OF SQ FT OF CAST IRON RADIATION PER SECTION (STANDARD SPACING 1¾")		
NO. OF TUBES PER SECTION	HEIGHT	SQ FT OF RADIATION PER SECTION
3	25	1.6
4	19	1.6
	22	1.8
	25	2.0
5	22	2.1
	25	2.4
6	19	2.3
	25	3.0
	32	3.7

HEATING SYSTEMS FOR HOUSES

Cast Iron Baseboard Heating Systems: 4 — Baseboard Rating Tables

Table 5 — TYPE R — LOW HEIGHT

Length of Assembly Ft	Rating Sq Ft*	Rating, Btu/Hr., at Various Average Water Temperatures									
		215 F	210 F	205 F	200 F	195 F	190 F	185 F	180 F	175 F	170 F
2	2.5	600	570	520	510	490	460	440	410	390	360
3	3.75	900	850	810	770	730	690	660	620	580	550
4	5.0	1200	1140	1080	1030	980	920	870	820	770	730
5	6.25	1500	1420	1360	1290	1220	1160	1090	1030	970	910
6	7.5	1800	1710	1630	1540	1470	1390	1310	1240	1160	1090
7	8.75	2100	1990	1900	1800	1710	1620	1530	1440	1360	1280
8	10.0	2400	2280	2170	2060	1960	1850	1750	1650	1550	1460
9	11.25	2700	2560	2440	2320	2200	2080	1970	1860	1740	1640
10	12.5	3000	2850	2710	2570	2450	2310	2190	2060	1940	1820
11	13.75	3300	3130	2980	2830	2690	2540	2410	2270	2130	2010
12	15.0	3600	3420	3250	3090	2940	2770	2620	2470	2320	2190
13	16.25	3900	3700	3530	3350	3180	3010	2840	2680	2520	2370
14	17.5	4200	3990	3800	3600	3430	3240	3060	2890	2710	2550
15	18.75	4500	4270	4070	3860	3670	3470	3280	3090	2910	2740
16	20.0	4800	4560	4340	4120	3920	3700	3500	3300	3100	2920
17	21.25	5100	4840	4610	4380	4160	3930	3720	3510	3290	3100
18	22.5	5400	5130	4880	4630	4410	4160	3940	3710	3490	3280
19	23.75	5700	5410	5150	4890	4650	4390	4160	3920	3680	3470
20	25.0	6000	5700	5420	5150	4900	4620	4370	4120	3870	3650
21	26.25	6300	5980	5700	5410	5140	4860	4590	4330	4070	3830
22	27.5	6600	6270	5970	5660	5390	5090	4810	4540	4260	4010
23	28.75	6900	6550	6240	5920	5630	5320	5030	4740	4460	4200
24	30.0	7200	6840	6510	6180	5880	5550	5250	4950	4650	4380
25	31.25	7500	7120	6780	6440	6120	5780	5470	5160	4840	4560
26	32.5	7800	7410	7050	6690	6370	6010	5690	5360	5040	4740
27	33.75	8100	7690	7320	6950	6610	6240	5910	5570	5230	4930
28	35.0	8400	7980	7590	7210	6860	6470	6120	5770	5420	5110
29	36.25	8700	8260	7870	7470	7100	6710	6340	5980	5620	5290
30	37.5	9000	8550	8140	7720	7350	6940	6560	6190	5810	5470

Table 6 — TYPE R — HIGH HEIGHT

Length of Assembly Ft	Rating Sq Ft*	Rating, Btu/Hr., at Various Average Water Temperatures									
		215 F	210 F	205 F	200 F	195 F	190 F	185 F	180 F	175 F	170 F
2	3.5	850	810	770	730	690	650	620	580	550	520
3	5.3	1270	1210	1150	1090	1040	980	930	870	820	770
4	7.1	1700	1610	1540	1460	1390	1310	1240	1170	1100	1030
5	8.8	2120	2010	1920	1820	1730	1630	1550	1460	1370	1290
6	10.6	2550	2420	2310	2190	2080	1970	1860	1750	1650	1550
7	12.4	2970	2820	2680	2550	2420	2290	2170	2040	1920	1810
8	14.2	3400	3230	3070	2920	2780	2620	2480	2340	2200	2070
9	15.9	3820	3630	3450	3280	3120	2940	2780	2630	2470	2320
10	17.7	4250	4040	3840	3650	3470	3280	3100	2920	2740	2580
11	19.5	4670	4440	4220	4010	3810	3600	3400	3210	3020	2840
12	21.25	5100	4840	4610	4380	4160	3930	3720	3510	3290	3100
13	23.0	5520	5240	4990	4740	4510	4250	4020	3790	3560	3360
14	24.8	5950	5650	5380	5110	4860	4590	4340	4090	3840	3620
15	26.5	6370	6050	5760	5470	5200	4910	4640	4380	4110	3870
16	28.3	6800	6460	6150	5840	5550	5240	4960	4670	4390	4140
17	30.1	7220	6860	6530	6200	5900	5560	5260	4960	4660	4390
18	31.9	7650	7270	6920	6570	6250	5900	5580	5260	4940	4650
19	33.6	8070	7670	7300	6930	6590	6220	5880	5550	5210	4910
20	35.4	8500	8070	7680	7300	6940	6550	6200	5840	5490	5170
21	37.2	8920	8470	8060	7660	7280	6880	6500	6130	5760	5430
22	39.0	9350	8880	8450	8020	7640	7210	6820	6430	6040	5690
23	40.7	9770	9280	8830	8390	8000	7530	7120	6720	6310	5940
24	42.5	10200	9690	9220	8750	8330	7860	7440	7010	6590	6200
25	44.25	10620	10090	9600	9110	8670	8190	7740	7300	6860	6460
26	46.0	11050	10500	9990	9480	9020	8520	8060	7600	7140	6720
27	47.8	11470	10900	10370	9840	9370	8840	8360	7890	7410	6980
28	49.6	11900	11300	10760	10210	9720	9170	8680	8180	7690	7240
29	51.3	12320	11700	11140	10570	10060	9500	8980	8470	7960	7490
30	53.1	12750	12110	11530	10940	10400	9830	9300	8770	8230	7760

* Based on the common standard emission rate of 240 Btu per hour per sq ft at 215 F.

HEATING SYSTEMS FOR HOUSES

Convector Baseboard Heating Systems: 1—Typical Layouts

By William J. McGuinness

Professor of Architectural Engineering

Pratt Institute

AT this writing the use of baseboard convector heating in this form is relatively new. Speedy research is resulting in changes in the units, their ratings, etc. Before completing designs based upon the information contained herein, check with manufacturers.

Adaptability to Various Systems

Baseboard convectors are most frequently used in connection with the series loop circuit and using forced hot water. They can be used successfully in a two pipe forced hot water system or in a conventional one pipe forced hot water system, where they are connected individually like radiators. Another possible use is in two pipe steam systems. They are not adaptable to one pipe steam systems because of the difficulty of steam and condensate passing each other in the small pipes.

Series Loop, Forced Hot Water

The water flows through a series of convector baseboards and back to the boiler by the motive power of a pump. If limited to circuits not exceeding 30,000 to 45,000 Btu per hour heat loss, the temperature of the heating water does not drop greatly. Average temperatures of 200 F and less are used and the temperature drop in the system is usually designed as 20°. A number of such circuits are possible, supplied by a single main, picked up by a single return and adjusted by balancing valves. With this arrangement it is possible to use baseboard series loop circuits in quite large buildings.

Comfort

Like cast iron radiant baseboard, the tube and fin type, discussed here, is effective in maintaining a fairly constant temperature at the various height levels in a room. The lower portion of the wall above the baseboard is kept at a greater mean radiant temperature and adds to comfort. Convection currents are more distributed than in radiator systems and will result in less wall discoloration if the system is otherwise well designed. Response to a call for heat is as fast as that of any system.

Performance

Except for the series feature, the performance of a series loop, forced hot water system is similar to that of any hot water system using a circulating pump. The connections at the boiler are the same. For a complete diagram of suggested connections, the reader is referred to Time-Saver Standards, Forced Hot Water Systems: 1, Sept. 1949. There, all connections are shown including controls and domestic hot water. An improved control is shown here in Fig. 7. Instead of turning the circulating pump on and off by means of a room thermostat, this system provides continuous circulation at a water temperature which varies to suit the outdoor temperature. Smoother operation is the result of this process.

The baseboard system operates with the same or slightly better economy than a conventional radiator job of forced hot water. Maintenance is about the same, involving manual venting periodically of all the high spots instead of at each radiator. Automatic vents may be installed at an additional cost.

Pipe Expansion

Straight runs of over 30 ft are not recommended unless expansion is provided for by means of a door loop (if it occurs) or of an expansion loop placed horizontally in a partition or other available space.

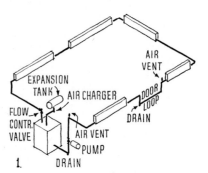

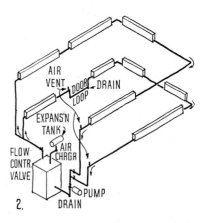

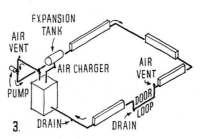

TYPICAL LAYOUTS FOR BASEBOARD CONVECTORS

1. Single circuit series loop.

2. Multi-circuit (2 story) series loop. Note balancing valves above pump.

3. Series loop, convectors level with or below boiler. Note recommended position of pump.

Notes: Examples are series loop and forced hot water, the most commonly used type. Drain all low points and vent all high points in each system.

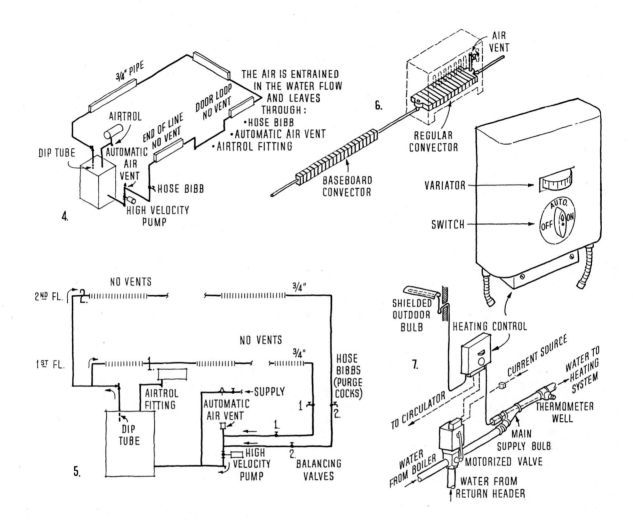

4. System using vents at boiler only. The Warren Webster Co., by using ¾ in. units and ¾ in. pipe, with high velocity circulator, maintains water speed between 2 and 5 ft/sec. At this rate air is carried back to boiler where it rises. Dip-tube prevents its re-entrance into system. It leaves through airtrol fitting. Air clinging to pump impeller rises and is exhausted by automatic vent. At start of season, hose bibb and supply valve (not shown) are opened. Pump is started. Air leaves through hose bibb. When a solid water stream flows, hose bibb is turned off.

No additional vents for door loops or at end of line are needed with this system.

5. Warren Webster 2-circuit system. Pre-season air purging is accomplished separately in circuits 1 and 2 by means of valves 1 and 2 and hose bibbs 1 and 2. To purge circuit 1, close valve 2, open hose bibb 1 and supply line. Pump until solid stream emerges from hose bibb 1. Then close hose bibb 1. Circuit 2 similarly vented. System then operates as described.

6. Combined use with regular convectors. Where scanty wall space precludes use of baseboard convectors, regular copper convectors and enclosures may be used in same circuit with some changes in the engineering design. Regular convector should be vented.

7. Controls. The Warren Webster control shown above operates automatically to vary water temperature supplied to base units, as set by outdoor temperature. With control unit switch set at "automatic," motorized valve mixes boiler water and return water to produce a temperature which is increased as outdoor temperature drops. At outdoor "design temperature" boiler water only is circulated Circulating pump runs continually and boiler water is kept at maximum temperature by an aquastat controlling fire. Variator permits a slight adjustment during automatic operation. "On" position of switch causes boiler water only to be passed, for a quick warm-up. "Off" turns off circulator.

HEATING SYSTEMS FOR HOUSES

Convector Baseboard Heating Systems: 3—Basic Data Table

By William J. McGuinness

MFR. & TYPE (Partial Listing)	SIZE (Inches) & MATERIAL		TYPES AVAIL. & DIMENSIONS		OUTPUT Btu/Hr/Lin Ft of Base at Water Temp. F					DETAILS R = Recessed NR = Non Recessed
	Pipe	Fins	Re-cessed	Non Re-cessed	170°	180°	190°	200°	215°	
DUNHAM			X Y (inches)	X Y (inches)						
BOTS	1 Steel	2¾ x 4 Steel	2½ x 10		562	636	722	807	948	METAL BACK. NO BOARD FIN. FL. X Y R
BOTSA	1 Steel	2¾ x 4 Alum.	2½ x 10		695	792	900	1005	1180	
BOTCA	1 Copper	2¾ x 4 Alum.	2½ x 10		735	835	946	1055	1245	
STERLING (Distrib. by H. B. SMITH)	1 Steel	2 x 4¼ Steel	1½ x 8	2⅛ x 7¾	370	420	470	525	600	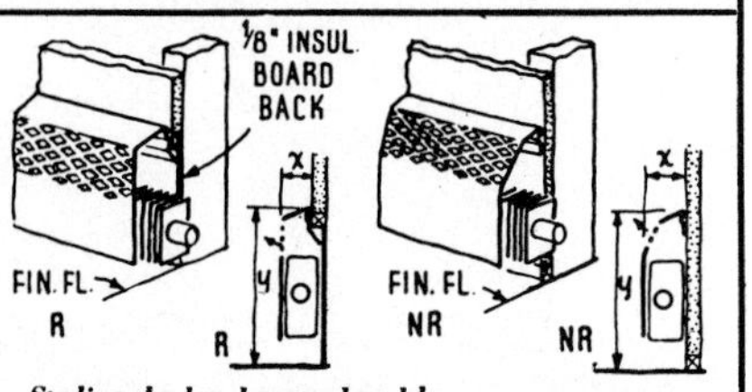⅛" INSUL. BOARD BACK FIN. FL. R FIN. FL. NR X Y *Sterling also has dampered models*
&										
U. S. RADIATOR Fin-Ray	1¼ Steel	2¾ x 4½ Steel	2¼ x 9	2⅞ x 8½	565	645	725	805	925	
WARREN WEBSTER HNL (*Heating Element Low*)	¾ Copper	2¼ Diam. Copper		2 x 8¼	310	350	400	450	*	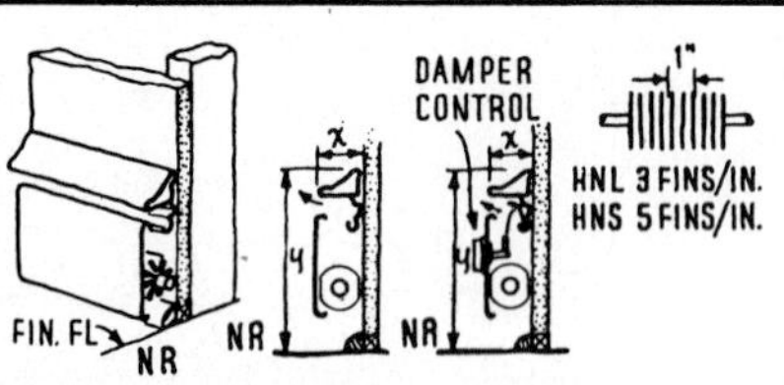DAMPER CONTROL 1" HNL 3 FINS/IN. HNS 5 FINS/IN. FIN. FL. NR X Y
HNS (*Heating Element Std.*)	¾ Copper	2¼ Diam. Copper		2 x 8¼	380	430	490	550	*	
					(*Depends on Fins/in.*)					
U. S. RADIATOR Comfort Ray	Steel Assembly See Detail		2 x 10 May be recessed		445	500	565	625	720	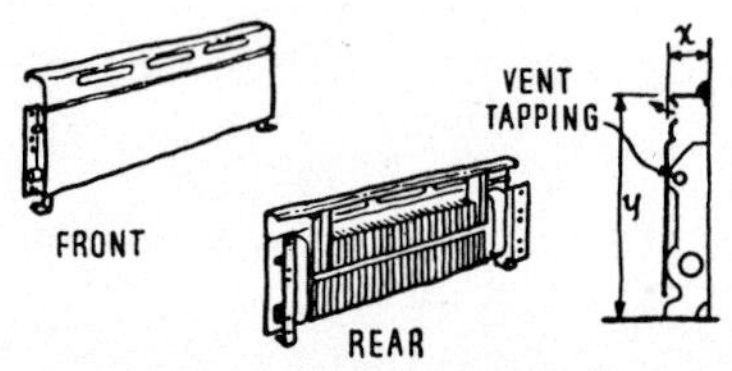VENT TAPPING FRONT REAR X Y
(*Note: This is a pressed steel unit more comparable to Cast Iron Radiant Baseboard. Systems are designed on that basis.*)										
VULCAN										STD. COVER / F.S. COVER
Standard	1 Steel	2 x 4¼ Steel	1⅜ x 8	2⅛ x 8	369	421	469	523	600	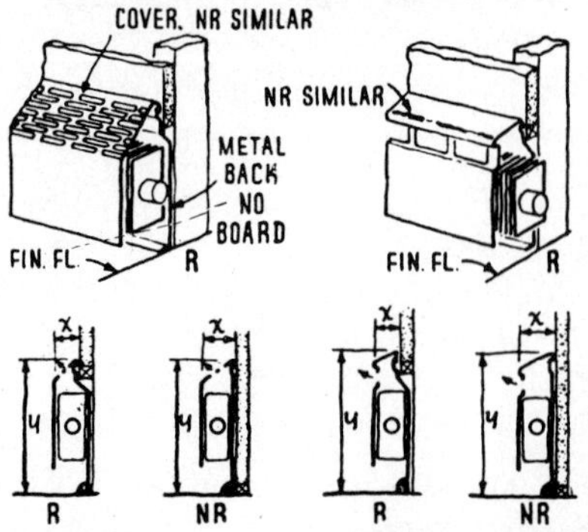COVER, NR SIMILAR NR SIMILAR METAL BACK - NO BOARD FIN. FL. R FIN. FL. R X Y R NR R NR
Standard	1¼ Steel	2¾ x 3¾ Steel	2⅛ x 8⅛	2⅞ x 7¾	568	648	721	806	924	
F.S. Cover	1 Steel	2 x 4¼ Steel	1⁷⁄₁₆ x 8⁷⁄₁₆	2¼ x 8½	341	389	433	484	555	
F.S. Cover	1¼ Steel	2¾ x 3¾ Steel	2¼ x 8½	2¹⁵⁄₁₆ x 8½	525	600	668	748	855	
F.S. Cover (2 high)	1 Steel	2 x 4¼ Steel	1⁷⁄₁₆ x 13	2¼ x 13	566	644	720	802	920	
F.S. Cover (2 high)	1¼ Steel	2¾ x 3¾ Steel	2¼ x 13	2¹⁵⁄₁₆ x 13	872	994	1110	1249	1420	*Dampered models also available* 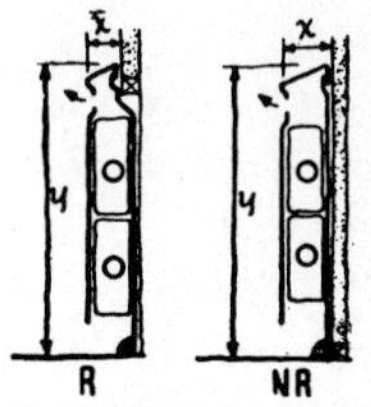X Y R NR

Notes:
1. *Vulcan uses aluminum & copper also. For ratings see literature.*
2. **Warren Webster does not recommend temperatures over 200 F.*
3. *The sq ft of radiation per ft of length may be determined by dividing Btu/lin ft output by standard heat emission in Btu/hr at temperature. Example: 600 Btu/hr/lin ft (at 215 F) ÷ 240 Btu/sq ft/hr = 2.5 sq ft of rad/lin ft.*

Convector Baseboard Heating Systems: 4—Design Of System

This is the second of two parts on convector baseboard heating, and presents a simplified design procedure for a typical small house installation. Part I, covering basic data and layouts of the system, appeared in the March 1950 Time-Saver Standards.

Room heat loss is computed in the same manner as for other conventional heating systems. The system is very economical of pipe since most of it is in the heated space. Credit can be taken for the heat emission of bare pipe behind base.

This and the finned areas of convectors make up heat loss in each room. Length of the convector will depend on its rating. Many designers feel that the lower output convectors are desirable because they come closer to filling up the length of the entire exterior wall, thus distributing heat better. A similar argument is offered for use of lower water temperatures. Convectors which discharge at the front cause less wall streaking but are slightly less efficient. Selection of pump and pipe sizes follows closely the usual procedure in designing radiator-type forced hot water systems. High points must be vented and low points drained. Convectors and loops are run level. It is advantageous for incidental piping to pitch to drains. Lengths obtainable vary with manufacturers, but usually units come in multiples of 6 in. The base which covers the unit can often be cut to exact size on the job. Controls are not possible within a circuit except by dampers in some models. The several circuits in a large system can be balanced with valves or zoned by the use of separate pumps.

DESIGN OF A SERIES LOOP, FORCED HOT WATER SYSTEM USING BASEBOARD CONVECTORS

Step 1. Compute hourly heat loss. This computation is the usual one and is not affected by use of baseboard convectors:

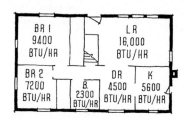

	Btu/hr heat loss
Living Room	16,000
Bedroom 1	9,400
Bedroom 2	7,200
Bath	2,300
Dining	4,500
Kitchen	5,600
Total	45,000 Btu/hr

Step 2. Establish average water temperature and temperature drop in system:

Average temperature	180 deg
Temperature drop	20 deg

Step 3. Compute gallons per minute (GPM) to be circulated at 20 deg drop to make up heat loss:

$$\frac{45,000 \text{ Btu/hr}}{9,600 \text{ (Factor)}} = 4.7 \text{ GPM}$$

For an explanation of step 3 and of factor 9,600 see Time Saver Standards, 2-Pipe Forced Hot Water Systems, Nov. 1949.

Step 4. Make layout and dimensioned pipe drawing to establish measured length and equivalent total length:

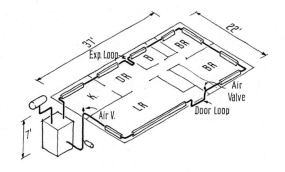

Actual Circuit Length:

Length	37
	37
Width	22
	22
Height	7
	7
	132 ft

Total equivalent length to include resistance of fittings, boiler, etc:

132 x 1.50 (add 50 per cent) = 197 ft

Say 200 ft.

HEATING SYSTEMS FOR HOUSES

Convector Baseboard Heating Systems: 5—Design Of System Continued

By William J. McGuinness
Professor of Architectural Engineering
Pratt Institute

DESIGN OF A SERIES LOOP, FORCED HOT WATER SYSTEM USING BASEBOARD CONVECTORS

Step 5. Select pump and establish "head" against which it must pump:

See Time Saver Standards, Nov. 1949, Booster Capacity, Chart 1.

A 1-in. pump will deliver 4.7 GPM against 5.5 ft of head.

Step 6. Select size of main:

Consult Time Saver Standards, Forced Hot Water Systems, Sept. 1949, Table 1 Sec. A, which also applies to this type of circuit. With an equivalent length of 200 ft and a head of 5½ ft, the pressure drop per ft will be 350 millinches.

Section "B" of this table shows that a 1-in. pipe will supply 59,000 Btu/hr at a 20 deg drop. This is adequate and a *1-in. main* will be selected. The capacity is found in the 350-millinch column.

Step 7. Select type of baseboard and by its output, compute the length required in each room:

For example, use Dumham "BOTS"; output at 180 F is 636 Btu/ft.

$$\frac{\text{Room heat loss}}{\text{Output/ft}} = \text{Length}$$

An "adjustment" (see below) is often used to increase the second and third divisions of the circuit 7½ and 15 per cent respectively. For this purpose, the circuit is divided roughly into 3 parts. The increase offsets the lower temperatures at end of line.

Step 8. Select expansion tank:

Btu Load	Tank Size
80,000/hr	8 Gals
150,000	15
180,000	18

An 8-gal tank is used.

Step 9. Select boiler:

Total heat loss of 45,000 Btu/hr and type of firing will be used in selecting boiler. Manufacturers make allowance for pipe-loss, pick-up and normal domestic hot water demand.

Step 10. Lay out system:

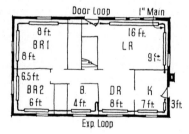

Notes: Heat emission of bare pipe has been neglected in this design, so system is slightly overdesigned.

Non-ferrous convectors can be used in series with fin-type baseboard elements. The size of these convectors is determined by their output rating at the average water temperature of the system.

180 deg average temperature is desirable for comfort and cleanliness. Higher temperature would make possible shorter units with resulting economy of installation.

Space	Heat Loss	Length "BOTS"	Adjust-ment	Revised length to be used
L. R.	16,000	25.0 ft	None	25.0 ft
B. R. 1	9,400	15.0	x 1.075	16.0
B. R. 2	7,200	11.5	x 1.075	12.5
Bath	2,300	3.6	x 1.150	4.0
D. R.	4,500	7.1	x 1.150	8.0
K.	5,600	8.8	x 1.150	10.0

RADIANT HEATING SYSTEMS FOR HOUSES: 1—Hot Water Systems

The author and editors wish to express appreciation to the following for their generous help and suggestions during the preparation of this study: Mr. George Lain, American Iron and Steel Institute; Mr. J. B. Fullman, A. M. Byers Co.; Mr. William P. Chapman, National Tube Company; Mr. Huson Jackson, Architect; Mr. D. L. Mills, Revere Copper and Brass, Inc.

Radiant Systems in General

Radiant or Panel Heating, which consists of making up heat losses by creating warm surfaces within the rooms, can have as its heating medium hot water, electricity or warm air. The response, economy and design differ somewhat. This discussion is limited to systems which use hot water and the design tables apply to residential installations only.

Human Comfort

The function of any heating system as it affects human comfort is to maintain a constant rate of heat loss from the body. The possible adjustments to regulate this loss are temperature of the air and temperatures of surrounding surfaces of spaces, air motion and relative humidity.

The latter two are confined largely to convection systems, but the proper relationship of the first two is the special province of radiant heating. By raising the temperature of the room surfaces, radiant loss from the body is retarded and the convective body loss can be increased by dropping the air temperature.

With a lower room temperature, the hourly heat loss from the room is reduced with a favorable effect on operating economy. The combined effect of warm surrounding surfaces and a lower air temperature is one which most people consider more comfortable and even invigorating. The "cold shoulder" effect is eliminated.

Other comforts are inherent in this system. Temperature distribution throughout the room is very uniform. This is especially noticeable in the constancy of the air temperature at various heights above the floor. Often the temperatures from floor to ceiling remain within 2 deg, while in other systems they often vary from 10 to 15 deg with cold floors and hot ceilings.

The absence of hot radiators prevents the "baked" sensation in the air and eliminates fast vertical convection air currents which cause dirt streaks on walls and ceilings. The relative humidity is slightly higher in radiant systems because of the lower air temperature.

Relative Economy

The comparative cost of radiant heating and other methods is quite special to the individual installation. In general, it is 15 to 20 per cent more costly to install, although some radiant installations have cost less than conventional ones. Structural savings, like the omission of basements and crawl spaces, can offset the extra cost of radiant heating.

Floor systems are often more economical to install than ceiling systems. Operating costs as already stated are usually less than in other heating systems because of the lower room temperature that can be maintained for equivalent comfort.

While there is a difference in the actual material cost of copper, wrought iron and steel, the total job cost will depend largely upon the facilities available for fabrication. This should be investigated locally.

Panel Location

Floor, ceilings and walls are available as possible panel locations. Walls are seldom used because of the difficulty in finding enough area to provide sufficient heat output. Their use is generally confined to auxiliary panels.

Fig. 1 illustrates the most commonly used ceiling and floor panel construction. For simplicity, this discussion will be confined to the use of these types. The floor slab which is more economical is well suited to basementless houses with concrete slabs on the earth. The mass of concrete surrounding the pipes has greater heat retaining qualities than the thinner plaster panels of the ceiling and therefore is appropriate to houses in which the call for heat is steady without fast fluctuations.

Ceiling panels, though more expensive than floor panels, are more truly radiant, have a greater permissable temperature and output, and will heat or cool off more rapidly upon demand. They are suitable for houses with much glass. Ceiling pipes must have at least one-half of their sur-

RADIANT HEATING SYSTEMS FOR HOUSES: 2—Hot Water Systems

By William J. McGuinness   Professor of Architecture, Pratt Institute

FIG. 1. TYPICAL CEILING AND FLOOR PANELS

Panel Details

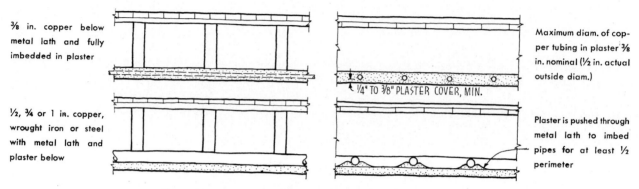

⅜ in. copper below metal lath and fully imbedded in plaster

½, ¾ or 1 in. copper, wrought iron or steel with metal lath and plaster below

Maximum diam. of copper tubing in plaster ⅜ in. nominal (½ in. actual outside diam.)

¼" TO ⅜" PLASTER COVER, MIN.

Plaster is pushed through metal lath to imbed pipes for at least ½ perimeter

Either of the above ceiling types will perform as shown in A, B and C below

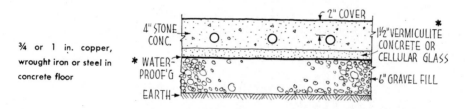

¾ or 1 in. copper, wrought iron or steel in concrete floor

2" COVER

4" STONE CONC.

* WATER-PROOF'G

EARTH

1½" VERMICULITE CONCRETE OR CELLULAR GLASS

6" GRAVEL FILL

Floor Panel Performance as shown in D and E below

Panel Performance (based on above details)

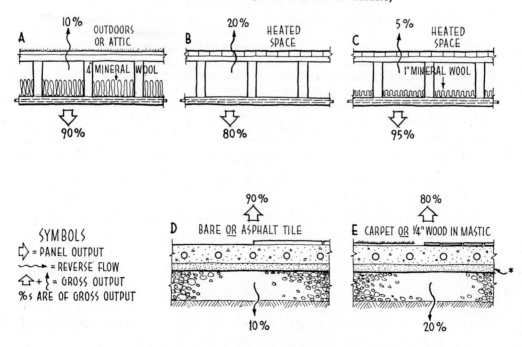

A — 10% OUTDOORS OR ATTIC — 4" MINERAL WOOL — 90%

B — 20% HEATED SPACE — 80%

C — 5% HEATED SPACE — 1" MINERAL WOOL — 95%

D — 90% BARE OR ASPHALT TILE — 10%

E — 80% CARPET OR ¼" WOOD IN MASTIC — 20%

SYMBOLS
⇨ = PANEL OUTPUT
⌇ = REVERSE FLOW
⇧ + ⌇ = GROSS OUTPUT
%s ARE OF GROSS OUTPUT

* Necessary only when slab is directly above ground water, heavy clay or rock. Otherwise may be omitted with negligible change in reverse flow.

faces imbedded in the plaster. Fig. 2 shows three types of houses and two choices for panel locations in each case. Either (a) or (b) is possible for the basementless, one-story house. The one-story house with basement is served by either (c) or (d). The two-story basementless house can use (e) or (f). For concrete slabs directly on the earth, floor coils in the concrete are preferred. If, however, large heat loss or the need for fast response indicates a ceiling panel, the problem of the cold slab-on-ground may be solved by carpet or auxiliary perimeter floor coils.

Coils and Grids

Sinuous coils (Fig. 3b) offer more resistance to the flow of water than grids but are easier to fabricate. They are almost universally chosen for residential work where coil lengths are not great enough to cause excessive friction. Grids find their largest use in industrial work where friction needs to be minimized in extensive piping.

Ferrous and Non-Ferrous Piping

The ruggedness of steel and wrought iron pipe recommends them for use in industrial jobs and for floor installation in residences. All connections within the panel must be welded. Copper tube, by its lightness and ease of bending, is well suited to ceiling installations. Solder consisting of 95 per cent tin and 5 per cent antimony should be used in sweat-fitting connections within the panel.

All of the materials mentioned will resist the corrosion commonly encountered. Since water is added in very small quantities, its corrosive action, if any, is quickly spent with little damage, and thereafter it is harmless. Corrosive action on the outside of pipes is a hazard which can be avoided by imbedment of pipes in weather-protected ceilings or in the concrete of slabs on dry, well-drained ground. Floor pipes must be kept out of the acid reaction of cinder fill.

While ⅜ in. copper tube is often set below metal lath and buried in the plaster and larger ferrous piping cast in concrete slabs, the order can be reversed. It is entirely possible to use

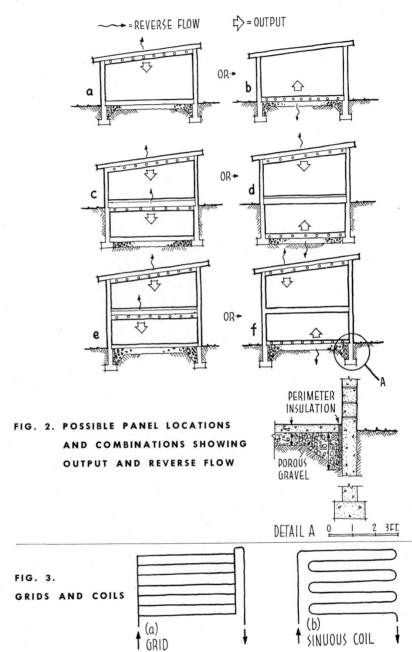

FIG. 2. POSSIBLE PANEL LOCATIONS AND COMBINATIONS SHOWING OUTPUT AND REVERSE FLOW

FIG. 3. GRIDS AND COILS

ferrous pipe (usually ½-in. dia or larger) connected to the soffit of joists with metal lath and plaster below, the plaster being forced through to partially imbed the pipes (one-half perimeter is enough). Likewise, copper tube may be used in floors if care is exercised in protecting it until the concrete floor is set. The heat-emitting qualities of the several pipe materials when imbedded in the panel are comparable.

Layout and Circuits

Radiant heating, more than any other system, must conform to the architectural and heating needs of the house. In layout work the following guides may be helpful.

(a) It is generally best when the warm ends of coils where the water starts are placed near glass or the perimeter of the house, and the cool ends toward the interior.

(b) Equalize as much as possible the length of all coils served by the same header. Short bathroom coils may be valved down later to avoid short-circuiting of the water.

RADIANT HEATING SYSTEMS FOR HOUSES: 4—Hot Water Systems

By William J. McGuinness   *Professor of Architecture, Pratt Institute*

(c) Keep the coil lengths within the recommended approximate friction limits.

Nominal Diameter	Coil Length Tube	Pipe
⅜ in.	120 ft	—
½ in.	150 ft	250 ft
¾ in.	250 ft	350 ft
1 in.	500 ft	500 ft

(d) The coils should be in a plane. Pipes must not cross within the panel. Maintain the spacing in all supply and return runs within the panel.

(e) Generally, the entire ceiling or floor is used instead of a small portion of those areas. Pipes may be spaced closely near the glass areas and wider near the interior.

(f) Place all balancing and vent valves in accessible places. They may be at the ends of coils, near headers.

(g) Effective insulation between ceiling coils and roofs is necessary to minimize reverse flow. The reverse flow to other heated space is credited to that space in designing other panels. This condition is illustrated in Fig. 2 (c) and (e). In both of these cases, the under-the-roof panels can have a reduced output. Fig. 1 (c) shows insulation used to diminish this flow if separate zoning and control of the upper story is desired. In this case, 1 in. of rockwool is enough; 4 in. are not needed.

(h) Ease of fastening ceiling coils is accomplished if the pipes run at right angles to the joists.

(i) In floor slabs, wire mesh is of some advantage in preventing cracks but is not essential if the earth is properly compacted.

(j) Avoid when possible, placing warm coil supply lines directly adjacent to cool return lines, particularly in plaster. Cracking may result if the temperature difference is large.

Basic Assumptions

It will be noted that this presentation is briefer than most of the texts and handbooks of design on this subject. It is well to state the limitations in its use and the assumptions upon which it is based.

1. Occupancy. Radiant systems may be used in a variety of structures. The design conditions in such varied occupancy as airplane hangars, gymnasiums, factories and houses differ widely. It is intended to present information for use in houses only. Large residences and 2 or 3 family houses may be included, but not enough data are given to design the heating for apartment houses.

2. Panel Type and Location. A great many different panel types are possible. For simplicity, two ceiling types and one floor type are suggested and the data given apply to them only. The ceiling panel output varies according to the insulation and the floor output according to the floor covering. For some additional cost, the response of floor panels may be improved and the reverse flow reduced slightly by the use of an insulating layer under the whole slab.

3. Perimeter Insulation. In all floor slab installations, it is assumed that 18 in. deep of 1 in. water-proof fibre board or cellular glass separates the slab from the concrete foundation wall and that the 6-in. gravel fill thickens to 18 in. at the perimeter. This, or its equivalent, is mandatory in good practice. See Detail A, Fig. 2.

4. Panel Surface Temperatures. Many systems of design establish first a required panel temperature and then select the conditions to assure it. Since there is much difference of opinion about desirable limits of temperature and indeed even about the probable output for any given temperature, *outputs* only are discussed and they are kept within safe limits.

5. Pipe or Tube Spacing. For fixed water temperatures and pipe or tube diameters, the output varies depending upon the linear ft of pipe or tube per sq ft of panel. Actual efficiency improves with wider spacings and decreases with closer spacings. Except in refined calculations, this may be neglected.

6. Units for Expressing Output. Design tables often read in output per sq ft of panel surface. Others read in output per linear ft of pipe. The latter system is chosen here but it is necessary that an arithmetic check be made on the output per sq ft of panel, so that it is kept within the stated limits.

7. Effect of Metal Surface Area on Output. For the same nominal diameter, ferrous pipes have a larger outside perimeter than copper tubing. Theoretically, a different output might be expected. An average output is stated in Table 1 which can apply to either material.

TABLE 1. Gross Output (including reverse flow)

Btu/hr/lin ft of pipe or tubing at avg. water temp. (135 F)
For other temps., apply correction factors shown below

Nominal tube or pipe Diam.-in.	PLASTER CEILINGS			CONCRETE FLOORS	
	Coil Location	Output Btu/hr/lin ft	Suggested limits tube or pipe spacing in. o.c.	Output Btu/hr/ft	Suggested limits tube or pipe spacing in. o.c.
⅜	Coils Below Lath	24	4½ to 9*	36	4½ to 12
½	Coils Above Lath	30	4½ to 9	43	6 to 16
¾		41	6 to 9	57	9 to 20
1		51	6 to 9	72	9 to 24

Important Note: The NET output, Btu/hr/sq ft of panel surface, must not exceed 75 for ceilings or 55 for floors unless special conditions justify it.
* Space in ceilings in excess of 9 in. may cause surface discoloration

CORRECTION FACTORS. For avg. water temps. other than 135 F, correct gross outputs as shown

Avg Water Temp (F)	100	105	110	115	120	125	130	135	140	145	150
Multiply gross output by:	.46	.54	.62	.69	.77	.85	.93	no change	1.08	1.16	1.22

FIG. 4. DESIGN ITEMS AND THEIR DETERMINING FACTORS

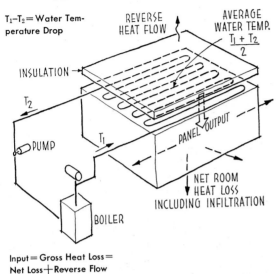

$T_1 - T_2$ = Water Temperature Drop

REVERSE HEAT FLOW

AVERAGE WATER TEMP. $\frac{T_1 + T_2}{2}$

INSULATION

T_2

PUMP

T_1

PANEL OUTPUT

NET ROOM HEAT LOSS INCLUDING INFILTRATION

BOILER

Input = Gross Heat Loss = Net Loss + Reverse Flow

FIG. 5. HEAT CAPACITY, FLOW AND FRICTION

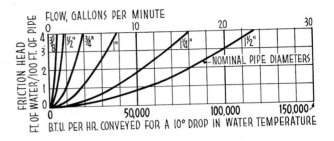

FLOW, GALLONS PER MINUTE

FRICTION HEAD FT. OF WATER/100 FT. OF PIPE

NOMINAL PIPE DIAMETERS

B.T.U. PER HR. CONVEYED FOR A 10° DROP IN WATER TEMPERATURE

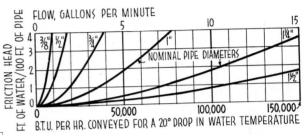

FLOW, GALLONS PER MINUTE

FRICTION HEAD FT. OF WATER/100 FT. OF PIPE

NOMINAL PIPE DIAMETERS

B.T.U. PER HR. CONVEYED FOR A 20° DROP IN WATER TEMPERATURE

ITEM	FIXED BY
Required Panel output Btu/sq ft/hr	Net room heat loss ÷ panel area High Limits (Btu/sq ft/hr) Ceilings 75 Floors 55
Actual Panel Output Btu/sq ft/hr	Avg water temp, pipe size, lin ft of pipe per sq ft of panel (Must not exceed above limits)
Reverse Flow	Kind of panel and insulation behind it
Gross Output (Entire Panel)	Net room heat loss (total panel output) plus reverse flow
Choice of Temp Drop	Size of piping (ceilings 20 deg, floors 10 deg)
Water Flow (gallons per minute)	Gross output and temp drop
Pipe Friction	Total equivalent length of pipe, water flow and pipe size
Pump Rating	Water flow (gal per min) and total friction in longest run (ft of head)
Boiler Rating	Gross output
Compression Tank Capacity	Water volume and temperature rise

8. Water Temperatures. Curves and tables are frequently issued for each of the possible average water temperatures with outputs varying accordingly. For brevity, Table 1 is based on 135 deg only. This temperature is chosen quite arbitrarily. The correction factors must be applied for all other temperatures.

9. Limitations on Table 1. It is apparent that the scope of Table 1 is such that conditions of temperature, size and spacing may be selected resulting in sq ft outputs above the ideal limits. It is understood that adjustments must be made to maintain these limits. The spacings are suggested only and can be varied except

for the upper limit of 9 in. for ceilings. Greater spacing is inadvisable in plaster.

10. Mean Radiant Temperature. This is an important item in many design manuals intended for use in a wide variety of structures. However, since this article is limited to residential design in which the MRT (average temperature of room surfaces) does not vary greatly, detailed calculations are not necessary. Table 1 is based upon an MRT of 70 deg which is on the safe side and usually results in a slight overdesign.

11. Heat Carrying Capacity of Pipes. The differing surface and inside dimensions of steel, wrought iron and copper affect somewhat their heat carrying capacities for the same nominal size. While Fig. 5 is based on the qualities of black iron pipe it can be applied without appreciable error to other materials.

Note. The effect of the above standardizations and short cuts have been well considered and they are in accord with acceptable practice. They may be used with confidence. Slight variations in performance can be adjusted by a change in water temperature or adjustment of flow by balancing valves.

RADIANT HEATING SYSTEMS FOR HOUSES — 6: Hot Water Systems

By William J. McGuinness

Professor of Architecture, Pratt Institute

This second installment in the series on radiant heating presents a simplified procedure for the design of a domestic hot water radiant system. A typical example worked out by this method will appear in the Time-Saver Standards for October 1951.

Designing a System

The following procedure is suggested.

1. Layout — Make a tentative layout of the system applying the foregoing principles.

2. Heat Loss — Compute the hourly heat loss from each room, including infiltration but omitting any loss through the surfaces selected to act as panels.

3. Adjustment — Reduce individual room heat losses by the amount gained by reverse flow from panels in ceilings below.

4. Establish the Required Panel Output — The panel in each room must give out enough heat to make up the losses found in steps 2 and 3. Divide this loss by the available panel area to find the required net output in Btu per hr per sq ft. Provide enough panel area to keep this output below 75 for ceilings and 55 for floors, otherwise discomfort or damage may result. If the ceiling is chosen, a portion of the floor may be added or vice-versa.

5. Find the Gross Output for Each Panel — Fig. 1 (a through e) (See Sheet 2, "Radiant Heating Systems For Houses," ARCHITECTURAL RECORD, August 1951) shows the relation of effective (panel) output and the additional reverse heat flow. Together they make up the gross output. Using the percentages for the selected type of panel, establish the gross output in each case.

6. Select a Water-Temperature Drop — When smaller temperature drops are selected, larger pumps are required, for a fixed length of coil and a given tube size. For ceiling installations, with smaller pipes and their greater resistance to flow, a 20 deg drop is suggested, while the larger pipes used in floors work well with 10 deg drops.

7. Select an Average Water Temperature — for a fixed MRT (here assumed to be 70 deg), the panel output depends upon the size of pipes, their spacing and the average temperature of the water. Critically high outputs are achieved only by large pipe, closely spaced and high water temperatures. It is best to provide enough panel area to keep the required outputs well within the prescribed high limits. Another conservative choice is to use a little extra pipe and a correspondingly lower average water temperature. A temperature of 130 deg is suggested as a trial temperature for ceilings. Temperatures

---

TABLE 2

Heat Carrying Capacity of Mains

Nominal Diam. of Main (pipe or tube)	Heat Conveyed in Btu Per Hour	
	For a 10 deg drop	For a 20 deg drop
1 in.	up to 35,000	up to 70,000
1¼ in.	35,000 to 70,000	70,000 to 140,000
1½ in.	70,000 to 100,000	140,000 to 200,000

TABLE 3

Compression Tanks

Net Heat Loss From Entire House (Btu per hr)	Capacity of Compression Tank (gallons)
Up to 50,000	15
50,000 to 100,000	18
100,000 to 150,000	24

over 140 deg should be avoided to prevent possible calcining of the plaster. For floors, a trial temperature of 110 deg is suggested.

8. Design the Critical Panel — Using the panel with the maximum required output, select a pipe size and average water temperature and, by means of Table 1 (See Sheet 4, "Radiant Heating Systems For Houses," ARCHITECTURAL RECORD, August 1951), find the length of pipe needed for the panel. Lay out the panel keeping the spacing within the limits suggested. Note that the table is based upon the gross output of the panel. The pipes may be spaced closely at the outside wall and increase in spacing toward the interior. Maintain the length of pipe required for the entire panel.

9. Design the Other Panels — Using the average water temperature of step 8, which must now remain constant for the entire system, find the length of pipe needed for the other panels, by the use of Table 1. Lay out the panels, indicating the spacing of the pipe. Generally one material — copper, wrought iron or steel — is used throughout one installation. If it is necessary to use two different average water temperatures, special equipment is needed. This should be avoided if possible.

10. Size the Mains — When a number of coils are served by a main it may be selected from Table 2 (See Sheet 6) on the basis of its heat-carrying capacity for the temperature drop selected for the system.

11. Compute the Water Flow — The required flow of water to make up the heat loss in the system is found by dividing the hourly heat loss by a factor dependent upon the water temperature drop. The flow is expressed in "gallons per minute" — GPM.

$$\text{For a 20 deg drop, Gpm} = \frac{\text{Btu/hr}}{10,000}$$

$$\text{For a 10 deg drop, Gpm} = \frac{\text{Btu/hr}}{5000}$$

Flow through any circuit can be found by dividing the heat loss in that circuit by the same factors.

12. Select a Pump — On the basis of the number of gallons per minute of water to be pumped through the system and the frictional resistance of the system expressed in "feet of water," a pump may be selected from Fig. 6. The frictional resistance is called "head" and is established as follows:

Trace the longest circuit through which water passes. Find the lengths of the main, the long coil and the return main. For each of these find the friction in ft per 100 ft of pipe from Fig. 5 (See Sheet 5, "Radiant Heating Systems For Houses," ARCHITECTURAL RECORD, August 1951). The total friction of each may now be found by multiplying the length by the unit friction. Add these and increase by 50 per cent to allow for the effect of boiler and fittings. With the total head and the total flow, select a pump.

13. Select a Boiler — The net rating of the boiler selected must at least equal the gross output of the system. In the usage of most manufacturers, there is enough capacity in a boiler so chosen to take care of normal domestic hot water needs. For unusual hot water demands, the capacity of the boiler must be increased accordingly.

14. Compression Tank — From Table 3 select a tank of the proper volume to permit expansion in the system.

FIG. 6. **Pump Performance Chart**

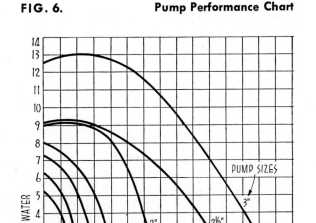

RADIANT HEATING SYSTEMS FOR HOUSES — 8: Hot Water Systems

By William J. McGuinness

Professor of Architecture, Pratt Institute

The third installment in a series on radiant heating, the following pages present a typical example using ceiling panels, and worked out by simplified methods presented in the Time-Saver Standards for August and September 1951. A similar example for a floor panel installation will appear in a subsequent issue.

This is a modern house, fully insulated and double-glazed. The floor slab rests on the ground, there is no cellar. An air space separates the insulated ceiling from a slightly sloping roof. Either ceiling or floor panels may be used. Example 1 uses ceiling panels. Carpet is used throughout.

1. Layout — Figs. 7 and 8 show the room use, size and area available for panels. While Fig. 9 is a final drawing summarizing the findings of the design, it is necessary in the preliminary stages to make several sketches resembling Fig. 9 in order to anticipate the most desirable location for the boiler, headers, adjusting valves etc. and the possible routing and location of coils.

2. Heat Loss — If the ceiling is used for panels, there is no loss from the room through this surface so it is not included in the net room heat loss upon which the panel net output is based. The gross output of the panel coil is later computed to include the reverse loss of the panel. The net loss in this case must include floor or perimeter loss, and of course, in all cases infiltration. Table 4 shows a convenient form for use as a work sheet in designing the system. Column 1 is reserved for the net hourly heat loss.

3. Adjustment — Since no heat flows from the back of a panel into another usable space, there is no adjustment to be made.

4. Net Output — If the net heat loss be divided by the available panel area in each room, the required output is arrived at in each case. This is listed in column 4 of Table 4. Since none of these outputs exceeds 75 Btu per hr per sq ft, it is unnecessary to plan for auxiliary floor coils in this example.

5. Gross Output — Fig. 1A (See Sheet 2, Time Saver Standards, August 1951) represents the condition of reverse flow in this house. The net output represents 90 per cent of the total heat loss from panels. By dividing the net output in each room by .90 the gross output of each panel is determined. This will finally establish the length of pipe or tube needed in each panel when the water temperature is chosen.

Fig. 7. Plan, Example 1.

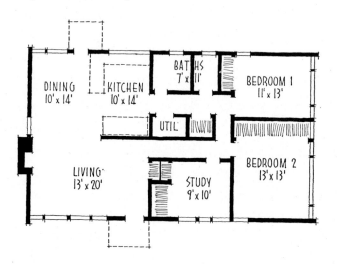

Fig. 8. Panel Areas Available, Example 1.

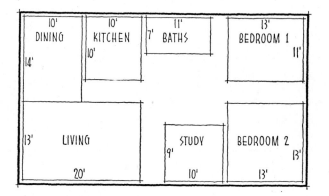

Fig. 9. Coil Layout, Example 1.

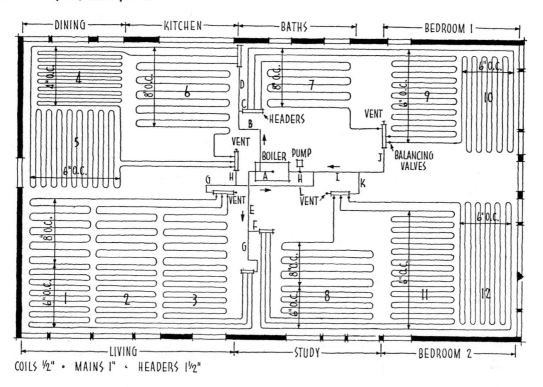

COILS ½" • MAINS 1" • HEADERS 1½"

TABLE 4. Design Work Sheet, Example 1.   *House shown in Fig. 7.*

General Design Data, Coil Location Ceiling   Average Water Temp. 135° F
Tube Size ½ Copper   Gross Unit Output, Btu/hr/ft of Tube 30†   Temp. Drop in System 20° F

Col. Nos.	1	2	3	4	5	6	7	8	9	10	11
	Net Room Heat Loss	Available Panel		Unit Output of Panel	Reverse Flow	Gross Heat Loss	Tube Req'd. Per Room	Sinuous Coils	Identification	Approximate Tube Spacing	
		Dimensions	Area							Trial	Final
	Btu/hr	Feet	Sq. ft.	Btu/hr/s.f.	% of Gross	Btu/hr	Feet	Number Per Room	Coil Numbers	Inches C. to C.	Inches C. to C.
Living	11,320	13 x 20	260	43	10	12,600	420	3	1,2,3	7	6 & 8
Dining	8,060	10 x 14	140	*57	10	9,000	300	2	4,5	5	4 & 6
Kitchen	2,860	10 x 10	100	29	10	3,200	107	1	6	10	8
Baths	2,560	7 x 10	77	34	10	2,900	97	1	7	8	8
Study	3,550	9 x 10	90	39	10	3,900	130	1	8	7	6 & 8
Bedroom 1	6,590	11 x 13	143	46	10	7,300	242	2	9,10	6½	6
Bedroom 2	8,200	13 x 13	169	49	10	9,100	303	2	11,12	6	6
Totals	43,160					48,000	1,599	12			
Notes	Not Incl. Ceiling Loss	See Fig. 8		Col. 1 ÷ Col. 3		Col. 1 ÷ .90	Col. 6 ÷ 30†	No coil to Exceed 150 Feet	See Fig. 9	See explanation in Text	See Layout Fig. 9

Critical Output (Not to exceed 75 for Ceilings)

RADIANT HEATING SYSTEMS FOR HOUSES — 10: Hot Water Systems

By William J. McGuinness

Professor of Architecture, Pratt Institute

6. Temperature Drop — The use of relatively small diameter tube in this installation suggests the use of a 20 deg drop in the water temperature. It is recorded as the design drop in Table 4.

7. Average Water Temperature — The critical output of 57 Btu per sq ft per hr in the dining area is quite moderate, therefore it is unnecessary to choose a high water temperature. 135 deg will be used.

8. Critical Panel — In order to avoid the close spacing that might be necessary with 3/8-in. tube at this moderate temperature, 1/2-in. nominal size tube is used, attached to the joists with metal lath and plaster below it. Table 1. (See Sheet 4, Time-Saver Standards, August 1951) shows 1/2-in. tube to have a gross output of 30 Btu per hr per lin ft of tube at the temperature of 135 deg. Dividing the gross heat loss from the dining space panel by 30, it is found that 300 ft of tube is required in this panel. Making the assumption that the tube will lie about 6 in. within the available panel limits, it is found that 5-in. spacing will provide the required length. For instance, if a tentative scheme called for 13 ft long tubes in the dining area, there would have to be 300 ÷ 13, or 23 lengths. The distance between the outer and inner tube would be 9 ft or 108 in. 108 ÷ 22 spaces is about 5 in. Of course, two coils are needed because 1/2-in. tube may not exceed 150 ft in length. Also, closer spacing is indicated near glass. Finally, the job would do well to confine itself to two or three standard spacings. This job is adapted to the use of 4-, 6-, and 8-in. spacing. A little study of the dining area and some more arithmetic result in coils 4 and 5, which together provide the required length of tube. Each designer will improvise his own

system. Simplicity of layout, ease of fabrication, plan-readability, uniformity of tube size and spacing are all important. Note that the coils start at the glass and at the perimeter with hot water supplied through header at the termination of main branch "D." Balancing valves and a vent precede the header which feeds return main "H."

9. Other Panels — Having established that the critical panel can operate with the spacing as chosen (4 in. is about the minimum possible spacing) it is possible to lay out the other panels, all of which operate at the average temperature of 135 deg, and in which the spacing of tube will be somewhat greater. The approximate tube spacings arrived at by the method already described can be entered in column 10 of Table 4. and standard spacings worked out and listed in column 11. Coils 9 and 10 use 6-in. spacing instead of 6 1/2 and therefore fill less than the panel area. Coil 6 uses 8-in. spacing instead of 10

and also uses a little less panel area than was planned. In each case the lin ft of tube must be as shown in column 6 of Table 4. and must divide into multiples of 150 ft.

10. Size the Mains — Table 2. (See Sheet 6, Time-Saver Standards, September 1951) shows that a 1-in. main will supply up to 70,000 Btu per hr in a system using a 20 deg drop. Since our total gross heat load is 48,000 Btu, a 1-in. main is satisfactory and is used in that size to supply all the headers.

11. Water Flow — Dividing 48,000 Btu by the factor of 10,000 for a 20 deg drop, the hourly pumping rate is found to be 4.8 gal. per min.

12. Select a Pump — The friction through the longest circuit expressed in feet of head must be determined before the pump may be chosen. The following arrangement of computation is convenient. The flow is that through coil number 12 from the

TABLE 5.

Tube Identification	Heat Conveyed	Tube Size	Actual Length	Friction Ft/100 Ft Tube	Friction Head Ft
A	48,000 Btu	1 in.	2 ft	1.8	.036
E	25,600	1	5	.5	.025
F	13,000	1	2	.2	.004
1/2" to coil	4,550	1/2	33	.4	.132
Coil No. 12	4,550	1/2	151	.4	.604
1/2" to header	4,550	1/2	12	.4	.048
K	13,000	1	2	.2	.004
I	23,200	1	8	.4	.032
H	48,000	1	2	1.8	.036
					.921

(From Fig. 5)

boiler and back. See Table 5, Sheet 10, for example worked out.

Adding 50 per cent for the effect of the friction of the fittings, boiler, flow-control valve, the total friction is .921 x 1.50, or 1.38 of head.

With a delivery of 4.8 Gpm and a head of 1.38 ft, it is apparent from Fig. 6 (Sheet 7, Time Saver Standards, September 1951) that any of the pumps shown will be satisfactory, since the curves of performance for all of them lie above the point of intersection of the two known characteristics. It is well to use a 1-in. pump as a minimum size, and it is chosen.

13. Boiler — The connected load for heating is 48,000 Btu per hr, and a boiler selected to carry this load together with the demands for domestic hot water.

14. Compression Tank — A tank of 15 gal. capacity will be satisfactory, as shown in Table 3 (See Sheet 6, Time Saver Standards, September 1951).

General

Fig. 10 shows how to trap the entrained air at the end of the coils so that it may be vented automatically from the header. An overflow protects the plaster. At this point, adjusting (balancing) valves are accessible, together with purge cocks for the purpose of bleeding or blowing out the air at the beginning of operations. The whole must be insulated against freezing and heat loss. Fig. 11 shows the more important of the boiler connections. For simplicity, the domestic hot water facilities have been omitted in the sketch. This and the other boiler controls are very largely as shown for hot water heating in TSS article on hot water heating, ARCHITECTURAL RECORD, September 1949.

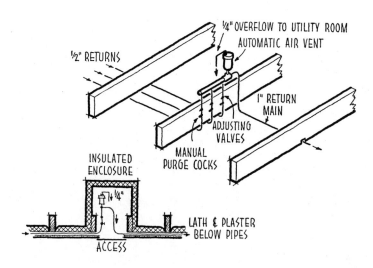

Fig. 10. Return Header Arranged for Venting and Adjustment, Example 1.

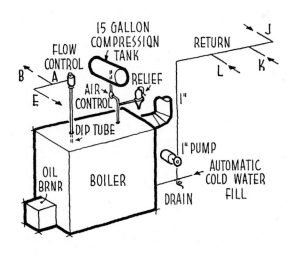

Fig. 11. Boiler Connections, Example 1.

RADIANT HEATING SYSTEMS FOR HOUSES—12: Hot Water Systems

By William J. McGuinness

Professor of Architecture, Pratt Institute

The fourth installment in a series on radiant heating, the following pages present a typical example using floor panels, and worked out by simplified methods presented in the Time-Saver Standards for August and September 1951. A similar example for a ceiling panel installation appeared in the October 1951 issue.

Example 2 — Floor Installation

This example illustrates the design of a system of floor coils for the heating of the same house (Fig. 12) as shown in Fig. 7, TSS, Oct. 1951, Sheet 8. The house is still assumed to be fully insulated and double glazed. Carpets may, in this case, be eliminated with some advantage to the operating economy.

1. Layout

The available panel areas are shown in Fig. 13. Coils should not be run below any fixed equipment such as kitchen floor cabinets. The bathroom panel might have been made smaller to avoid the area of bathtubs, although they are good transmitting surfaces and some piping below them assures comfort while bathing. Fig. 14 is a final summary of the design. Preliminary sketches resembling Fig. 14 should be made to study the possible location of coils and equipment and the routing of mains.

2. Net Hourly Heat Losses

Column 1, Table 6, lists the heat losses from the several rooms. For the use of floor coils, they include the losses through glass, walls and ceilings as well as infiltration of air. Perimeter floor loss is not included. The reverse flow from the pipes to the ground is later added to establish the gross heat loss (column 7, Table 6) from which the linear feet of pipe is selected for the coils.

3. Adjustment

Because this is a one-story house, there is no gain in any heated space from heat flowing in by reverse loss from a panel in a room above or below. Adjustment is not needed.

4. Net Output

It is well to keep the net output in Btu per hr per sq ft of panel below 55 in floors. Columns 1, 3 and 4 (Table 6) establish this output in the case of each room. The dining room is critical at 55 and should be considered first.

5. Gross Output

The water circulated through the pipes must bring in enough heat to make up the net heat loss from the rooms and also the reverse loss to the ground. Fig. 1, TSS, Aug. 1951, Sheet 2, expresses the approximate reverse loss for various floor coverings. Columns 5, 6 and 7 of Table 6

Fig. 12. Plan, Example 2.

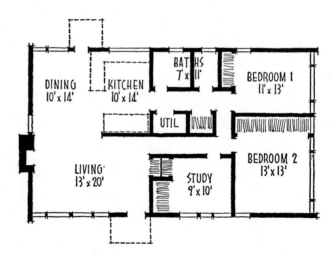

Fig. 13. Panel Areas Available, Example 2.

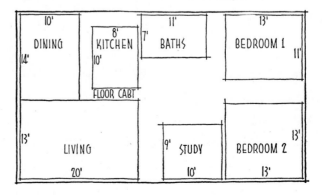

Fig. 14. Coil Layout, Example 2.

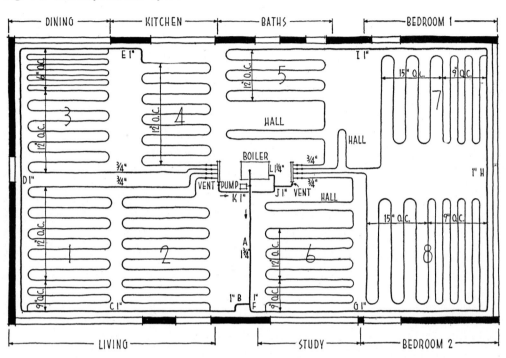

TABLE 6. Design Work Sheet, Example 2								House shown in Fig. 12			
General Design Data		Coil Location—*Floor*				Gross Unit Output, *Btu/hr/ft or pipe*—53††					
		Pipe Size ¾ in. wrought iron or steel				Avg. Water Temp. *130° F* Temp. Drop in System *10° F*					
Col. Nos.	1	2	3	4	5	6	7	8	9	10	11	12
		Available Panel		Unit Output of Panel	Floor Covering	Reverse Flow	Gross Heat Loss	Pipe Req'd. Per Room	Sinuous Coils	Identification	Approximate Pipe Spacing	
	Net Room Heat Loss	Dimensions	Area								Trial	Final
	Btu/hr	Ft	Sq Ft	Btu/hr/ s.f.	Material Selected	% of Gross	Btu/hr	Ft	Number Per Room	Coil Numbers	Inches c. to c.	Inches c. to c.
Living	11,440	13 x 20	260	44	Carpet	20	14,350	270	2 @ 135	1, 2	11	9 & 12
Dining	7,700	10 x 14	140	55†	Asphalt Tile	10	8,550	160	1	3	9	6 & 12
Kitchen	3,250	8 x 10*	80	41	Asphalt Tile	10	3,620	68	1	4	13	12
Baths	2,740	7 x 10	70	39	Ceramic Tile	10	3,050	58	1	5	12	12
Study	3,760	9 x 10	90	42	¼ in. wood in mastic	20	4,700	88	1	6	11	9 & 12
Bedroom 1	6,300	11 x 13	143	44	Asphalt Tile	10	7,000	132	1	7	12	9 & 15
Bedroom 2	8,100	13 x 13	169	48	Asphalt Tile	10	9,000	170	1	8	11	9 & 15
Totals	43,290						50,270	946	8			
Notes	Not incl. floor perimeter loss	*Exclusive of floor cabinets		Col 1 ÷ Col 3		See Fig. 1 TSS Aug.'51 Sheet 2.	Col—by .80 or .90	†† Col 7 ÷ 53	L.R. Divided for equalization	See Fig. 13	See Text	See Layout Fig. 13

† *Critical output, (not to exceed 55 for floors)*   †† *From Table 1, TSS, Aug. '51, Sheet 4. 57×.93=53 Btu/hr/ft of pipe*

RADIANT HEATING SYSTEMS FOR HOUSES — 14: Hot Water Systems

By William J. McGuinness

Professor of Architecture, Pratt Institute

show the method of arriving at the gross heat loss for each space.

6. Temperature Drop in the System

Pipes of wrought iron or steel ¾ in. in diameter will be used for the coils. In these relatively large pipes the friction is small and the water can be pumped through them quite rapidly. A small temperature drop can be expected and 10 deg is chosen.

7. Average Water Temperature

A trial computation was made using 110 F as the average water temperature, and it was found that the pipe spacings in the dining area were too small. A temperature of 130 F was then chosen and is used here. Table 1, TSS, Aug. 1951, Sheet 4, gives the output per ft of ¾ in. pipe as 57 x .93 = 53 Btu/hr at 130 F.

8. Critical Panel

If the gross heat loss of the dining area be divided by the output per ft of pipe (53 Btu), it is found that 160 ft of pipe are required. This works out to an average spacing of 9 in. on center. This is in accord with suggested spacings in Table 1, TSS, Aug. 1951, Sheet 4. To overcome the greater loss near glass, the pipes will be spaced 6 in. on center near the glass and wider as the coil recedes from the glass. 6 in. is greater than the closest possible spacing of ¾ in. pipe as determined by the minimum bend radius. Comments under the item "Critical Panel", TSS, Oct. 1951, Sheet 10, may be helpful in layout and study.

9. Other Panels

Columns 8 through 12 in Table 6 are a summary of the trial and final spacings based upon the required total linear footage for all coils. Coils up to 350 ft in length are permissible

using ¾ in. wrought iron or steel pipe. It will be seen that all of the proposed coils are less than this length, resulting in a simpler coil layout than that of Example 1. In that example, 12 coils were used instead of 8 because of the smaller tubing chosen. The living room requirements are met by two coils or lengths comparable to those in other rooms.

10. Size of Mains

Mains A and L convey more than 35,000 Btu per hr. Reference to Table 2, TSS, Sept. 1951, Sheet 6, results in the selection of 1¼ in. mains at these two points. All other mains can be 1 in. because their capacities are less than 35,000 Btu. The mains are shown in heavy lines on Fig. 14.

11. Water Flow

Sufficient water must be pumped to make up the gross heat loss. Dividing the gross heat loss of 50,270 Btu

by the factor 5000 for a 10 deg drop, 10 gallons per minute is found to be the necessary rate.

12. Selection of a Pump

The pump size will depend upon the rate of pumping and the friction head through the longest circuit (Coil 3) expressed in ft of water. The path of the water and the friction of each pipe length may be traced in Table 7. The resulting head of 2.38 ft of water makes no allowance for fittings and equipment for which 50% is commonly added. 2.38 x 1.50 = 3.57 ft of water, total friction head. If these coordinates (10 G.P.M. & 3.57 ft) are plotted on Fig. 6, TSS, Sept. 1951, Sheet 7, it will be seen that in this small system the usual minimum pump size of 1 in. is adequate.

13. Boiler

The hourly requirement of this house under design performance is 50,270 Btu for the gross connected heating load. A boiler must be se-

TABLE 7, Friction in the longest run (Coil 3)

Pipe Identification	Heat Conveyed	Pipe Size	Actual Length	Friction Ft/100 ft Pipe	Friction Head, Ft
A	50,270 Btu	1¼ in.	19 ft	1.8 ft	.34 ft
B	26,520	1	5	2.0	.10
C	19,350	1	18	1.2	.22
D	12,180	1	36	.4	.14
Coil 3	8,550	¾	170*	.8	1.37
K	26,520	1	8	2.0	.16
L	50,270	1¼	3	1.8	.05
Total					2.38 ft
Notes	Fig. 13 & Table 6	Table 2, TSS Sept. '51 Sheet 6.	*160+ 10 ft to header	Fig. 5, TSS Aug. '51 Sheet 5.	

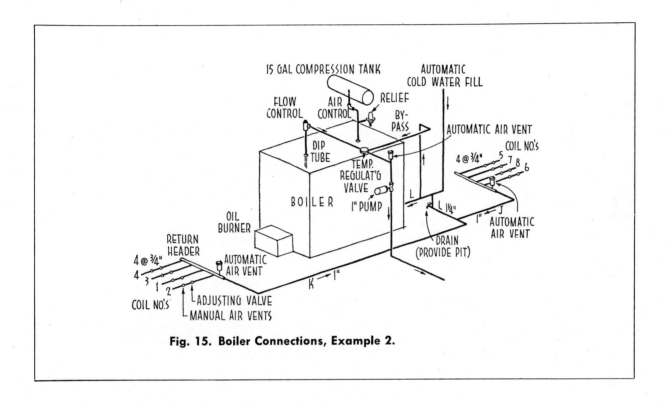

Fig. 15. Boiler Connections, Example 2.

lected to carry this load and also meet the demand for domestic hot water.

14. Compression Tank

A 15 gallon tank will permit the required expansion of the water in this system according to Table 3, TSS, Sept. 1951, Sheet 6, since the *net* heat loss is less than 50,000 Btu/hr.

Boiler Connections

The piping arrangements at the boiler are pictured in Fig. 15. For simplicity, some of the boiler controls, valves in the piping and domestic hot water connections have been omitted. The boiler will deliver water through main A at 135 F and it will return through L at 125 F. This is necessary to achieve the 130 deg average water temperature and the 10 deg drop. The bypass from the

return line and the temperature regulating valve permit the boiler to operate at 180 deg or more, assuring a temperature high enough for domestic hot water (135 is not enough). The hot water of the boiler is mixed with the cooler return water to produce the supply water at 135. This mixing arrangement is needed in most cases where domestic hot water is generated by the same boiler. It would have to be used if domestic hot water were desired from the boiler in Example 1, Fig. 11, TSS, Oct. 1951, Sheet 11. The actual piping might be a good deal more compact than that shown in Fig. 15 resulting in the inclusion of the vents and adjusting valves within the utility room. Otherwise, the adjusting valves would have to be in a recess in the floor covered by an access plate. The automatic vents would have to be above the floor in a partition or utility space.

All vents and controls must be accessible.

Venting and Adjustment

The dip tube prevents air from favoring a path through the main. It collects in the air chamber of the compression tank. Entrained air in the supply and return mains is exhausted by the automatic air vents at high points in the supply main and return headers. The manual air vents are petcocks which can be opened and the air purged from one circuit by closing off the others and pumping through the open circuit only until the air is driven out. This may have to be done at the beginning of operations. The adjusting valves may be used to cut down the flow to coils which are overhot. Care should be taken not to constrict the general flow too much, but only to equalize or balance it.

RADIANT HEATING SYSTEMS FOR HOUSES—16: Controls

By William J. McGuinness, Professor of Architecture, Pratt Institute

CONTROLS

Basic Assumptions

If domestic hot water need not be generated from the same boiler, the boiler may be used to deliver water at the lower temperature needed for radiant panels. However, since most modern installations produce both water for heating and domestic hot water from the same plant, it will be assumed that the boiler water temperature must be kept at about 180 to 200 F, and that some mixing device is needed to produce water in the usual range of about 100 to 150 deg for use in the radiant panels. The second assumption· is that the fuel used is gas or oil, rather than coal. The systems of control described apply to these two fuels. The third assumption is that high- and low-limit aquastats are used to operate the automatically controlled gas or oil fires to keep the boiler water at a fairly constant temperature for use in the mixing devices.

Water Temperature Control

The common method of delivering water of the temperature required is to mix some of the hot water from the boiler with the cooler return water from the radiant coils. Fig. 16 shows three methods for doing this. The first of these uses gate valves, which may be adjusted manually to deliver water at the correct temperature. An improvement on this scheme is seen in the second example where a thermostatic mixing valve is used. It can be set to deliver water at any desired temperature provided the boiler water temperature is higher. Either of these is suitable for use with a circulator which operates at intervals to make up the heat losses as required. The third arrangement in Fig. 16 is a blending valve which constantly changes the temperature of the water delivered in accord with the dictates of indoor and outdoor bulbs, as described later. This valve is used with a circulator which operates continually, except that, occasionally, it is turned off for brief intervals when the room temperature exceeds that set for it. The graph in Fig. 16 shows two typical points on the curve of operations for such a

Fig. 16

Three methods of adjusting temperature of water for coils

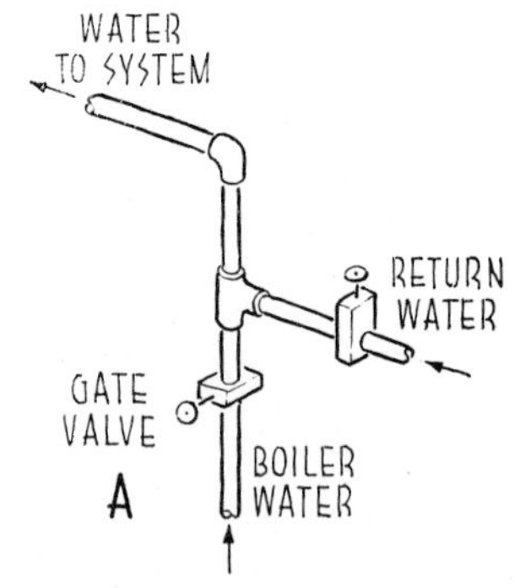

A

Valves on return water and boiler water can be adjusted manually to deliver water to coils at proper design temperature. System works quite satisfactorily with intermittent use of circulator

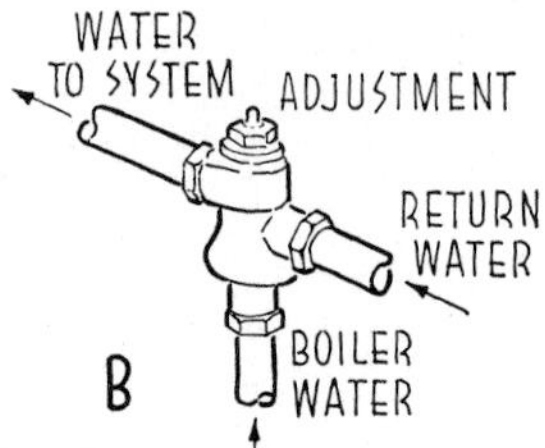

B

Temperature control valve with thermostatic element will assure delivery of water at any predetermined temperature, provided boiler water temperature is higher. It is an improvement over "A" at some additional expense

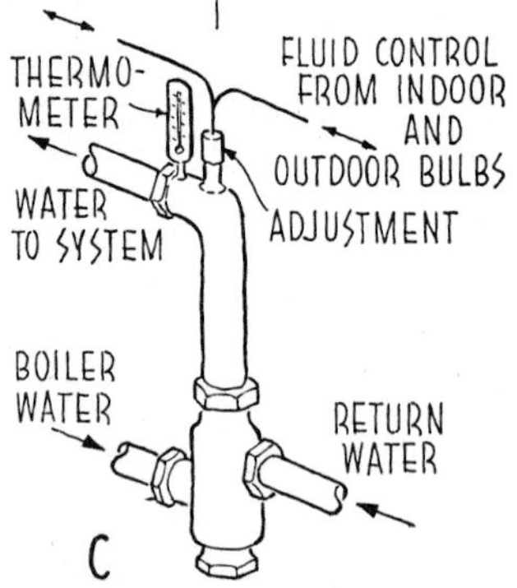

C

When circulator is run continuously, temperature of water delivered to coils can be changed by this automatic blending valve. Control is by indoor and outdoor bulbs

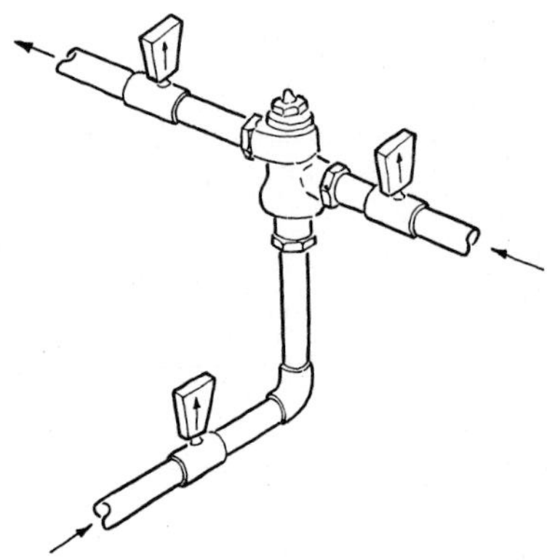

In any system, liberal use of thermometers is recommended as an adjustment aid

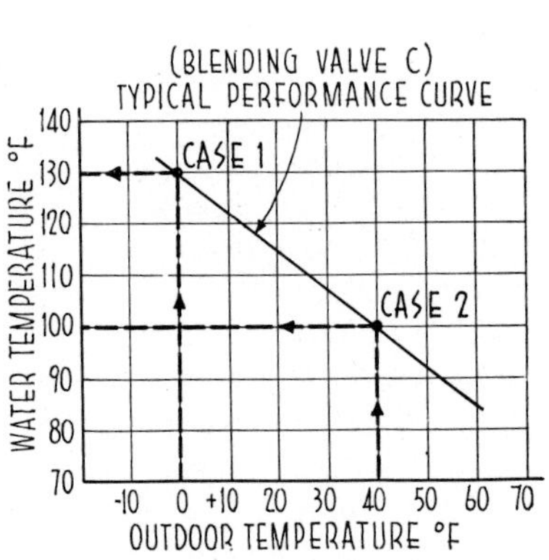

Case 1. Design conditions. Water delivered at design temperature (130° F) when outside temperature is 0° F

Case 2. Mild weather. Water delivered at lower temperature, in this case 100° F, when outside temperature is 40° F

Fig. 17 Control Devices (*See Fig. 18 for combined uses*)

1. Aquastats

High and low limit immersion aquastats in the boiler water turn fire on and off to maintain water temperature high enough to generate domestic hot water, and for use in radiant coils after mixing

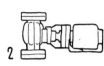

2. Circulating Pump

Intermittent use with fixed water temperature or continuous use with varying water temperature are two usual schemes. In both cases, room thermostats or room controls generally stop circulator when room temperature is adequate

3. Thermostat

For intermittent circulator use, thermostat turns circulator on when heat is called for, and off when satisfied. This type with no automatic night set-back is often used when lower temperature is inadvisable at night, as in concrete floor slabs. Heavy slabs recover slowly from low temperatures

4. Clock Thermostat

The temperature of ceiling panels can be lowered at night (morning recovery is fast). For this purpose, clock thermostat can be used. For use in connection with outside anticipator, it can be electronic

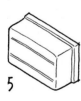

5. Averaging Thermostat

In large houses, it is sometimes advisable to average the temperature at which thermostat operates. This one acts in tandem with main thermostat and the average temperature of the two is used. In ceiling systems where panels cool off unevenly, this is a good equalizing device

6. Outdoor Anticipator

This device is part of an electronic system. Together with thermostat and (in floor systems) immersion bulb in return water, it operates circulator. This anticipates cooling off of house by sensing a drop in outdoor temperature before inside thermostat does. It is placed on a north wall

7. Cycler

It is evident that with multiple controls, fire and circulator would be turning on and off at short intervals. Cycler assures periods of operation not less than three or four minutes

8. Immersion Bulb

In floor slab systems, this is set into return water to sense any drop in temperature. It operates together with outdoor anticipator to turn on circulator when needed. The outdoor anticipator varies control point of immersion bulb

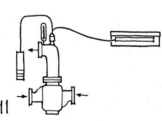

9. Outdoor Bulb

Before inside devices can observe change in outside temperature, outdoor bulb operates. When outdoor temperature drops, a contracting liquid opens valve at boiler water supply, increasing temperature of mixed water. With outside rise, reverse occurs. It is placed on a north wall

10. Indoor Bulb

This is operated by the room control. When room temperature exceeds setting of room control, it warms indoor bulb electrically. Indoor bulb then delivers an expanding liquid to blending valve. This tends to close boiler water opening in blending valve, reducing temperature of water delivered. If room temperature continues to rise, it shuts off circulator

11. Blending Valve

Continuous use of circulator demands varying water temperature. Increased temperatures of either indoor or outdoor bulb cause an expanding liquid to depress mechanically the valve which admits hot boiler water to mixture. This reduces temperature of water delivered to system. With decreasing bulb temperatures, hotter water is delivered

12. Room Control

About the size of a thermostat and with similar setting dial, this control operates as described in (10) (Indoor Bulb). It is upper limit control only, outdoor bulb taking care of operating system when temperatures drop. Room control senses radiant and convective changes as well as changing room temperature. Flush type is also available

GLASS

200 ± Btu
Per Sq. Ft.
Per Hour

13. The Sun

In solar houses with much glass on the south, sun is part of heating system and is more than adequate to heat house. Interior heating system, or at least the south zone, must turn off when sun is operating

RADIANT HEATING SYSTEMS FOR HOUSES—18: Controls

By William J. McGuinness, Professor of Architecture, Pratt Institute

valve. Case 1 occurs when the outside temperature is zero (design temperature in many localities). In this case, the water is delivered at 130 deg, which could be the design temperature called for at this critical condition. At the milder outdoor temperature of 40 deg, the water is delivered at 100 deg, which is sufficient to make up the smaller heat losses which occur at this higher outdoor temperature.

Systems of Control

Two important influences in selecting a control system are the thermal lag of the panel and the amount of glass facing south, which makes solar heating a part of the heating system. For houses having little glass and employing ceiling coils, fixed proportions for water mixing are possible with intermittent use of the circulator, controlled by a simple electric thermostat. The mixing may be as shown in Fig. 16, A or B. Ceiling coils have a fast response. They heat quickly and cool quickly. This house is little influenced by changes in the intensity of sunshine. See Fig. 18 (A) for this arrangement. The use of floor coils in concrete in this kind of house would preclude the possibility of night set-back because of the thermal lag. Otherwise, the control could be the same. Outdoor control might be of some advantage in this case if budget permits.

In solar houses receiving much heat gain from glass on the south, the use of outdoor controls is recommended in all cases, and they are most necessary with the use of floor coils. It is necessary to anticipate the heat that will come from the sun and to shut off the system before this heat is received. Conversely, when the sun is about to set and outside temperature drops, it is well that the system start in response to an outside sensing device early enough to replace the effect of the sun when it sets. The additional importance of anticipating outside temperature changes by regulating the temperature of coils in concrete slabs is obvious because of their greater thermal lag.

Fig. 18 Recommended Control Systems For Radiant Panels

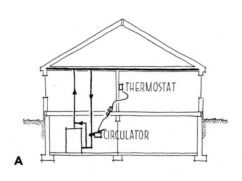

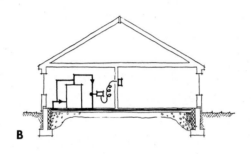

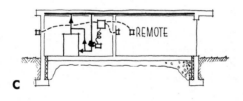

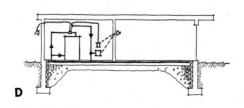

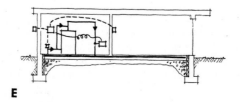

A. Conventional House, Ceiling Panel

Glass represents about 10 to 20 per cent of wall areas, orientation is unimportant. Circulator is operated intermittently by clock thermostat which can serve for night set-back. Outdoor controls not needed

B. Conventional House, Floor Panel in Concrete Slab

Glass and orientation same as case "A" above. Plain thermostat without night set-back operates circulator intermittently. A radiant-and-convective type room control, Item 12, Fig. 17, is slightly preferable. Outdoor controls are of some advantage. If used, they could be as in cases "D" or "E" below. Night set-back not recommended because of slow return of slab temperature

C. Solar House, Glass on South, Ceiling Panel, Electronic Controls

Electronic relay amplifier receives signals of outdoor anticipator and of thermostat-set comprising clock thermostat and averaging thermostat remote from it. Through a cycler assuring at least 3 or 4 minutes operation, circulator is controlled by amplifier for intermittent operation

D. Solar House, Glass on South, Floor Panel in Convective Slabs, Blending Valve Control

Outdoor bulb and combination of room control operating indoor bulb regulate blending valve. Room control location is same as for thermostat. Temperature of water varies to compensate for varying temperatures. Circulator operation is continuous unless indoor bulb cannot cool slab quickly enough, in which case room control turns off circulator. No night set-back. *Note: System may be used for ceiling panel as in case "C" without change except night set-back may be added*

E. Solar House, Glass on South, Floor Panel in Concrete Slab, Electronic Controls

Electronic relay amplifier receives signals of outdoor anticipator, a plain thermostat (no night set-back) and an immersion bulb in return water. If one indicates temperature drop, circulator is started. Immersion bulb helps prevent lag in floor slab systems. A cycler is used

Selecting A System

In Fig. 18, electronic and mechanical systems are shown for the control of radiant panels. In general, the electronic systems use a fixed water temperature adjustment with intermittent circulator operation, while the mechanical systems use a blending valve and continual circulator operation. Each has its particular merits. The electronic system is inexpensive and very sensitive. The system of continuous circulator operation has the advantage of adjusting closely to the actual heat loss from the house. By some it is thought that continuous operation is a distinct advantage in floor slab panels and in larger installations, both situations where, because of great thermal capacity, the panels would not be flexible enough to follow quick changes in heat delivered to coils.

ZONING

Selection of Zones

In modern solar houses the first zone to pick is the no-sun zone. This is shown in Fig. 19 on the north side of the house. This zone receives no sun during the day, and at low outdoor temperatures the heating panels might operate all day. Under these same conditions and when the sun is shining, all south zones might be turned off. A further split could be between the sleeping and living wings. This is possible only when ceiling systems are used, permitting night set-back. Further zones might be suggested by remote, isolated wings or second stories. In these cases, the north sides of isolated wings or upper stories should still be separately zoned if the south receives much sun during the day.

Piping For Zone Control

The piping shown in Figs. 11 and 15 (see Time-Saver Standards Sheet 11, October 1951, and Sheet 15, January 1952) for single zone systems would have to be modified for multi-zone operation. For instance, in a three-zone system such as shown in Fig. 19, a header would be needed to receive the mixed water. The three mains serving the zones would each start through a separate flow-control valve. The piping for each zone would run separately and return as a zone-return-main from each of the zones. A circulating pump would serve each individual zone-return-main before the return water was assembled in a master return header.

Controls for Zoning

A full set of controls is required for each zone. In the house shown in Fig. 19, three sets of controls are needed. A ceiling system is assumed. If the controls were electronic, they would comprise three each of: clock thermostat, averaging thermostat, outdoor anticipator, and electronic relay amplifier. If continuous operation were selected, the controls would comprise three each of: blending valve, outdoor bulb, indoor bulb, and room control. In either case, three pumps and three flow-control valves would be needed.

Fig. 19 Zoning Layout for Large Solar-Type House

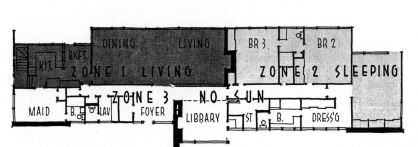

Plan: Courtesy of Daniel Schwartzman, Architect

INDEX